THE SUCCESSFUL VOLUNTEER ORGANIZATION

Getting Started and Getting Results in Nonprofit, Charitable, Grass Roots, and Community Groups

Joan Flanagan

Contemporary Books, Inc.
Chicago

Library of Congress Cataloging in Publication Data

Flanagan, Joan.
   The successful volunteer organization.

   Includes bibliographical references and index.
   1. Voluntarism—United States.   2. Associations,
institutions, etc.—United States—Management.   I. Title.
HN90.V64F55   658′.048   81-66080
ISBN 0-8092-5838-2   AACR2
ISBN 0-8092-5837-4 (pbk.)

Copyright © 1981 by Joan Flanagan
All rights reserved
Published by Contemporary Books, Inc.
180 North Michigan Avenue, Chicago, Illinois 60601
Manufactured in the United States of America
Library of Congress Catalog Card Number: 81-66080
International Standard Book Number: 0-8092-5838-2 (cloth)
                               0-8092-5837-4 (paper)

Published simultaneously in Canada by
Beaverbooks, Ltd.
150 Lesmill Road
Don Mills, Ontario M3B 2T5
Canada

Contents

Acknowledgments

The W. Clement & Jessie V. Stone Foundation is a pioneer among foundations in offering expert advice and technical assistance to volunteer organizations as well as providing financial support. The staff provides consulting services to hundreds of volunteer organizations, and receives requests for help from thousands of others. To meet this need, the Foundation Board agreed in 1978 to launch a project to prepare a comprehensive "how-to" manual to help charitable organizations become more efficient and more effective.

At the same time, I was directing a national technical assistance program based on my book *The Grass Roots Fundraising Book.* More than 1,400 volunteer leaders and staff attended workshops to learn how to raise more money. I discovered that most groups' fund-raising problems were the result, rather than the cause, of weak organizations. So I tried starting the workshops with a session called "How do you build an organization worth raising money for?" Although it was not grammatical, it was very effective! I decided to write a book on this topic to help nonprofit groups build organizations that their communities want so much that fund raising becomes a pleasure. So when the W. Clement & Jessie V. Stone Foundation asked if I would prepare a manual for volunteer organizations, I immediately said yes! This book is the result.

In addition to Donna J. Stone, who is the president of the W. Clement & Jessie V. Stone Foundation, I want to recognize the contributions of the excellent foundation staff. They all helped make this book a reality. Maree Bullock, executive director, gave the leadership to make the project a reality. Jessye Payne served as project coordinator. Ray Murray and Gloria Varona gave their experienced advice and consulting skills. Librarian Kathy Hamilton helped find the best books and resources. Linda A. Hazlewood and Nancy Babich helped to type mountains of drafts; Helen Reif typed the final manuscript. Lawyer Richard Golden reviewed and improved Chapter 9 on lobbying. Special recognition must go to Karen Brownlee, who helped with the research, administration, typing, and preparation of the entire project.

Over the last six years, I have talked to more than 2,000 community leaders who are doing the work and getting results in volunteer organizations. For the last two years, I have systematically looked for the answers to the question posed by organizer Jane Beckett: "How do you change a crusade into a serious, permanent organization?" Here are the answers that work. None of this advice is original. All of it is tested principles developed by outstanding citizens to help their own communities. You know who you are, because I have shamelessly stolen all your best ideas. Thanks for the advice — keep it coming!

Most of all, I want to thank my family and friends for their enthusiasm and support. I couldn't have done it without you.

JMF
1981

The W. Clement & Jessie V. Stone Foundation

Donna J. Stone

The story of the W. Clement & Jessie V. Stone Foundation is the story of riches that multiply when they are shared. Mr. and Mrs. W. Clement Stone dream of a world where each person can realize his or her potential and contribute to the welfare of mankind. The W. Clement & Jessie V. Stone Foundation motivates, inspires, and assists people, programs, and organizations.

The foundation is distinguished by three characteristics:

- principles of positive thinking
- action grants for positive change
- advice, counsel, managerial support, and fund-raising advice to charitable organizations

This book was commissioned by the foundation to help people begin or succeed in charitable organizations. The project involved two years of research, testing information, and organizing and writing material so it is accurate and easy to use. We are proud to share this work, for by strengthening voluntary organizations we can make a better world in which to live.

As the founder of the National Committee for Prevention of Child Abuse, I know by personal experience that ordinary citizens *can* make an enormous difference in solving many of the serious problems facing us today. In starting the National Committee in 1972, I had a goal, a borrowed office, determination, motivation, and a plan worth working for — the eradication of child abuse. Most people told me that it *could not* be done!

By 1981, the National Committee has grown to become an effective national organization with its own offices, more than twelve skilled national staff members, a national public awareness campaign supported by ninety million dollars of public service advertising, and a growing network of state chapters and local coalitions establishing multiple grass roots volunteer prevention programs.

The National Committee is actively working to motivate concerned citizens to become involved in child abuse prevention programs. Child abuse is an important national problem. The National Committee set a goal — to respond quickly to this serious problem — and has achieved it. Your group may not need or want to be as far-reaching in its goals. But I know that *you* can set *your* goal and *achieve* it if you follow the guidance in this book and are a positive thinker.

Dare to aim high! Two national conferences in the early seventies concluded that Americans did not realize child abuse was a problem in their country. Our priority, therefore, was to heighten awareness of the problem, its incidence, and the causes of child abuse. The National Committee was the only national organization with the single goal of primary prevention of child abuse.

A friend introduced me to The Advertising Council staff in New York. I shared my dream and my goal with them. They said they also had identified child abuse as a major problem and were seeking a national organization to assist them in their interest and effort.

With their help and counsel, the National Committee grew to qualify for a full media public service campaign: car cards; billboards; and television, radio, and printed ads. People *believed in us.*

To our delight, Campbell Ewald, Inc., our volunteer advertising company, was awarded an international prize for our campaign as "the best public service announcements in the world." The public service announcements are now appearing in many foreign languages. Our efforts now have a worldwide impact.

I know from my own work with the National Committee and many other charitable organizations that what makes an organization successful is one man or woman with the positive conviction that his or her idea will succeed. You may call it willpower, determination, or stubbornness. In any case, you can and will reach your goals if you believe you can, decide you can, and take action to achieve them. The results of volunteer efforts in the United States have been astounding. The practical advice in this book will make it easier for you along the way.

How You Can Achieve Success

W. Clement Stone

When asked to write the introduction to *The Successful Volunteer Organization*, I realized from my many years of experience as a lecturer, author, and teacher in the Art of Motivation with PMA (Positive Mental Attitude) that the greatest service I could render to you, the reader, would be to help you identify, personalize and use the principles Joan Flanagan included in her manuscript. After all, that was Joan's purpose in writing the book.

It occurred to me that an article I'd written for the June 1981 issue of *SUCCESS, The Magazine for Achievers* could, with a small number of changes, help you achieve your purpose in reading this book. The article was titled "How to Help Your 'Self' with a Self-Help Book."

Have you ever read a self-help book and described a certain passage, or the book itself, as "very moving"? Well, if so, how far did you move? How fast did you move? When you stopped moving, where were you—the place you started from or the place you wanted to be?

*My questions probably seem a play on words . . . that is exactly
what they are. But there is a definite point: If the book was so
"moving" . . . did it move you to constructive mental or physical
ACTION? If not, you did not put your "self" into self-help.*

Currently, there is a barrage of self-help books on the market.
Some helpful . . . some harmful — physically, mentally, morally.

The most important of all literature is what I term "inspirational
self-help action" books . . . books that motivate you to motivate
yourself to achieve anything in life you desire, in principle, that
doesn't violate the laws of God or the rights of your fellowmen. The
most effective among these tell you specifically what to do and
HOW TO DO IT in an interesting style that makes good reading.
And something more: They motivate you to apply the proven
principles they contain. There are many books in this category. A
few that come immediately to mind are *The Autobiography of
Benjamin Franklin . . . How I Raised Myself from Failure to
Success in Selling* by Frank Bettger . . . *Think and Grow Rich* by
Napoleon Hill . . . *Success Through a Positive Mental Attitude*
coauthored by Napoleon Hill and me . . . *Language in Thought
and Action* by S. I. Hayakawa and . . . *I Dare You!* by William
Danforth.

LEARN HOW TO RECOGNIZE AND APPLY PRINCIPLES

There are tens of thousands of persons who have read inspirational self-help action books . . . magazine and newspaper
articles and editorials designed by the writers to motivate the
readers to motivate themselves and others to desirable ACTION
. . . but nothing happened to them. This is understandable. Why?
Because throughout the history of education, two principles that
every man, woman, and child should learn and apply were not
taught in our school systems until recent years. They are (1) HOW
TO Recognize, Relate, Assimilate, and APPLY Principles in the
behavioral sciences such as psychology, the study of the human
mind — the functioning of the brain and nervous system; and (2)
HOW TO motivate yourself and others at will to achieve any
desirable goal. A student in psychology will receive a high grade

merely for memorizing principles. He or she is not taught to AP-PLY them.

Everyone does, to some extent, recognize principles, techniques, systems, methods, and formulas . . . and everyone does motivate himself or herself and others. There are many courses on motivation, but they are for specific purposes rather than the essence whereby an individual can set high goals—even in the possibility of the improbable—and achieve them. He or she can meet serious problems and solve them by learning and applying what I term "the essence of motivation."

THE HUMAN COMPUTER

The computer was designed from the brain and nervous system. You—and every living person—do absolutely nothing unless it begins with the conscious or subconscious mind or the interaction of the two. Those who know HOW TO are able to use their conscious mind to tap the known and unknown powers of the subconscious. It would, therefore, be advantageous to you to seek the necessary knowledge and instruction on HOW TO convert the unlimited potential power of your human computer to actual power.

IF THEY CAN DO IT, YOU CAN DO IT, TOO!

I learned at an early age HOW TO Recognize, Relate, Assimilate, and APPLY Psychological Principles and . . . HOW TO motivate myself at will and others to desirable action by applying them. Combined Insurance Company of America, of which I am founder and chairman, is the largest company of its kind in the world due, in great part, to the fact that our sales and administrative personnel have been taught and have learned to respond to and use these principles. If they can do it, you can do it, too!

Motivation is that which induces action or determines choice. It is that which provides a motive. A motive is the "inner urge" only within the individual which incites him to action, such as a passion, emotion, instinct, tendency, habit, mood, impulse, desire, or idea.

MEMORIZE FOR A PURPOSE

Take yourself, for example: If you lacked cold-canvass experience, you would be timid or afraid to call store-to-store or office-to-office without appointments. Our representatives cold canvass. They are taught to memorize, *for a purpose,* such verbal self-suggestions—which I call self-motivators—as SUCCESS IS ACHIEVED BY THOSE WHO TRY AND MAINTAINED BY THOSE WHO KEEP TRYING WITH PMA . . . WHERE THERE IS NOTHING TO LOSE BY TRYING AND A GREAT DEAL TO GAIN IF SUCCESSFUL, BY ALL MEANS TRY WITH PMA and . . . the self-starter: DO IT NOW! Repeating DO IT NOW! fifty times in the morning and fifty times at night for a week or so indelibly imprints the self-starter DO IT NOW! in the subconscious so that it flashes to the conscious mind in times of need (any time you may be tempted to procrastinate). *The purpose is to develop the habit of ACTING immediately.*

REASON VERSUS ACTION

When DO IT NOW! flashes into the conscious mind of one of our representatives—after he has developed the habit of immediately responding by getting into ACTION—he enters the place of business. When he interviews a person, he may be figuratively shaking inside because of the emotion of fear. He learns to neutralize this fear through voice control by: speaking loudly . . . rapidly . . . emphasizing important words . . . hesitating where there might be a period or comma or other punctuation in the written word . . . keeping a smile in his voice so that it won't be gruff and . . . using modulation.

When the butterflies stop flying in his stomach, he can talk in a conversational tone, unafraid because the emotion of fear has been neutralized. It works one hundred times out of one hundred with experience. For while the emotions are not always immediately subject to reason, they are *always immediately subject to ACTION.*

APPLY YOUR "SELF" TO SELF-HELP BOOKS

There are ten major points to keep in mind when studying—

instead of only reading—an inspirational self-help action book to help you discover and employ principles that will motivate you to ACTION.

1. Write down the goals you would like to achieve or the desires you wish to bring into reality. One of the most effective methods is to answer the following question: If you had a magic wand and could have anything you wanted that didn't violate the laws of God or the rights of your fellow men, what would it be? In addition to your major, definite goal, you could list minor, nonconflicting objectives that might occur to you. IMPORTANT: When you sincerely establish a definite goal, you are more apt to recognize and apply that which will help you achieve it.

2. Imagine yourself already in possession of your objective. In your mind's eye, actually visualize the achievement of your goal. In the August 1978 issue of *SUCCESS,* Denis Waitley wrote in an article titled "Visualize Your Way to Success": "Winners see the act of winning before it ever happens. Winners act like winners, imagining with pictures, feelings and words the roles they want to play. They give themselves a preview of coming attractions. What you 'see' is what you get!

"Individuals behave and perform not in accordance with ability or reality but in accordance with their perception of reality. How individuals feel about themselves is everything, for all that they ever do or aspire to do will be predicated on that all-important self-image."

3. Keep an open mind. Read as if the author were your personal friend . . . speaking to you and you alone. What are the reasons for reading in this manner? When you do, you will pay attention to the author's advice as you would to that of a personal friend responding to your request; you will react personally, warmly, and affirmatively. In fact, you will engage in thinking time. As you read, there is direct communication from the author to you, similar to that when studying the contents of a letter from a dear friend.

One more thing . . . follow instructions and advice. Some inspirational self-help action books that you will encounter will have their own directions, instructions, and programs. Above all else, take advantage of the author's experience, and put these programs to use (experiment now by following the instructions in this article).

4. Pay attention to what the author is trying to tell you. Concentrate on what you are reading. If you have trouble concentrating, take a brief break, walk, or short nap, or move to a quieter environment.

5. Recognize, Relate, Assimilate, and APPLY Principles. All inspirational self-help action books contain hidden treasures that you can find for yourself. How? By Recognizing, Relating, Assimilating, and putting into ACTION principles, ideas, and techniques that apply to YOU.

You *Recognize* a principle, idea or technique when you find yourself saying, "Hey, that's for me!!!" — when you *know* you have run across something that applies to you. You *Relate* that principle, idea, or technique to yourself when you answer these questions: "What does this mean to me?" or "How does this apply to ME?" or "How can I use it?" You *Assimilate* a principle, idea, or technique when you incorporate it into yourself — when you make it become part of you. And you put the principle, idea, or technique into ACTION when you *get MOVING* — when you follow through with *ACTION*.

6. Read with pen in hand. Underscore that which is important or applicable to you. Put a question mark next to items that you don't fully understand for future clarification. One value of underscoring is that you can review the essentials of the book quickly. You will also find it advantageous to write out parts that you have underscored to memorize as you review.

Of course, you will make notes on a separate piece of paper as you read, jotting down ideas you wish to remember and, most importantly, those ideas that flash in your mind . . . including answers to some question or unsolved problem.

7. Use suggestion and autosuggestion as tools to develop mental habits. In *Webster's New Collegiate Dictionary, suggestion* is defined as "the process by which one thought leads to another, especially through association of ideas; a means or process of influencing attitudes and behavior . . ." and *autosuggestion* is defined as "an influencing of one's own attitudes, behavior, or physical condition by mental processes other than conscious thought."

In *Success Through a Positive Mental Attitude,* Napoleon Hill and I state: "Conscious autosuggestion and self-suggestion are synonymous, and are contrasted with the word autosuggestion, an unconscious activity. Autosuggestion automatically sends messages from the subconscious to the conscious mind as well as to parts of the body. The subconscious mind is the seat of habit, memory, inviolable standards of conduct, etc."

8. *Memorize* the self-motivators and quotations that you decide are important to YOU or . . . develop your own. When you commit to memory certain important principles . . . commit yourself to them. This is one inherent aspect of self-suggestion that will help insure your success. The idea here is that developing self-suggestion forces you to develop mental *habits* . . . right mental habits. When a desirable mental activity becomes a *habit,* it becomes an extremely powerful tool.

9. Take thinking time, planning time, and study time . . . with regularity. What is the true value of thinking, planning, and study time? Merely reading an inspirational self-help action book will entertain you but may not motivate you to ACTION. If you engage in time for thinking, planning, study, and self-inspection with regularity—preferably daily—you can move right up to full effectiveness. Take thinking and study time to reflect upon what you have been reading. Take planning time to formulate your plans—how you are going to go about achieving your goals, setting deadlines, and planning your schedule to get into ACTION!

Finally, the most important point to keep uppermost in mind when reading an inspirational self-help action book:

10. MAINTAIN YOUR POSITIVE MENTAL ATTITUDE—PMA! I cannot overemphasize that keeping your attitude POSITIVE is what will make the big difference. Maintain the right attitude: Recognize that YOU are the MOST IMPORTANT LIVING PERSON, as far as You are concerned. Keeping this in mind will insure your future success!

PUT YOUR "SELF" INTO SELF-HELP

This introduction is intended to motivate you to learn HOW TO motivate yourself to desirable ACTION. Each of the ten points to help you get out of inspirational self-help action material what the author wants to share with you can be reduced to a few words. You may want to write them on a bookmark, and review them whenever you open *The Successful Volunteer Organization*. The same system will help you discover success principles in any form of inspirational self-help action material . . . books, newspaper or magazine articles, films, lectures, sermons, etc.

PUT YOUR "SELF" INTO SELF-HELP . . .
GET MOVING NOW!

How to Use This Book

Volunteer organizations are a vital part of American life. Throughout our history, foreign visitors have marveled at how resourceful Americans have pulled together to create effective committees to solve their own problems. Ever since the Colonial times, Americans have used community organizations they control to get results they want.

We can call on our greatest resources—our own time, money, and intelligence—to create and maintain organizations to meet our needs. Whether our goal is support for a new widow, rehabilitation of an old building, fairer taxes, a safer workplace, original theater, or teaching children to read, it is the groups we run ourselves that get the best results. Government agencies, social workers, experts, and professionals cannot and will not do it for us. We must do it for ourselves.

This book is written for the leaders of volunteer organizations. Whether you are the president of a well-established organization or the founder of a new nonprofit group, this book will give you tested advice to do your work better. The advice comes from interviews with thousands of successful leaders. It has all been done by other citizens in community organizations. It *can* all be done by you!

The advice is divided into four sections. Part 1 explains how to start a new tax-exempt nonprofit organization. Part 2 tells how to build a self-sufficient organization with loyal members, popular programs, and reliable income. Part 3 shares tested advice on the administration of a nonprofit organization. Part 4 offers scores of books and resources to give you even more advice!

If you want to start a new organization, begin at the beginning of the book and read all the way through. If you want to improve an organization that has already been organized as a tax-exempt nonprofit corporation, begin with Part 2, "Getting Results," and read the chapters that discuss your immediate interests.

Part 1, "Getting Started," gives step-by-step advice to anyone who wants to start a new tax-exempt nonprofit organization. Even if you are now only one person with a good idea for a useful community organization, you can make that idea a reality. Learn how to make sure that your community wants this kind of organization, how to form a planning committee, choose a structure, and set up dependable funding. Find out where to get professional advice for free and how to handle all the legal work necessary to make the group into a tax-exempt nonprofit cor-poration. "Getting Started" will help the founders of a new non-profit organization make sure their group gets the best possible start.

Some chapters in Part 1 include a section called "Starting in the Middle." This is advice for the president, treasurer, or concerned board member of an organization that is already operating but has never finished all of the necessary legal work. If you think that the foundation of your organization is incomplete or incorrect, "Starting in the Middle" will tell you how to get from where you are to where you want to be.

Part 2, "Getting Results," tells leaders foolproof ways to build a better organization. In a successful volunteer organization, the decisions are made in a group and carried out in a group. But one person needs to be the motivator to get the group to decide on a plan and then to make the plan happen!

Part 3, "Getting Organized," is tested advice on managing the money and records of a volunteer organization. The secretary and the treasurer get detailed advice on their responsibilities, and the entire board gets advice on making budgets and long-range plans. You will learn how to use time lines and calendars to get control of your money and your work. "Getting Organized" is for all leaders who want to make their organizations more efficient.

Part 4, "Getting Advice," tells you where to get free publications and services from your local, state, and federal government agencies. The Bibliography describes the best publications available for community leaders. They are all good values, easy to read, and easy to use for more complete advice on what to do and how to do it.

ADAPT THE ADVICE

I have shared the tested ideas that get the best results for the most groups. Anyone who wants to see his or her group succeed can do any of this. Of course, you do not need to follow every word slavishly. You can adapt the ideas and improve upon them to get better results using your own best resources: your own leaders.

First, read this book yourself, and think about how to use the advice for the group you want to start or improve. Then share it with the other people who share your goals. Discuss what ideas you can use with the opportunities you have today. This may spark some suggestions of other organizations you know that excel at certain activities. If so, research how the other groups have already done what you want to do. Combine useful ideas from this book, advice from other experts, and your own common sense.

Thousands of community leaders know that all it takes to make a group succeed is *one* person who *wants* to do it. If you want to make your organization prosper, decide to do it, and then create a plan to make it happen. Begin with your own willpower, use your creativity to make a plan, and use your courage to put the plan into action.

You do not need any special training or education to do any of this. All you need is the courage of your convictions and the desire to make your group succeed. When I began the research for this book, I sent out a questionnaire to the leaders of five hundred successful nonprofit groups to ask their advice. I asked them to tell me the factors needed to make a group succeed. Because several of my own heroes and heroines of community organizations have very magnetic personalities, I suggested that one essential ingredient for success was charismatic leadership. Virtually every leader who answered the questionnaire crossed out the word *charismatic* and wrote in *dedicated*. Everyone said that what you need to succeed is a leader who is serious, who *wants* to do the job, and who will persist until it gets done. Personality and sparkle are less important than *desire* and *determination*.

All of this can be done by any group, whether or not it hires paid staff. If you are all volunteers, you can still do everything in the book. If you are the leaders of an older group that has paid staff but wants the board to do more, you can learn how the elected leadership on the board can run your own organization. If you *are* paid staff, give this book to the leaders and members; then challenge them to try out the advice.

The way to benefit from this book is to *use* it! Read the ideas, think about how they would apply to your organization, adapt them to fit your opportunities, and then *use* them. Study what works and what does not, make new plans, and try again. Nothing happens because of people who read; something happens because of people who read, think, plan, persuade others to join in their plan, and then *act!* Do it now!

Part I
Getting Started

1

Dos and Don'ts

To find out what makes successful community leaders, I interviewed the founders of hundreds of the best nonprofit organizations in the United States and Canada. I asked them, "What would you tell someone starting a new organization?" or "What do you wish that someone had told *you* when you were starting?" The advice they shared was remarkably consistent; they often used the very same words, such as "Do it now!"

Here is the advice from other people who have founded successful organizations. If you adapt it to your project and your people, it should save you from mistakes and accelerate your progress. Of course, you may also invent some ideas that are even better than the ones here!

The best way to get good at this is to *do* it! If you are scared, you are normal, so take this suggestion from the Citizens Information Service. They wrote it as advice on parliamentary procedure, but it holds true for anyone learning any new skill for a new organization:

"'But it scares me to think about it. I'll look foolish if I make a mistake.'

"Surely you're scared the first time. Being brave only means that you have done it before. What gets this all together is practice, practice, for both members and officers. It's like learning to drive a car; you can read a book, listen to a lecture, watch somebody else

1

drive. But you won't really know how until you get in the car, turn the key in the ignition, put your hands on the wheel, swallow hard, say a little prayer, and back out of the driveway."[1]*

DOS

1. Do it now!
2. Have fun! Plan the fun and make it happen often.
3. Start where you are right now with who you are right now. The "authorities" may tell you that someone else could start this group if he or she were as diplomatic as Benjamin Franklin, as creative as Walt Disney, as eloquent as Sojourner Truth, as energetic as Mother Jones, and as blessed as Mother Teresa. But *you?* You may be told "You're too . . . ," or "You're not . . . ," or "You're just a . . . ." (Fill in the blanks.) Ignore this "advice" and go right ahead. Be realistic about the talents you lack, but only so that you can recruit people with those talents — not to talk yourself out of trying something new.
4. Dare to be different! Try something new. If it does not work the first time, change it and try it again. Anybody can copy someone else. It takes courage to attempt a new idea.
5. Take time to think about what you are doing and why you are doing it. Writing a column for your newsletter is one good way to do this. You have to plan time to think about your work and why it matters, so you will keep feeling good about it and yourself.
6. Keep your program activities going while you organize your group. If you let yourself get wrapped up in the novelty of meeting lawyers and neglect the original purpose of the group, there will not be any members around to *be* the organization once you get the paperwork completed. Remember that any legal work is just a means to an end, so keep working on the important things, too.
7. Focus! You will find that as more people learn about your group, many of them will want to tell you what to do. Thank them for their good ideas, and start a list of "proposals for future action." Learn to say no, (or at least to say not now) nicely. If you try to be everything for everybody, you end up being nothing for anybody.
8. Ask for money from people right from the start. Sometimes founders are afraid to ask for money until they have "done"

* Superior numbers refer to the notes listed in Chapter 25.

something. But by then your members are used to getting a free ride and will say, reasonably enough, "We won the first fight without my money, didn't we? Why do I have to pay now?" If they get the organization for free, they will not respect it as much as if they pay for it. Do not insult your program by giving it away.

9. Pick a program that you can accomplish! Jonathan Kozol, founder of one of the first free schools, says, "Pick battles big enough to matter, small enough to win."

10. Trust the group process. The group will be better than you are. As you discuss your goals in the group, the meetings will build trust between the members. Hearing other people and having them listen to you will make everyone more confident about expressing opinions and discussing them until everyone is satisfied.

11. Ask for the best leaders! Go to the top! Believe you are the best, and ask the best people to join you. Also, keep the group open enough so there is always room for new people. Get the best you can, and then get better. If this includes people who are even better than you are — wonderful!

12. Set a standard of hard work. After cleaning the sinks in the new office, Ada Addington, founder of Horizon Hospice, commented, "I wouldn't ask someone *else* to do it." Never ask someone else to do something you will not do yourself. If this means asking for a big donation, cleaning up after the barbecue, or working Saturday night on the hot line, do it yourself before you ask someone else. Keep on doing the dirty work even after you are president so that everyone will see that it is important.

13. Be yourself! As Nicholas von Hoffman says, "Nothing is so reassuring as a person who acts like himself. If you don't know who you are, stay out of organizing until you do, and are willing to accept yourself as yourself. When you do, you will find that other people will."[2]

14. Keep your priorities straight! Donna Stone, founder of the National Committee for Prevention of Child Abuse, says, "Put your home first. You have to set up a human support system, people you can count on when the chips are down. You have to create it, set it up, or take it with you." Heather Booth, founder of the Midwest Academy, says, "Organize your family." You need roots to give you the courage to keep going. You have to make it happen. It will not happen by itself.

DON'TS

1. Don't wait to set up books! Jack Wuest, founder of the Alternative Schools Network, says, "You've got to anticipate, like a shortstop. Don't just let things happen. Get a structure and books right away to give you control."

2. Don't think you can do it all yourself. Never work alone. It is not effective, healthy, or fun. If you cannot find other people who want to work on this idea now, leave it until a better time. As one lady in Arkansas put it, "After you've knocked your head against the wall long enough, you realize it's *your* head." You need other people. If you do not have them, do not go on.

3. Don't be afraid to ask for help. It takes courage to admit you need help and brains to ask for it. In her autobiography, Jane Addams tells how her father consoled her as a child because her friends claimed they understood predestination, but she did not: "He said . . . that it did not matter much whether one understood foreordination or not, but that it was very important not to pretend to understand what you didn't understand and that you must be honest with yourself inside, whatever happened. . . . Mental integrity above everything else."[3]

4. Don't put your money into an office, furniture, or equipment too early. Get these things for free or do without them, but do not tie up limited resources. Mary Jean Tully, founder of the National Organization for Women (NOW) Legal Defense and Education Fund, says, "Free is easier than cheap." Her group was given a free office in Manhattan by a cosmetic company. Karl Menninger's "Villages" program found free office space in a Topeka motel. Many groups start with free offices in churches. My friend Clifford Swick says, "Buy what you don't need, and pretty soon you'll need what you can't buy."

5. Don't depend on just one source of money. Independence comes from diversity in fund raising. Never let one big grant put your fund-raising efforts to sleep.

6. Don't waste your leaders' time in somebody else's meetings. It is tempting to join coalitions and attend conferences so that you can be one of the "in" crowd and know all the gossip. But there may be no payoff for your own people. Founders have to have a one-track

mind during the first year. Always ask, "Will this build *my* organization? Will *we* get more members or better leaders?" If the answer is no, send a social member as your delegate.

7. Don't be stalled because you lack certain skills. If you have the abilities, get the skills. If you really want to see this organization become a reality, you will find someone to teach you what you need to know. Cesar Chavez tells about the nights after his first job organizing small meetings in people's homes in Oakland: "After a house meeting I would lie awake going over the whole thing, playing the tape back, trying to see why people laughed at one point, or why they were for one thing and against another. I was also learning to read and write, those late evenings. I had left school in the seventh grade after attending 67 schools, and my reading wasn't the best."[4] If you do not have the abilities, recruit someone who does.

8. Don't expect to be appreciated. Your reward is a job well done. No one ever will tell you that you did a great job on the bylaws or in setting up the bank account. Lavish praise on your co-workers, but do not get discouraged because you do not get it yourself.

9. Don't give up!

SUCCESS

I asked founders to think about the most successful organization they had ever known. What did they think contributed most to its success? The top ten answers, in order, were:

1. Clear goals.
2. The will to succeed.
3. Focus on a limited number of goals.
4. Plan and timetable to reach goals.
5. Tangible victories.
6. Exciting programs.
7. Fun.
8. Strong board of directors.
9. Dependable income.
10. Up-to-date bookkeeping.

FAILURE

I asked them to select the "factors most likely to cause the failure of an organization." The top ten killers, in order, were:

1. Unclear or contradictory goals.
2. Lack of the will to succeed.
3. Conflict of interest.
4. Boring programs.
5. No plan or timetable to reach goals.
6. Out-of-date or inaccurate bookkeeping.
7. Too little money.
8. Too many goals.
9. Lack of dedicated leaders.
10. Lack of paid staff.

2

From One Person's Idea to a Planning Committee

"I shall be telling this with a sigh
Somewhere ages and ages hence:
Two roads diverged in a wood, and I—
I took the one less traveled by,
And that has made all the difference."
— Robert Frost
The Road Not Taken

Let us say that you have a good idea for a new nonprofit organization for your community. It may be a child care center, a chamber choir, or a community organization. What matters is that you want it and you are willing to work to make it happen. You already may know other people who want to help. But even if you are only one person with a good idea, if you have faith in yourself and faith in your work, you can make this idea a reality. This book is going to share with you tested ideas other leaders have used to create successful organizations.

In the first stages of your work, you will find and involve other people in your project. This group then can find out if your community wants and needs this organization. If you are needed, you can create a planning committee to make your idea into a permanent organization.

How do you start? You probably have never had a chance to start a group before. But you probably have belonged to nonprofit groups. Some of these made a big difference in your life; a few of them just wasted your time. What can you learn from them that will help you to achieve your goal?

Think about your own experiences with other nonprofit organizations. What made the group succeed or fail? What made you personally effective and happy in the organization? What can you copy for your new group? Write down these goals. Then start the research and planning you must do to make this vision come true.

PLANNING

Now that you have decided to begin a new organization, you must think about the three Ps: partner, purpose, and plan. Write down your ideas on each of these.

A Partner

Although outstanding individuals often have created successful corporations alone, in the nonprofit world it is usually better and certainly more fun to work with a partner. Besides, looking for a partner is a good way to find out if anyone other than you is interested in your idea. The best partner is someone who has many of the skills and interests you lack.

Keep looking until you find a partner. If no one wants to help you, then consider giving up your project, at least for the time being. See if you can join another group already working on a similar project. But if you find a partner, you are ready to begin work on your purpose and plan.

A Purpose

The statement of purpose, sometimes called a mission statement, gives you a chance to say exactly what this group wants to do. The statement may also include what the group will not do. For example, the Metropolitan Milwaukee Fair Housing Council (MMFHC) states its purpose as: "The purpose of the MMFHC is to promote fair housing throughout the Milwaukee Metropolitan Area by guaranteeing all people equal access to housing opportunities and by creating and maintaining racially and economically integrated housing patterns."[1]

The Parent and Childbirth Education Society (PACES) says, "Our mission is to promote good parenting from prenatal through the preschool years through an expanding program of educational and supportive services."[2]

Keep the statement of purpose as short and simple as you can. This is the group's reason for existing. Your tactics, whether filing lawsuits or running a lending library, are means to an end and should be left out of a statement of purpose. Leave yourself room to grow and change. Your job is to write a clear, simple statement that will reflect the goals of the group and still allow healthy diversity within the group. If one person thinks "good parenting" is mothering twenty-four hours a day, and another person thinks it is affordable, quality child care for working parents, both can belong to the same organization in good faith.

The statement of purpose allows everyone, including newcomers, to share the ideals that inspired the founders. Especially if your group is growing quickly or is very busy with many activities, the people involved must sometimes be reminded of *why* you are doing this work. The statement of purpose is, educator Ralph Tyler says, "The difference between one man who says 'I'm laying bricks,' and another man who says, 'I'm building a cathedral!'"

A Plan

Create a plan for your organization the way a reporter writes a news story. Ask the basic questions: Who, what, when, where, why, and how? Then ask, how much?

WHO

This is the most important question. Who are you? You already have written down your skills and recruited a partner who has the talents you lack. Now you should engage in some frank discussions about "Why are we doing this?" What do you expect to get out of the organization for yourselves? What are you willing to give to it?

What will be the cost in time taken from family, job, and other activities?

Next, you should ask, "Who else will want to join us?" Think of other people with this interest or problem and of their friends and families. Then, ask who you want in the organization because he or she has skills you need. These people will complete your core group, which will take the first steps toward creating your organization.

Last, ask who will oppose your plan. This list might include anyone who will lose money, feel threatened, be embarrassed, or be inconvenienced by your organization. Once you have made a list of possible opponents, decide how they will affect your work. You may want to make sure that potential opponents do not know about your group until you are strong enough to withstand opposition. Or you may want to go to already existing groups and explain that you want to cooperate, not compete.

WHAT

This is your purpose. Now is the time to be specific about what your group intends to accomplish. Break your larger goals into specific tasks. Decide exactly what you intend to achieve. Use numbers and dates if you can. For example, the parents' group might say, "We will recruit and train twenty-eight people so that there will be four volunteers per day on the parent hot line beginning in September."

WHEN

This is a calendar for the next year. The future will not be exactly as you plan, but your yearlong plans will become more accurate as you gain experience. Block out all the dates you can for the next year. Write down specific activities and goals for the next month, including any meetings, conferences, or hearings you want to attend. Also write down important family dates and holidays so that you save time for your family, friends, and yourself.

WHERE

Where means where and with whom you will work for the first year. If you are starting a tenants' organization, your *where* may be one building. If you want to stop the construction of a new highway, your *where* is the proposed path of the expressway, plus the people who will have to pay for the highway. If you want to save the whales, your scope could be international.

When you start, you should decide what you can do in your own community, even if your issue is international. The people you will work with must see results, or you will have trouble keeping them. It is better to make one community garden out of the vacant lot on the corner, and get it *done,* than to plan the greening of America and end up with only plans.

WHY

This should already have been spelled out in your statement of purpose. You may think that your reasons for starting the group are self-evident, but it is still important to write the reasons down, to clarify them for yourselves, and to explain them to others.

HOW

How refers to the activities that will work best and that you like best. Of course, you may change your methods as you go along because you will get better at this part of planning with more experience.

HOW MUCH

This is an estimate of how much your organization's activities will cost. Even a simple group will have expenses for phone calls, paper, and stamps. Keep a record of all your expenses. To cover these expenses, you may decide to pass the hat at larger meetings or to charge admission to cover meeting costs. After you have chosen a structure for the organization, you can let people become members and charge dues. But in the very early stages of your group, you will have to depend on contributions from people in the community. By asking for money, you will find out how much your audience really likes the idea of the organization. You also will show that the founders are serious about getting the organization together. If you want to create an independent organization that is accountable to your community, you should take two important steps immediately. First, ask for money from the people who want and need your group. Second, find one responsible person to take charge of the organization's finances, handle the money, and prepare a written statement of income and expenses each month.

Use the planning guide at the end of this chapter to write your statement of purpose and work plan for the core group. Continue to revise and improve the plan as you get more information and better ideas. Then begin to test your plan in the community.

RESEARCH

The core group can begin to hold a series of small public meetings to discuss your idea for an organization. You may find that more and more people want to join the discussions, that they are willing to contribute money to cover expenses, and that community leaders encourage the project. Then you have to answer one more important question:

Can This Organization Be Avoided?

First, find out what other organizations exist in your area. Do this research yourselves so that you have accurate, current information. Like your own, other organizations are only the people who make them up, so you have to meet the people in charge. Make your own assessments of other groups and the work they do.

To find out who else is working in this field, one member of your group could research local projects through local newspapers, the United Way, sympathetic foundations, popular politicians, the community referral service, or the telephone book. Another person could look for similar organizations in the rest of the state. A third person could explore national projects through national media, associations, and larger foundations.

Once you learn what other organizations are operating in your community, ask yourself, "Can this organization be avoided?" There are five possible answers.

YES

The organization you want already exists. Fortunately, you can join this group. The easiest way to start an organization is to be "adopted" as a new committee by an existing group. Then you can use the facilities and systems of the existing group to ask for money, handle phone calls, or hold meetings. Later, you may find that people want to give you money, that your leaders want to continue, and that the group needs to be an independent organization. Then you can become a separate group with the blessing of the parent organization.

YES, BUT

Similar groups exist, but they are not directly competitive. Perhaps you feel that the size, style, or budget of existing groups excludes you or your constituency. After checking these groups *in person,* see if you can work with them to launch a program that will complement theirs. For example, there may be a good after-school sports program on the West Side for Spanish-speaking children, but nothing on the East Side for Chinese-speaking kids. The older group shares its expertise with you to help you get your group started.

YES AND NO

You are not satisfied with the status quo. Another organization already exists, but you believe you can do the job better. You will have trouble convincing others of this, however. They are likely to say, "The Youngstown Young-at-Hearts have served our senior citizens for twenty-seven years. Why can't you join them? How are you different?" Analyze your answer carefully. Are you starting your own group just because you cannot get along with the people in the other group?

If you are convinced that you have a better way of solving a problem or delivering a service, test the market by asking others to give you money. If people will pay, they want your group. If no one is willing to give you money, you know that they are getting what they want somewhere else. So there is no need for you to start another group.

NO

You are the only game in town. But be cautious. It may be that nothing else exists because no one else has had this idea. But it could be that no one else has implemented this idea because nobody *wants* it. The only way to find out if people want this program is to *ask* them. If they give you time, money, or their endorsement, they want it. Otherwise they do not want what you are selling. Do not waste time and energy trying to start an organization that your community does not want.

NO, BUT

Finally, you may start to sell one idea and discover that your community wants something else. In that case, decide if you want to change your plan. For example, the staff at Southwest Women Working Together found that they could get federal funding for a day-care center. They thought a day-care center would be a good program for their community. Then they went door-to-door in their neighborhood, asking women if they wanted to help plan a day-care center. They found that the women had chosen to be mothers and housewives and wanted to raise their own kids at home. They did not want a day-care center. They *did* want group activities once a week for their preschool children and training in parenting for themselves. So the group designed a once-a-week tot-lot. The tot-lot was so successful that the group started two more tot-lots on other days of the week, then helped a local church start a fourth tot-lot.

By talking to people, you will learn what your community wants. You already know what you want to do. If your purpose and plans match the needs of the community, you will have a winning combination, an organization that cannot "be avoided."

PLANNING THE PLANNING COMMITTEE

Your research probably will take at least three months. If you also are involved in other activities or if your group likes to have lengthy discussions about the research, it may take longer. Once you have proved that your community both needs and wants this group, then it is time to create a planning committee.

So far, your core group could operate as informally as it liked. It could have open discussions with anyone who showed up at meetings. But once you decide that you want to create a serious, permanent organization, the group has to give itself a more formal structure. From here on, it will be making legally binding decisions. The members of the group will be legally responsible to the state and federal governments and morally rsponsible to each other.

You will have to decide how often you want the planning committee to meet, who else to invite to join the committee, and how to divide the work. Be sure to allow yourselves plenty of time, and get all the advice you can from local people who have started other organizations.

Your work will be easier if you divide it up so that everyone knows who is responsible for doing what jobs. At a minimum, you should choose one or two people to chair the committee (a chair or co-chairs), someone to handle the money (a treasurer), and someone to take notes and write letters (a secretary). Make sure that all the people in the organization realize that the people now in these jobs will serve only as long as the planning committee is in existence, to plan the permanent organization and do the legal work. When you hold the first annual meeting of the permanent organization, the members of the organization will elect officers to speak and work for the organization. Thus the planning committee is replaced by a legal board of directors. Call the members of the planning committee *temporary treasurer, secretary of the planning committee,* and so forth, so that no one thinks they are in that job forever.

HOW TO HANDLE THE MONEY

You should already know how much money you are spending as a group. Individual committee members may have been paying some expenses out of their own pockets. Other expenses may have been reimbursed from money collected at some meetings.

As the public meetings get larger, the mailing list gets longer, and people drink more coffee, the planning committee will want to keep better track of the finances and share the financial burden of the organization with more people. Individuals should pay for their personal expenses such as carfare, but the cost of the organization should be shared by everyone who participates. By asking others to share the cost of running the group, you make new people think of the organization as "our group" rather than "their group." The planning committee may vote to ask for money at every public meeting and to ask for money from other individuals who support the group.

At first, you will have to handle money in cash. This is all right as long as you do not receive much money or pay many bills. But it is critically important to keep complete, written records. See Chapter 19, "The Job of the Treasurer," for advice on setting up books. Once you have done the necessary legal work, your board of directors can open a checking account and a permanent accounting system.

The planning committee can now begin to plan a strong, permanent organization.

THE WORK AHEAD

Giving birth to a healthy new organization is like giving birth to a healthy new baby. It will take you about nine months just to get the baby born. The experience is full of challenges you can never imagine when you start. It will cost a lot of money, certainly more than you expect. The group's development depends on more than just two people. If you succeed, the group will take on a life of its own, which will make you happy and sad at the same time. Most of all, the care and love you invested in the beginning will pay off many times over in the long run.

As you go along, you will learn a lot of new skills and new words. Remember that everything you are doing has been done successfully by other community leaders in the past. Like a parent, you will learn to do by doing. Seek advice from volunteers, lawyers, accountants, bankers, and organizers. But remember, this is *your* baby. It is worth your time and trouble to discuss each step, understand each step, and make group decisions. If you control the creation of the group, you will be able to explain it to others and reorganize it fairly and efficiently as the group grows and changes.

PLANNING GUIDE FOR A NEW ORGANIZATION

Our statement of purpose is:

Our work plan is:

    Who:
    What:
    When:
    Where:
    Why:
    How:
    How much:

Steps to getting from one person's idea to a planning committee

THE FOUNDER WILL:

1. Have a good idea for a nonprofit organization.
2. Decide to make it a reality.
3. Find a partner.
4. Write a statement of purpose.
5. Write a plan.
6. Introduce the idea at a series of small meetings.
7. Research existing community organizations to see if you can avoid starting a new group.
8. Test your idea by asking for time and money from your community. If people give you their own time and money, they want this organization.
9. Expand the core group into a planning committee, if people want the organization.

THE PLANNING COMMITTEE WILL:

1. Elect temporary officers.
2. Divide the work.
3. Adopt a system to handle money and keep written records.

3

Choosing a Structure

> ". . . an orderly life is the surest path to happiness . . ."
>
> — Alexis de Tocqueville
> *Democracy in America*

As the planning committee introduces the idea of your organization to the community, it will gradually involve more people and expand its activities. As the organization grows, you will find that you need to make more decisions and do more work. Unless you want your organization to remain a small discussion group, you will need to consider how to create a structure to get the work done in a way that is both fair and effective. Even a small group needs to decide who will make decisions and how to divide the work.

Most groups begin with an informal structure that develops naturally from meeting to meeting. The people who are the natural leaders will propose ideas, choose people to help, and begin working in loose committees. A few people who have the most time and commitment will do most of the work and make most of the decisions. As the work load expands, they will discover that they want a more formal structure for their organization in order to get more accomplished. The larger the organization and the more ambitious its goals, the more important it is for the planning committee to choose a structure for the organization.

WHY HAVE A STRUCTURE?

A structure is a means to an end. It is a planned, conscious effort to create a system so that each person can participate fully in the organization, every part of the group performs effectively, and the leadership is responsible to the people involved. A structure guarantees that the organization will be flexible enough to involve many different people, encourage each person's growth, permit a variety of activities, and still remain true to the philosophy and vision of the founders.

Structure will make the organization last. You will not have to make the same decisions over and over. The founders can choose procedures and policies based on the mission of the group, then pass them on to future leaders. A structure gives you the means to pass on the history of the organization.

Structure will promote trust. When you begin, each person may be able to do all jobs and make all decisions. But, as you grow, the amount of work you will want to do will require you to divide the work between individuals or committees. The more you divide the work into pieces, the more each piece is dependent on the others. If each person can understand the responsibilities of each person and each committee, everyone will feel more confident about his or her own role in the organization and give more to others doing other jobs.

Structure helps you grow. A volunteer organization depends on participation from many people. Citizens join because they want to do something worthwhile for their community. It is easier to recruit new members and get them involved in a meaningful way if everyone knows how the organization operates and where each member belongs in the group.

Structure creates opportunities for leaders to develop. You already have people with common sense and the courage of their convictions. By making them accountable to the people in the organization and responsible for a certain piece of work, you will enable them to develop their confidence and competence as leaders.

People want and need leadership. Any organization must have leadership to get where it wants to go. Choosing a structure that enables leaders to lead will help your organization get the results it wants.

WHAT TO CONSIDER

The planning committee can take several meetings to talk about the structure that will make this organization work best. After you decide on a structure, test it. Try the system out for three months or more. If it works well, you can write your structure down in your bylaws, a document that contains the rules for running your organization.

Every organization will have different needs, depending on who joins, who leads, and what it wants to accomplish. Here are some questions to help you choose a permanent structure for the group.

1. What is our mission? What do we want to do? What do we need to do? What should we do first?

2. Who are we? Who is in this group now? Who would we like to join the group? Who are the leaders? Whom would we like as leaders? How can we design our group so that people will want to join and leaders will get a chance to lead?

3. To whom are we accountable? What are the responsibilities of the leaders? Who chooses the leaders? How do they choose leaders? Who makes decisions? Who gives them authority to make decisions? Who can speak for the organization?

4. Who does the work? How will we divide the work? How can we share work? How can we teach new people the skills we already have?

5. How will we raise money? How can we get money from the people who need and want this program so we remain accountable to our own community?

6. Can we change? Can we make a structure that is flexible enough to change when our members, goals, or community changes?

As the planning committee decides the answers to these questions, it will be creating a first structure for the organization. But the planning will continue throughout the life of the organization. Each new group of officers will reconsider the strengths and weaknesses of the structure based on the needs of the current members and goals. Fortunately, a good structure will allow you to change your programs while keeping the original vision and the overall mission chosen by the founders.

A successful volunteer organization stands out from other organizations because of two features. First, its decisions are made by a group of leaders chosen by the people who participate in the organization. This group of leaders usually is called the board of directors. Second, the leaders are directly accountable to the people who participate in the organization. The leaders take this responsibility very seriously and work hard to be sure that their decisions are based on the wishes of the community. The most reliable way to guarantee that the leaders are accountable to the people who make up the organization is to raise money directly from those people. The most popular way to do this is through membership dues, but several other systems also will guarantee that the people involved literally own the organization. A strong board of directors and a community funding base are the foundation for a successful volunteer organization.

WHAT IS A BOARD OF DIRECTORS?

If your group is very small, all participants can make all decisions. But once it gets bigger, all of the people who participate in the organization will have to choose representatives to make decisions for the group. The leaders who are responsible for making decisions for the organization as a whole are usually called the board of directors. They also may be called the trustees, the executive committee, the steering committee, the congress, the governing board, or the council.

Boards range in size from three to sixty, but a total of eight to twelve people seems to work best. A typical board is made up of the officers who are chosen to do specific jobs (such as the president, vice-president, treasurer, and secretary) and several members who are empowered by the people in the organization to make decisions. Most boards are established to make decisions; plan programs; raise and spend money; maintain property; hire, supervise, and fire staff; speak for the organization; and lead the people involved. A board is created because the founders know from experience that a group's collective knowledge and experience is always superior to an individual's judgment. Any democratic body, from your board of directors to the Congress, is based on the principle that most of the people will make the right decision most of the time.

HOW TO GET A BOARD OF DIRECTORS

Successful leaders of successful organizations stress that you *get* the best people to serve on your board by *asking* the best people to serve on the board. Be proud of yourselves and your goals, set high standards for the board, then ask the best people to be on the first board. Aim high, and you will be pleased with the response.

Many people recommend a board made up of one-third affluent people, one-third volunteers, and one-third professionals—the three Ws: wealth, work, and wisdom. Everyone agrees that diversity makes a stronger board and more interesting meetings. You may want to set other, more specific qualifications for the people who will serve on the board. Ideally, a board member should be someone who:

1. Is committed to the mission of the organization.

2. Raises money for the organization; that is, this person asks others for money and gives according to his or her means.

3. Is recognized by the people in the organization for his or her honesty, enthusiasm, courage, and common sense.

4. Attends meetings regularly.

5. Is willing to work hard.

6. Knows about the issues, the problems, and the solutions.

7. Commits himself or herself for a complete term of office.

8. Recruits new members and helps each one find a place in the group.

9. Believes in democracy and majority rule. Enthusiastically supports the group's decisions, even when he or she is on the losing side.

10. Wants to serve on the board.

Ideally, your leaders should work their ways to the top by succeeding at committee work. If you do not have active members or committees, but still need a board (for example, if your group is a theater), you will have to choose board members based on the work these people have done for other organizations. You need doers, so look for people who get results. You can get advice for free from anyone.

WHOM DO YOU NOT WANT ON THE BOARD?

You may want to make some decisions about whom you would *not* like on the board. You may make a general rule — for example, that no one with a conflict of interest may serve on the board. Or you may want to be more specific. For example, many self-help groups prohibit professionals from serving on the board, although they are welcome to participate in other ways. You might want to exclude the following.

1. Anyone who never has and never will raise money for your group. Raising money is the acid test of leadership. If someone is serious about the organization, he or she will raise money. As the Junior League says, "The three Gs of board membership are: get, give, or get off."

2. Anyone with a conflict of interest, which means that he or she has reasons to make decisions that might not be in the best interest of the organization. If someone has a job or another volunteer commitment that would affect the way he or she would vote, do not choose that person for your board. You want people who always consider *only* what is best for your organization.

3. Anyone who is on the paid staff. No matter how much the members of the board like and respect the staff, it is not possible for someone to make decisions in the best interest of the organization if his or her livelihood will be affected by those decisions.

4. Anyone who "wants to learn more about you." Such a person can be conducting a self-serving research project for a diploma, be a skeptic who wants to see "how they really run this outfit," or, at worst, be a spy. Students want to observe and analyze, but leaders stand out because they want action. Make rules allowing members, staff, students, press, and outsiders to observe nonfinancial board meetings. But you have no reason to give them a vote.

5. Anyone you *hope* will give you a lot of money or anything else

"once he or she gets to know us." You do not have to exclude rich people. If they have given you their time and talent as well as their money, you should be eager to have them on your board. But leadership in your organization should result from past performance rather than future potential. Giving Morris Megabucks a place on your board will not necessarily make him give you money. Sometimes board membership will make him reluctant to give as much as he otherwise would out of fear of dominating the group. You get what you ask for. If you ask someone to serve on your board, you will get service; if you ask for money, you will get money. Be realistic about what you really want from Morris. Do you want his time or his money? Or both? Then ask.

Similarly, do not be in a hurry to add to the board individuals — such as press or celebrities — who are seen as having something special to offer your group. Famous people may be glad to help you now and then, but they are unlikely to do the monthly work of the group. If you want to use their names, ask them to serve on an honorary board. If you want their advice now and then, ask them to serve on an advisory board (a group of people who give you advice). If you start an advisory board, tell each member *exactly* what you want from him or her. For example, you might ask an editor to edit your annual report or ask a lawyer to help you negotiate a lease for an office. The members of the advisory board are selected on the basis of what they know, and they are asked to share their expertise when called upon. They are *not* expected to raise money or attend regular meetings. See Chapter 4 for more advice on advisory boards.

SOME SUGGESTIONS FOR YOUR BOARD OF DIRECTORS

Here are some suggestions for organizing your board that have worked well for other grass roots organizations. You may want to use some or all of these ideas.

The board is made up of the officers of the organization and others who have been chosen for the board. Each person has a specific term of office, usually one to three years. A leader may serve as a member of the board, then as an officer, and then rotate off the board. Rotating leaders off the board creates room so that new talent can move up. Because everyone knows the system rewards hard work and ingenuity, you will get more vitality, enthusiasm, and creativity out of all your members and leaders.

Co-chairs and President

The top elected officials of the organization may be called the co-chairs if there are more than one. Or you may have a president if you have only one top official. This officer leads the organization. He or she speaks for the group, chairs the board meetings, sets the pace for the board by raising money first and consistently throughout his or her term, inspires the group to reach immediate goals, and challenges the other leaders to set long-range goals.

Co-chairs work well in many ways. Having co-chairs doubles your leadership. It gives you two people to talk to the media, two people to listen to the members, and two people to raise money. In addition, sharing the work is more fun for the chairs.

Co-chairs can divide the work between themselves according to their talents. If both people are good at chairing meetings, they can divide the agenda so each chairs the parts he or she likes best. This speeds up meetings. If only one is a good chair, that person can focus on internal matters such as chairing meetings and committees, while the other focuses on external duties such as public speaking.

The advantage of having a president is that one person is clearly identified as the group's public representative and decision maker. A good president will succeed by making everyone else in the organization succeed. This is in the president's immediate self-interest (because one person can only do so much), as well as in his or her long-range self-interest (because there will be good leaders to nominate for president the following year).

Vice-President

You may want one or more vice-presidents. In some states you may legally combine the vice-president's job with another job. For example, you can make one person vice-president and treasurer. In many organizations, the vice-president serves as the president-elect. That way the vice-president has a year in which he or she can observe and plan his or her term as president, then automatically become president. The vice-president also is ready to take over if the president cannot finish his or her term.

You can create several vice-presidents to make sure that a variety of people are represented at the top level of your organization. For example, many civic organizations create vice-presidencies by professions, so that they have vice-presidents from the clergy, medicine, business, and so forth. Some large community organizations create a vice-president for each major issue in which the organization is involved. This usually guarantees that different issues and kinds of people are represented. For example, the land use vice-president may be a middle-aged farmer, the mass transit vice-president may be a young city professional, the schools vice-president may be a young suburban parent, and the senior citizens vice-president will be a senior citizen. In large cities, by creating vice-presidents who represent geographic districts, you can usually guarantee minority and ethnic representation on your board.

The Treasurer

The treasurer is in charge of finances, including tax reports. He or she must prepare an up-to-date financial report for each board meeting, chair a quarterly meeting in which the budget is compared to actual income and expenses, and prepare annual financial reports. The treasurer is *not* in charge of fund raising. Fund raising requires an aggressive salesperson, whereas the ideal treasurer is a fastidious record keeper, an unflappable diplomat, and a conservative manager. He or she should be the voice of caution in the organization. Without a doubt, the treasurer's job is the most thankless in the short run but the most important in the long run. See also Chapter 19, "The Job of the Treasurer."

The Secretary

The office of the secretary is the most flexible of the top jobs, and a creative secretary can mold the job to fit his or her style and talents. In most states, a secretary is legally required to send written notices of board meetings to the members of the board. He or she also must take accurate minutes of board meetings, send them to all board members, and preserve a signed copy for the audit and history. Many secretaries also handle most internal communication, serve as liaison with other organizations, handle correspondence, and act as historian. See also Chapter 18, "The Job of the Secretary."

Other Board Members

The board usually has other members in addition to the officers. One system is to have twelve board members elected for three-year terms on a rotating basis; that is, four people are elected each year, serving three-year terms. Elect twelve people to the first board. Then decide by lottery which four people will have one-year terms, which four will have two-year terms, and which four will have three-year terms. This way you only have to find four good people each year. It is difficult to find people who will commit themselves for three years, but those who will are serious about the organization. A three-year term also allows board members to try long-term projects and make them work.

There are many advantages to adding new blood to the board every year. Best of all, you will get a regular supply of "dumb" questions that begin, "This may be dumb, but . . . ," such as "Why are we doing this?" or "How do you know it works?" These may seem dumb to the asker, but they are enormously valuable to the other people on the board. Candid expression of confusion from the new people will force all members of the board to consider just exactly what it *is* doing!

Secondly, if you promote from within your own membership, after the first few years, you will have more and better people to choose from for the board. When you start the board, you may have to choose the twelve people who want the job out of the total group of twenty. After the first three years, you may have a total membership of four hundred, and fifty veteran committee chairs who already have proved their commitment to the organization and their ability to get results. Putting new people on the board inspires every ambitious member of the organization to work harder so he or she can get there, too!

In the same way, if you recruit board members from outside your membership, you will be able to get better board members as the founders leave and make room for new talent. An organization that has been operating for a few years has a record of accomplishment. It can appeal to more people than can a brand-new organization that has only high hopes to offer. Many of the people who have the most to give your organization will take a "wait and see" attitude during your first few years. As you work, it will become obvious that you know what you are doing, that you get results, and that you are accountable to the people in the community. Your track record becomes your best recruiting tool. As the original members rotate off the board, they can make way for people with more power, money, and followers to join the board. People who never would have joined your organization after three months may be eager to be board members after three years.

COMMUNITY FUNDING BASE

Once you have designed a board of directors to make the decisions for the group, the second step to planning a structure is to plan a dependable way to collect money from the people who will benefit from your program. This is the best way to assure that the leaders will be accountable to the community. As long as you know that the people who need and want your organization are willing to pay for it, you will know you are doing the right thing.

The most popular way to raise money from your own community is to ask people to join the organization as members and to pay dues. Dues are a set amount of money each member pays every year to belong to the group. You may have more than one category of dues—such as dues for individuals, families, students, and senior citizens—or a sliding scale setting dues according to people's incomes. Many groups also accept work in lieu of money; for example, if you work five hours a month for the organization, you may waive your dues payment if you choose.

DUES

Dues are the most popular way of raising money for volunteer organizations because they are the most effective, dependable, and democratic way to raise money. The advantages of dues for your group are:

1. Dues identify your constituency. The people who pay dues to become members are people who want your organization. Members who pay dues believe in your mission.

2. Dues validate your program. They prove that your community wants this program.

3. Dues promote growth. More people provide more money to do more work, which will attract more people.

4. Dues increase the investment and involvement of the membership. If they pay in, they stay in.

5. Dues can make the organization financially self-sufficient. They can reduce or eliminate your dependence on outside money. Grants run out and government programs shut down, but income from dues is renewable. You can plan and carry out your program every year, as long as you are pleasing your members.

6. Dues require clear, current financial accounting to the members. If I pay my dues and ask my neighbor to pay his or her dues, then I will demand a report so that I know what happened to the money.

7. Dues remind the members every year at renewal time what it costs to operate the organization, and what the members get in return.

8. Dues give you an accurate way to find your real leadership, because membership sales can be traced. Power in any organization goes to the people who bring in the most money. Especially in the beginning, it is easy to let the best talkers persuade you that they should be the leaders. But the people who sell memberships are the leaders who really care about the organization and have followers. Selling memberships gives you a chance to let the real leaders rise to the top.

9. Dues give you an accurate way to choose where to use your resources. If you need to decide which program to do, where to expand, or where to assign staff, you can always test competing programs or neighborhoods by selling memberships. If new people buy memberships when you talk about chemical wastes, but not when you talk about the sewer system, you know to allocate your

resources to the chemical waste campaign, but not to the sewer
system campaign. If the Roxbury neighborhood buys memberships,
but Somerville does not, then expand to Roxbury and leave
Somerville for later.

10. Dues are fast. You can begin to collect money as soon as you
begin the membership drive.

OTHER SOURCES OF MONEY

If your organization does not have a dues-paying membership,
you can create some other system to ask the people who benefit to
pay a set amount of money each year. Because money is the fuel for
your organization, you want to create a fund-raising system that
produces renewable money each year, rather than depend on
sources that will run out. One popular renewable money source is
pledges, which are promises to pay a certain amount of money per
time period. Many churches use a pledge system that is renewed
each year during a "stewardship campaign" that stresses the
responsibility of each member to pay his or her fair share of the
church budget. Many churches recommend the member give 10
percent of his or her income, so when the income goes up, so does
the pledge. This system works best for churches, because they offer
their members what they want most, and churches can collect at
least fifty-two times a year. It works less well for institutions that are
less vital to people's lives and meet less frequently.

Many performing arts organizations use season subscriptions as
their renewable money source. They sell the entire season in advance, so that they have money to prepare the productions and are
not as vulnerable to changes in weather or current events as they
would be if they depended on single-ticket buyers. Get Danny
Newman's lively book *Subscribe Now!* for all the "how to" from the
master of subscription sales. It is listed in Chapter 24, "Bibliography and Resources."

Many organizations use an annual fund-raising drive as a
dependable source of money. A very well-organized volunteer team
calls or writes each giver each year to ask him or her to renew and
increase the donation he or she made last year. This is copied from

big institutions like colleges and hospitals, but it can be adapted to
work for a smaller group, too.

Some groups use a combination of systems to get money from the
people who benefit from their services. For example, a preschool
may charge tuition on a sliding scale; run an annual campaign to
ask their alumni, alumni's parents, and regular supporters to give
money; put on one or two annual fund-raising benefits; and assess
the current parents to cover any deficit. If the members of the current board of the preschool know they will have to make up the difference between the budget and the fund-raising results, they will
work harder and plan better all year to raise the money the school
needs.

BYLAWS

Once the planning committee has chosen a structure, tried it out,
and decided it will work well for this group, you can write your
bylaws. The bylaws contain the "rules governing the internal affairs
of an organization."[1] The bylaws of a government are called a
constitution. Some nonprofit organizations also call their bylaws
their constitution, or they divide the rules so that part is called the
constitution and part is called the bylaws. Whatever you call them,
take time to think about them and write them down for three
reasons.

The bylaws will tell everyone in the group what the rules are and
what each person is expected to do. They will set a standard for
future officers so that they will be expected to work the way the
founders did. Finally, the federal government requires a signed
copy of your bylaws as part of your application for a tax exemption.

The bylaws also will affect how much control you personally
retain. Because you are investing time, money, and emotion in
starting this organization, you may want to guarantee certain
responsibilities for yourself or someone else. The fairest and safest
way to write bylaws is to discuss frankly each person's interests and
how to combine those interests with the committee's responsibility
to the organization as a whole. Bylaws create a fair system to define
the power of the first officers and to transfer that power in an or-

derly fashion to future officers. It is perfectly all right for you to say that you want a certain office or that you hope to see the group organized in a certain way. The bylaws will be better if each person says honestly what he or she wants for himself or herself and the entire organization.

What Goes into Bylaws?

The Citizens Information Service of Illinois publishes *The Whys, Whats, and Whos of By-Laws,* which includes the following questions you should ask yourselves when you write your bylaws.

1. What is the full, official name of the organization?
2. What is the purpose of the organization?
3. Who can become members of the organization?
4. What dues, if any, must be paid?
5. When will meetings be held, and how often?
6. How many members must be present for business to be done?
7. What officers will be necessary, how shall they be chosen, and how long shall they serve?
8. When will elections be held?
9. How shall committees be chosen?
10. What are the duties of the officers?
11. How can the bylaws be changed?

This booklet is available in both English and Spanish and includes information on how to write, adopt, and amend bylaws. For ordering information, see the list of recommended reading at the end of this chapter.

How to Get Sample Bylaws

Ask similar nonprofit organizations for a copy of their bylaws. If you are part of or want to be part of a national association, the national office may be able to provide sample bylaws. You also will find sample bylaws in the appendixes of books listed at the end of this chapter.

Legal Requirements

The sample bylaws suggest provisions you might like to include in your bylaws. State law tells you what you *must* include in your bylaws. Ask the secretary of state's office for a copy of the laws governing nonprofit corporations. This free booklet will tell you what must be included in the bylaws of any nonprofit corporation in your state. For example, the law may require a minimum number of directors and specify the duties of the officers.

Make a list of the legal requirements for your bylaws; then decide how you want to meet those requirements. Discuss what else you would like to include in your bylaws. Think about how you want the group to operate and then how to make that happen.

Making It Final

As you discuss what you want, write the points down. Try to keep them as short and simple as possible. Chris Nugent of the Citizens Schools Committee said, "We tried to think of how we would like the organization to be run if everyone on the board dropped dead today. We wanted to leave just the important structure — for example, how to elect officers — and leave out everything that could be changed, such as, 'The president will chair such-and-such committee.' "

Now ask a lawyer to review what you have done to make sure that the language meets the current federal, state, and local laws. Include a way to amend the bylaws as necessary. Good bylaws will stand the test of time, but also may be improved by amendments.

After everything is down on paper, send copies to everyone on the planning committee. After final changes, the planning committee can vote to approve or ratify the bylaws. This takes place at the first official business meeting, as explained in Chapter 8.

STANDING RULES

Many organizations write both bylaws and standing rules. The bylaws are the permanent rules of the organization. They remain the same regardless of who holds office or what the programs are. The standing rules are written, public rules stating how the people who are in the organization today want to do business. They can be changed according to the needs and wishes of the current members. Usually, standing rules cover such details as date, time, and place of committee and board meetings.

Standing rules are easy to change whenever the people change. For example, you may have a standing rule that the president and treasurer sign checks. But at the annual meeting, the group elects a treasurer who is not always in town to sign checks. The board can change the standing rule so that the president and the treasurer or secretary sign the checks. This way, you do not have to revise the bylaws every election.

STARTING IN THE MIDDLE

What if you are a new member of an old board, or a new officer of an organization that has been around for a while? You believe that the group could be improved by changing the structure. How do you rewrite the bylaws?

First, you have to find them. If the bylaws are not in the files, ask former officers or the group's lawyer if they know of any bylaws. If the organization has ever applied for a federal tax exemption, the application should have included a copy of the bylaws. The nineteen Internal Revenue Service (IRS) Key District Offices keep copies of all applications. Call the IRS, listed in most telephone directories, or call the IRS toll-free number for your state listed in Chapter 23. They will direct you to the correct Key District Office. Ask them to send you a copy of the by-laws the group filed with its application for tax-exemption.

The IRS Key District Office is the only government agency that should have a copy of the organization's bylaws. Even if the group has not applied for federal tax exemption, it may have applied to incorporate in the state as a nonprofit corporation. If the organization has been incorporated, ask the secretary of state or your county recorder of deeds for a copy of the Articles of Incorporation, the document filed by the founders when the organization incorporated. This will give you the names and addresses of the first board of directors. Try writing to these people. Ask if they remember writing any bylaws and if they know where you can get a copy of them.

If the group was never incorporated, it may still have bylaws, a constitution, or some other set of rules by which it operates. Ask your predecessors if they remember bylaws. The secretary or the lawyer would be most likely to have a copy.

If you cannot find a copy of the bylaws or other rules, and you cannot find anyone who remembers writing any, use the process discussed earlier to create them.

If you can find a copy of the bylaws, circulate copies to all of the officers. They should include a section on how to revise or amend the bylaws. If they do not, use whatever system you ordinarily use to make decisions. Try to find someone who served on the original committee to explain why the original bylaws were written the way they were. Decide what you want to keep and what you want to change. Sometimes the original bylaws may be so out-of-date that it would be easier and faster to write a new set. In this case, use the process described earlier.

In any case, when you are writing or rewriting bylaws for an existing organization, you will know what does *not* work. That tells you what to change. Many groups have more than one set of bylaws in their lifetimes. A group will try out one system, outgrow the system, change its constituency or goals, find better examples, and write new bylaws.

Caution

Give the system a chance before you tamper with it. Although it may be new to you or not the same as your last organization's, it may work well for this group of people at this time doing this work. Try to be creative with what you already have before you change it. If most of the officers prefer the current system, learn to live with it, because you do not want to lose your best leaders along with the old system.

To use the timeless eloquence of repairmen, "If it ain't broke, don't fix it."

SAMPLE BYLAWS

The following include sample bylaws from a variety of organizations:

Arts Administration. Tem Horwitz. Chicago Review Press, 215 W. Ohio St., Chicago, IL 60610. $7.95. See Appendix 4, "By-laws of Arts Group, Incorporated." These are designed for a performing arts group with a board of sixteen elected by themselves. There are no members.

The Bucks Start Here. Kathleen M. Fojtik. The Domestic Violence Project, Inc., 1917 Washtenaw Ave., Ann Arbor, MI 48104. $6. See Appendix A, "Constitution and By-Laws of the NOW Domestic Violence Project and Spouse Assault Fund, Inc.," designed for a social service agency with a board of nine elected by a dues-paying membership.

How To Start A Rape Crisis Center. Rape Crisis Center of Washington, DC, P.O. Box 21005, Washington, DC 20009. $4. See Appendix 2, "By-laws," designed for a rape crisis center with a board of trustees of fifteen elected by the members. Members are "volunteers who have completed training, contributed consistently to the activities of the Center for at least six months, initiate and participate in special projects of the Center, and attend General Monthly Meetings on a regular basis. . . . Members are not required to pay dues."

Whys, Whats and Whos of By-laws. Q-9. Citizens Information Service of Illinois, 67 E. Madison St., Chicago, IL 60603. 40¢. Includes sample bylaws and sample standing rules for a local community council with an executive committee of four elected by the dues-paying membership. En Español: F-20. *Hablando De Estatutos.* 40¢.

Working By-Laws for a Consumers' Cooperative. NASCO, Box 7293, Ann Arbor, MI 48107. $1. Copy of bylaws for a large, multiservice cooperative with a board of twelve elected by the dues-paying members.

STEPS TO DEVELOPING A STRUCTURE

THE PLANNING COMMITTEE WILL:

1. Decide it wants a structure to enable the people involved in the organization to work together in a way that is fair and effective.
2. Consider the mission, goals, people, funding, decisions, and accountability.
3. Plan a tentative structure. Try it out. Make improvements until you develop a structure that everyone likes.
4. Develop an effective board of directors.
5. Develop a dependable funding base from the community.
6. Collect sample bylaws.
7. Ask for advice from an experienced lawyer and founders of other community organizations.
8. Write, review, and revise the bylaws.
9. Ratify the bylaws at the first annual meeting. See Chapter 8 for more advice.

4

How to Find Professionals to Help You for Free

"I get by with a little help from my friends."
—John Lennon and Paul McCartney

Once you have designed your board and written rules for the organization, you can work on the legal papers necessary to become a corporation and get a tax exemption. Before you take this step, however, you should recruit some experienced professionals to give you advice. Legally you can do all of this work yourself, even if you are not a lawyer or accountant. But you will be safer if you find a good lawyer and a good accountant to help you. This chapter includes some general advice on how to find professionals, how to get them to help you, and how to work with them so they will want to go on helping you.

WHO THEY ARE

Professionals are workers with special skills, education, and experience who excel at a certain job. Some professionals, such as lawyers and accountants, charge high hourly rates for their services. Others, such as travel agents and insurance agents, are paid a commission on what you buy. Professionals such as bankers, secretaries,

38

and organizers are paid a regular salary. Others, such as writers and artists, may work on a free-lance basis and are paid by the job. Some experts, volunteers, may not be paid at all. All of them may not think of themselves as professionals, but they are included in this section because they know things that you will want to learn. How can you find and work with all the professionals who have skills the organization needs?

HOW TO FIND PROFESSIONALS

First, poll the members of your board and committees to find out what talents and experience they already have. Second, ask them whom they know who would help the group. Third, ask other non-profit organizations whom they recommend. Fourth, ask your key advisors whom they recommend. Only a handful of people in each profession have both the skills and the inclination to help nonprofit organizations, so they often run into each other. Lawyers, accountants, bankers, and insurance agents have business reasons to know each other, so if you can find one, he or she often can recommend the others.

You also can ask clergy, politicians, your own neighborhood association, local colleges, or the community hot line. Last, try the person who does this work for your employer or a referral service run by the local professional association. These are last resorts because they probably will direct you to someone who has worked only with paying customers and who may lack the ability or desire to help a group with little or no money.

How do you get a professional to help you? Ask! You get what you ask for, so discuss exactly what you want in your planning committee. Get someone who has experience working with nonprofit organizations. Guarantee this by asking for referrals from other nonprofit groups. You may have to be very specific.

If you want to give your business to an auditor who is black or female, say so. If you need a lawyer who speaks Polish or specializes in immigration law, say that. If you want an insurance agent who lives in your community, say it. You may learn that no one in your community fills your bill. But if you do not say what you want, you will not get what you want.

WHY YOU NEED PROFESSIONALS

In building a successful organization, there are things you *want* to do and things you *have* to do. Professionals will help you do a better job with both. They can be teachers or workers.

If, for example, you want to publish an excellent newsletter, you need professionals as teachers. You want the help of a photographer, a graphic artist, an editor, an advertising salesperson, a circulation director, and someone who understands bulk mailing. Ideally, these people should volunteer for a limited time to train your volunteers. Each expert should work on the first few issues with someone from the organization serving as an apprentice. Then for a few issues, your members should work with the professional available to answer questions and give advice. This works well because the professionals have an incentive to teach well: when they succeed they are *through*.

Professionals can also do the work that you are legally required to do, but are unable to do yourself because you lack experience, education, or a state license. For example, an experienced lawyer should review your application for a tax exemption from the IRS. A good certified public accountant (CPA) is required to fill out government tax reports. In some states, you may be required to have your books audited by an auditor licensed by your state.

HOW TO WORK WITH THEM

The first rule to follow in working with professionals is to make their job easy. Large law firms and accounting firms bill paying customers from $25 to $150 an hour. When lawyers and accountants give you their time, you should show some appreciation of what this time is worth.

An architect, advertising copywriter, doctor, business executive, or any other professional who helps you also should be treated with respect. Consider a time donation by a professional just as you would a financial donation. You want this to be the first of many donations, so you want to work hard to develop a good, long-term relationship. Do your share of the work. Before a meeting, read all the material, decide what to ask, write down questions, and collect all the papers you need. Be on time to the meeting, get right to the point, write down all of the answers, and ask if you left anything out. Always ask about anything you do not understand.

Each professional uses special words that become a normal part of his or her conversation. After a while, he or she forgets that not everyone understands these words. So you have to *tell* a professional when something is not clear to you. Keep asking him or her to explain until you are sure you understand.

After the meeting, write down what you learned and send a copy with a thank-you note the same day. Ask the professional to check that you understood his or her advice. Be sure he or she gets your newsletter, press releases, and research so that he or she is kept up to date on your activities. Invite him or her to open meetings, conventions, and special events. As he or she learns the importance of your work and gets to know your members, he or she will be proud to donate time to your group.

WHAT TO DO WITH THEM

Before a professional agrees to help you, decide what your relationship will be. You have a number of choices, depending on the makeup of your group, the interest of the professional, and the job you need done.

1. Put the professional on the board. If your board is made up of a variety of community people, you may want to put professionals on your board so that they are directly involved in making decisions. You can do this if the professionals truly are interested in your program and want to serve the group without pay.

You cannot put a professional on the board if he or she is supposed to work for the board as a whole, as does your lawyer. Also, some professionals such as newspaper reporters and auditors may wish to retain their independence from your organization. You particularly cannot put a professional on the board if he or she will make money from his or her work with you. This rule might apply, for example, to an insurance agent or a contractor. Smart groups that want to stay in business state in their bylaws that a member of the board may not make money from the group.

2. Create an advisory board. An advisory board is a group of peo-

ple who give you advice. They are recruited because they are good at what they do, care about your work, and want to help you. But they are not voting members of the legal board.

Members of the typical advisory board may do business with the group. They are not involved in the day-to-day work, so they can give better advice; they do not have to do as much work as the members of the board of directors. Many groups plan for twice as many members on the advisory board as on the board of directors. So, if the board of directors has twelve members, the advisory board could include up to twenty-four members. Advisors could include a lawyer, a certified public accountant, a banker, an insurance agent, a travel agent, a business executive, a lobbyist, a state representative, a minister, a social worker, a secretary, a doctor, a fund raiser, a graphic artist, and experienced leaders of other successful community groups.

The advisory board may meet on its own as a group, or it may serve as a talent bank "on call" to meet specific needs of the officers. You will find it easier to recruit top people if their terms of office are limited to two or three years.

3. If you need only a few professionals, consider making them consultants. Give each one a specific job and title. The lawyer can serve as special counsel to the board, the writer can service as editorial consultant to the publicity committee, and the secretary can serve as administrative consultant to the secretary.

4. Hire the professionals. Simply plan your budget so you can buy the skills you want. Paying someone gives you more control over the quality of the work and the ability to get it done on time.

LAWYERS

Although it is not a legal requirement, it is well worth it to get an experienced lawyer to review your applications for nonprofit incorporation and federal tax exemption. A lawyer who has done this work before will be familiar with the language, forms, and procedures of the government agencies. He or she will know the latest court and IRS decisions that affect your work.

The lawyer's job is to help the founders do all the legal work properly and to make sure that your decisions are stated in words that have legal meaning for the courts and government. It is *not* the job of the lawyer to make your decisions for you. If the board does most of the work itself, you will have the satisfaction of mastering a new skill, you can explain the legal structure to newcomers, and you can make any changes needed in the future.

How to Find a Good Volunteer Lawyer

Ask for one. Specify that you need a volunteer lawyer with experience in getting nonprofit incorporation and federal tax exemption for new groups. You must say clearly at the beginning that you need a *volunteer* lawyer for your nonprofit organization. In legal jargon you need a *pro bono* lawyer. This is short for *pro bono publico*, which literally means "for the good of the public" and commonly means "works for free."

More than three hundred city and state bar associations run lawyer referral services to direct customers to lawyers who pay the bar an annual fee to get referrals. The service is usually advertised in the Yellow Pages under "Attorneys" or "Lawyers." Tell the referral service about your members and work. Ninety-five of the lawyer referral services have special no-fee or low-fee panels. Some services offer special programs for people who are deaf, homebound, prison inmates, juveniles, military personnel, rural dwellers, senior citizens, or students. Others provide special panels to work on problems involving immigration laws, legal-fee disputes, malpractice problems, and mental health or commitment.

You may find that the referral service has no lawyer on its list who will work for free. Then you must look elsewhere. Some cities have alternative bar associations such as the Chicago Council of Lawyers, which is "primarily concerned with justice and the advancement of the law—not the advancement of lawyers." This organization publishes a directory listing legal-service centers in the county by geographic area and by specialty—such as class action, domestic violence, or food law. Some lawyers' organizations are designed to help a specific population. For example, sixteen cities have groups such as the Bay Area Lawyers for the Arts, which helps artists. Seven cities have groups such as the Boston Lawyers Committee for Civil Rights Under Law that are able to help incorporate and get tax exemptions for groups composed of poor people, minorities, or women. If your group is composed entirely of poor people, the legal-aid office or the Legal Assistance Foundation may be able to help.

Once your group is incorporated and tax-exempt, do you still need a lawyer? Yes. In fact, some people say that you need a lawyer even more once you finish the organizational work. Tem Horwitz, director of Lawyers for the Creative Arts, says, "Your lawyer is most valuable to you for ongoing legal functions. For example, he or she can help you with leases, contracts, taxes, collecting bad debts, and negotiating with employees, unions, or landlords. Because your lawyer is not involved in your day-to-day business, she or he can be more objective about your needs and more aggressive negotiating on your behalf."

ACCOUNTANTS

Accounting is like housekeeping: no one notices if you do it right, but it will cause trouble if you do it wrong and can lead to disaster if you do not do it at all. In order to make sure that the accounting is done and done right, recruit an accountant to help you design a good system right at the start!

What Is a Certified Public Accountant?

A CPA is an accountant who is licensed by your state. CPAs consider themselves the professionals of their business. The requirements for becoming a CPA are different in each state, but a CPA usually has to complete a certain amount of schooling, pass a test given by the state, and spend a certain amount of time working for a CPA.

Some people are called *accountants,* and some states have *public accountants.* They have similar education and work backgrounds, but they have not passed the state CPA test. If you are referred to them by a successful nonprofit organization, they may be able to help you with your year-round accounting. But most states require that you hire a CPA to do an audit.

Role of the CPA

Ideally, you will find a CPA who cares about your work, is part of your constituency, and is willing to give his or her time to serve as your treasurer. If you can do this, you can combine the jobs of treasurer and volunteer CPA.

You may not be able to find such a person. In this case, elect as treasurer one of your own people who is willing to learn the job. Then recruit a CPA who is sympathetic to your work, respects your people, and is willing to give his or her time. This person can serve as assistant treasurer, special advisor to the treasurer, or as a member of the advisory board.

How to Work with a CPA

If none of your members is a CPA, how should your officers work with a CPA who has volunteered to help you?

Like your lawyer, the CPA can help you with the things you want to do and with the things you need to do. Obviously, you first want to have enough money to run your program. The CPA can teach you how to prepare a budget, which is a plan for how the money will be spent. The CPA can teach you how to write monthly and quarterly reports for committees and the board, so that leaders know if they are working within their financial plan.

In the beginning the CPA can help you set up your bank accounts, books, and financial records. Later, he or she can advise the board on taxes, personnel policies, investments, loans, contracts, mortgages, and long-range financial planning.

THINGS YOU NEED TO DO

Your CPA can help you do what you legally must do in order to run an effective nonprofit organization. Missing or avoiding important deadlines will make it hard to plan, and will cost you money in fines. Learn to do things right the first time.

If you hire and pay staff, you will have to meet deadines for paying taxes to the state and federal government. This becomes routine once you get the system set up, but the CPA will make sure you set up the system. Best of all, the CPA can give you all the reasons why your payroll taxes must be paid *in full, on time, every time* by recounting the grisly stories of now-extinct organizations that did not do this.

The last thing the volunteer CPA can help you with is your audit, which is an inspection of your books by an independent accountant. Consider it a cost of doing business, and plan it into your budget and annual work plan. Some states require audits for some nonprofit organizations, some funding sources require audits before they give you money, and some national organizations require audits of their local affiliates. Your volunteer CPA can help you set up your books and records so that the audit will be relatively easy, fast, and less expensive.

Ethically, a CPA may not audit his or her own work, nor the work of another person who works for the same accounting firm. But the volunteer CPA can help you hire an independent CPA and help you plan the work necessary before, during, and after the audit. See Chapter 21 for more information on the value of an annual audit.

How to Find a CPA

Try to find a CPA who already does volunteer work for a successful nonprofit organization. Although a CPA is unlikely to be able to volunteer to work for more than one group, he or she may be able to refer you to another CPA who would be interested in helping your group. Your banker, lawyer, or insurance agent may be able to refer you to an experienced CPA. Ask all the members of your board, too. Some accountants' professional associations may be able to help you. Ask a CPA or look in the phone book. A professional association is likely to be listed under the name of your city or state, as in "Kentucky Society of Certified Public Accountants." Some professional associations have "nonprofit committees" that can help you. Some cities also have accountants and firms that specialize in nonprofit work, such as the Accounting Aid Society of Detroit. Ask local nonprofit groups for referrals and recommendations.

OTHER PROFESSIONALS

Many professionals can help you throughout the year. It is well worth your time to look for people who will care about your organization and your goals. You are giving them an opportunity to use their talents and education to build an organization that will accomplish important work in your community. Be bold! Ask for introductions to the best professionals in your town, and ask them to donate their time and talent to your group.

The Banker

A good banker can help you in many ways. It is his or her job to know about money and to know other people in town who know about money. A banker can help you with all of your banking and give advice on investments, taxes, loans, mortgages, and contracts. Once you have proved that you will be around for the long run, a banker can help you set up your "planned giving," a way people can leave you money in wills and trusts.

The Insurance Agent

A good insurance agent can help you get the insurance you need. He or she can advise you on the best package of insurance to cover the board and the volunteers now and can sell you more insurance if you open an office or hire staff in the future. Some small nonprofit groups now benefit from participating in local or national insurance pools, and some large nonprofit groups have chosen to become self-insured. Ask local nonprofit organizations to recommend good insurance agents.

The Business Executive

A business executive is usually someone who can sell and convince other people to sell. He or she knows how to help an organization get results. Executives like to see growth in their company, in their profits, and in their coworkers.

You want to learn and copy these talents so that your group will thrive. In the beginning, the planning committee may have grand but *vague* plans. When you are ready to stop talking and start doing, an experienced businessperson can teach you how to convert your goals into measurable results. A vague goal would be "We really ought to educate the community about our issue pretty soon." A specific plan says, "Over the next six months, we will create a speakers' bureau to train four teams of speakers and book them at the top thirty colleges, civic organizations, and churches."

The Secretary

If you do not hire a secretary, you should immediately recruit an experienced secretary to help you. He or she can help you design your files so that anyone can easily retrieve anything that could be needed. Even if your files are now in two cardboard boxes in the president's basement, you should set them up to be useful. A secretary also can help you find a way to save and retrieve the names, addresses, phone numbers, jobs, and volunteer commitments of people interested in your organization.

The Veteran Volunteer

With luck, several members of your board have served on the boards of other successful volunteer organizations. However, you may be starting a group whose members by definition do not have that experience—for example, teenagers, ex-offenders, or recent immigrants. In that case, ask someone you trust, such as your rabbi or pastor, to introduce you to someone who has served effectively as an officer of a local nonprofit group. Ask the veteran volunteer to meet your officers and share ideas on meetings, committees, and programs. Also ask this volunteer to introduce your officers to officers of other successful groups.

GOOD PARTNERS

Finding and working with committed professionals will be rewarding for you and the professionals. You will gain the expertise and talents you need to reach your goals. The professional will gain the satisfaction of using his or her training and experience to help an exciting and innovative project. Best of all, the community will gain a more competent and more effective organization.

STEPS TO FINDING AND WORKING WITH PROFESSIONALS

THE PLANNING COMMITTEE WILL:

1. Decide whom you want.
2. Ask other nonprofit groups for recommendations of experienced professionals.
3. Decide how the professionals will fit into the structure of your organization.
4. Ask the best professionals to help you for two years.
5. Make the professionals' jobs easy. Do your homework, be punctual, take notes, and ask questions until you understand.
6. Send a personal thank-you note immediately after every meeting!
7. Put the professionals on your mailing list, and invite them to all special events and meetings.

5

Should Your Group Become a Tax-Exempt Nonprofit Corporation?

"Hope is the magic ingredient in motivating yourself and others."
— Napleon Hill and W. Clement Stone
Success through a Positive Mental Attitude

As your planning committee defines the purpose of the organization and sets its goals, you soon will have to consider creating a legal framework for the group — that is, you may want to incorporate. If you are only a small group of individuals, each of whom pays his or her own expenses, and you have no desire to grow, you probably do not need to incorporate. However, once you plan an ambitious program that will require handling large amounts of money and involve large numbers of people, you will benefit from doing the work necessary to convert the planning committee into a tax-exempt nonprofit corporation.

This will require several steps that are outlined here in a chart and explained in detail in the next chapters. Carefully consider each step, particularly how much it will cost and how long it will take. Also consider the alternatives, especially the possibility of becoming a for-profit corporation. Some organizations, such as theaters or counseling services, can choose to be either for-profit or nonprofit, depending on the goals of the founders. But for most volunteer community organizations, becoming a tax-exempt nonprofit corporation is best.

WHY INCORPORATE?

First you must become a corporation in your state. Legally, a corporation has a life and identity of its own separate from the humans who make it up. It is a legal "entity," or "something that exists independently." Thus the corporation, as a legal entity, becomes legally responsible for the business your organization conducts. In addition, future leaders of the corporation are legally required to obey the bylaws. If you incorporate, the group's name is protected. No one else can use the corporation's name to capitalize on your successes.

From the business standpoint, as a corporation your organization will be organized as are most other businesses in your community. When you work with these businesses or their employees, the organization will seem more serious and permanent to them.

Organizationally, incorporating gives you a chance to think about the organization as an entity with a life of its own. Although this can be painful, like having your children grow up and begin lives of their own, it should also be satisfying. Incorporating gives the founders a chance to discuss what they want the organization to become and also to recognize that they will not control the organization forever. With this important groundwork laid, the early leaders and staff of your organization will be able to move on without having to fear that the organization will change drastically if they leave.

Being a nonprofit (also called "not-for-profit") corporation does *not* mean that you must lose money or break even every year. You can bring in more money than you spend, as long as you do not treat this extra money as profits and use it for the benefit of the individuals who started the corporation. Any money left over after the bills are paid must be invested in the present or future work of the organization.

WHY BECOME TAX-EXEMPT?

The tax exemption means that the corporation does not have to pay corporate income taxes to the federal government. In order to get a tax exemption, you have to tell the Internal Revenue Service (IRS) that your organization will serve a purpose that the IRS considers qualified for tax exemption. You must limit the amount of money you spend on lobbying (any activities intended to influence politicians). If the corporation goes out of business, all of its assets must be given to another tax-exempt organization.

The financial benefit of tax exemption is that wealthy individuals and foundations are more likely to give you money. If you qualify, donors may deduct their donation from the income on which they pay taxes. Foundations may give you grants without endangering their own not-for-profit tax status. U.S. tax laws benefit individuals and foundations that give money to tax-exempt nonprofit organizations. As the IRS says, "Our Federal Government recognizes that donations to religious, educational, charitable, scientific, and literary organizations have contributed significantly to the welfare of our nation; and the tax laws are designed to encourage such giving."[1]

Organizationally, deciding whether to seek a tax-exemption will force you to discuss how much lobbying you want to do and in what ways. Of course, this decision can change every year.

Steps to Become a Tax-Exempt Nonprofit Corporation

Table 5-1 shows you each step to take to transform your committee into a tax-exempt nonprofit corporation. Each step is described in detail in the chapter listed after that action. Fortunately, the organization will receive many benefits from each step in the process, both legally, in terms of your relationships with outsiders, and organizationally, in terms of the advantages for the organization itself. Use this Table and Table 5-2 to help the planning committee schedule its work for the first year.

TABLE 5-1
Steps to Become a Tax-Exempt Nonprofit Corporation

Action	Legal Benefits	Organizing Benefits
Choose a structure and plan a board. Chapter 3	Step toward getting state nonprofit incorporation.	Makes you discuss who you want to lead the group and how you want them to work with members, committees, and staff.
Write bylaws. Chapter 3	Step toward federal 501(c)(3) income tax exemption.	Makes you decide on rules to make the group work best.
Recruit volunteer professionals. Chapter 4		Gives you experienced advice.
Obtain federal identification number from the IRS. File Form SS-4. Chapter 6	Gives the government a number, similar to an individual's Social Security number, for all records from your group. Needed for forms to open a corporate checking account in a bank. Needed for federal 501(c)(3) income tax exemption. Needed for all federal, state, and local tax forms.	

TABLE 5-1 (Continued)
Steps to Become a Tax-Exempt Nonprofit Corporation

Action	Legal Benefits	Organizing Benefits
Hold first annual meeting. Chapter 8	Step toward state nonprofit incorporation and federal 501 (c)(3) income tax exemption.	Enables you to ratify bylaws, elect officers and a board, approve Articles of Incorporation, choose a bank, and collect money to put in the bank to open the organization's checking account.
Become a nonprofit corporation in the state. File Articles of Incorporation with secretary of state. Chapter 7	Legally makes you a nonprofit corporation in your state. Step toward getting federal 501(c)(3) income tax exemption. Step toward exemption from other federal, state, and local taxes. Step toward getting a nonprofit mailing permit.	Makes you decide your name, address, board, registered agent, and purpose. Future officers are legally bound to operate the group according to the bylaws and purposes. Limits liability of the group to assets of the corporation. Guarantees that no one else has your name now, and that no one else can use it in the future. May qualify you to get free banking services and other benefits.
File state certificate of incorporation with county recorder of deeds. Chapter 7	Records legal existence of new nonprofit corporation in county.	

TABLE 5–1 (Continued)
Steps to Become a Tax-Exempt Nonprofit Corporation

Action	Legal Benefits	Organizing Benefits
Open a corporate checking account. Chapter 19		Takes the organization's money out of the treasurer's home or private bank account. Is a businesslike way to pay bills. Produces a written record of all payments and deposits. Banker can give you advice on money and how to use it.
Open a savings account or investment plan. Chapter 19		Earns interest on money that you do not immediately need.
Obtain federal 501 (c)(3) income tax exemption from the IRS. File Form 1023. Chapter 7	Makes you legally exempt from corporate income taxes, although an annual tax report is still required. Makes you a legal "charity" so that people who give you money or items of value deduct the amount allowed by law from the income on which they pay taxes.	Makes you decide how much lobbying the group will do, the purpose of the group, what to do with profits, and what will happen to assets if the group goes out of business. This information also must be supplied as part of the "purpose" part of your application for incorporation in your state.

TABLE 5–1 (Continued)
Steps to Become a Tax-Exempt Nonprofit Corporation

Action	Legal Benefits	Organizing Benefits
	Makes you a legal "charity" so that foundations may give you money without endangering their tax-exempt status.	Gives you a good opportunity to discuss your strategies for getting people to make donations to you.
	May qualify you for exemption from other state and local taxes.	Gives you a chance to discuss what will occur if this group does not last.
	Step toward getting a nonprofit bulk rate mailing permit. (3.5¢ rather than 18¢ per piece in 1981.)	Requires an annual report that will force you to bring your financial records up-to-date every year.
OPTIONAL: Elect to make expenditures to influence legislation. File IRS Form 5768. Chapter 9	The IRS must measure the amount of lobbying you do based on percentages of dollars spent.	Makes you plan how much of your budget to spend on lobbying. Requires an annual report of dollar amounts spent on direct lobbying. Gives you accurate numbers to compare from year to year to help you plan.
Register as a charity with state regulatory agencies. Chapter 21	Makes you a legally registered charity in your state. Is supposed to protect the citizens of your state from fraudulent charities.	May require an annual report that will force you to update your records once a year. May also require an audit, which gives you the benefit of having an independent expert look at your records.

TABLE 5–2
Sample Costs and Time to Become a Tax-Exempt
Nonprofit Corporation (Cook County, Illinois)

Applications	Cost (1981)		Quoted Government Time
Order and receive forms and instructions from State and Federal agencies.	Phone calls or postage	.36	2 weeks
Articles of Incorporation (File with secretary of state, Illinois).	Filing fee Notary fee Postage	$50.00 .50 .18	1 week
Certificate of incorporation (Send to recorder of deeds, Cook County).	Recording fee Postage	11.00 .35	3 weeks
Federal identification number (File with IRS, Form SS-4).	Filing fee Postage	0 0.18	6 weeks
Federal 501(c)(3) income tax exemption (File with IRS, Form 1023).	Filing fee Notary fee Postage	0 .50 1.37	8 weeks
Decision to make expenditures to influence legislation (File with IRS, Form 5768).	Filing fee Postage	0 .18	6 weeks
Charitable organization registration and financial exemption questionnaire. (File with attorney general, Illinois).	Registration Notary fee Postage	0 .50 .69	2 weeks
	TOTAL:	$65.81	7 months

WHAT DOES IT COST AND
HOW LONG WILL IT TAKE TO BECOME
A TAX-EXEMPT NONPROFIT CORPORATION?

Becoming a tax-exempt nonprofit corporation will probably take less money but more time than you think it will take. Here is a chart that uses Cook County and Illinois figures to give you an idea of the time and money involved.

Remember that each state sets fees and requirements for becoming a corporation. The costs vary from one dollar to incorporate plus five dollars to record in Ormsby County, Nevada, to fifty dollars to incorporate plus eleven dollars to record in Cook County, Illinois. The state forms are all relatively simple to fill out.

The chart lists how long governmental agencies *say* that it will take them to process your application if it is perfect. If they have questions, these agencies may take longer to process your application.

Expect to spend a total of about nine months finishing the paperwork. You will finish sooner if you can get help from someone who has recently incorporated another tax-exempt nonprofit corporation.

WHAT ARE THE ALTERNATIVES?

This book is written to help your new community organization become a tax-exempt nonprofit corporation. But that is by no means the only form that your group can choose. There are other options that you should research further if you think that any would be better for you. They include the following.

1. Do not organize. Remain an informal discussion group and have each participant pay his or her own expenses. Because you are not asking for anyone else's money, you do not need a tax exemption; because you do not work with the public, you do not need a formal structure. The advantage is that you have to do very little paperwork and planning. The disadvantage is that you are frozen at the very small size and informal style you have right now.

2. Be adopted by an older group. Rather than do all this legal

work, find an established group that will let you be a subcommittee, task force, field office, or new project. Then you can focus on your program rather than on legal structures and applications. You can always decide to become a separate group at a later time.

3. Choose to become another type of nonprofit organization. There are two other common forms of organization that will make your group a legal entity. These also may apply for federal tax exemption.

The first is to become an *unincorporated association*. This is usually formed by filing the name of your group with the county clerk. The advantage is that no one else can do business under your name. The disadvantage is that the individual members of the group are still legally liable for the business of the group. Check with your county clerk for the application and how to proceed. In Cook County in 1980, the time required was about five weeks and the cost was about fifty dollars.

The second is to become a *cooperative corporation*. Every state has different laws regarding co-ops, so check with your secretary of state and with other co-ops in your state for the current laws. Historically, most co-ops are built on the following principles: one member, one vote; open membership; profits distributed to the members as refunds; education on cooperation for members; and membership control of the organization. Legally, if you choose to incorporate as a cooperative you may use the word *cooperative* in your name, and members explicitly retain certain rights. Symbolically, being a co-op makes you part of the international cooperative movement. The disadvantages are that it may be more difficult to receive a tax-exempt ruling from the IRS, and the labor-intensive style of operation requires a very energetic membership. For more information on incorporating as a cooperative, get *On Incorporation,* by John Achatz, available for $1.25 from the North American Students of Cooperation (NASCO), Box 7293, Ann Arbor, MI 48107.

Finally, you could become a *for-profit corporation*. If you plan to offer something to the public that could be successful enough to turn a profit, such as quality theater, counseling, or workshops, you could decide to become a for-profit corporation. The advantages are that you can earn profits, you can lobby as much as you like, and you can choose whomever you wish to receive the assets of the group if you disband. The disadvantage is that a for-profit corporation must assume the risk of losing money.

For more information on becoming a for-profit corporation, including a discussion of single proprietorship, partnership, and corporation, order *Incorporating a Small Business* (MA 223) and *Selecting the Legal Structure for Your Firm* (MA 231), available free from the Small Business Administration, P.O. Box 15434, Fort Worth, TX 76119.

You can see that making your organization a tax-exempt nonprofit corporation is no simple task. But if you take the work one step at a time, divide the tasks among the committee members, and ask for advice from veterans, it all will get done. Remind the committee that this work is a means to an end — a way to create a strong, permanent organization that will achieve your goals for your community. One day you will be revered as the founders, because you did the work that, once completed, will allow the group to flourish. So get started today!

6

Federal Employer Identification Number and Fiscal Year

"So teach us to number our days that we may apply our hearts to wisdom."

—Psalms 90:12

A federal employer identification number is to your organization as your Social Security number is to you as an individual. A nonprofit corporation must have one even if it has no employees, because it will need this number listed on an IRS application for tax exemption; on federal, state, and local tax reports; and on applications for checking and savings accounts.

You can apply for this number as soon as you decide that you want the organization to become a nonprofit corporation. The IRS says it takes about six weeks to assign you a number, so send the form in as soon as possible. It can even be sent before you apply for incorporation, if you like.

Call the Internal Revenue Service listed in your telephone directory or use the IRS Toll-Free number for your state listed in Chapter 23. Ask for Form SS-4, "Application for Employer Identification Number." This is a very simple form on which there are eighteen questions. See page 63. You must send two copies to the IRS. Be sure to make three photocopies for your own use before you send in the original Form SS-4. If you have not received your number from the IRS when you want to open a corporate bank account or file for a federal tax exemption, you can send the bank or the IRS a photocopy of the completed Form SS-4.

After about six weeks you will receive a letter telling you your organization's federal employer identification number. It consists of a two-number code for your state, followed by a dash and the code number for your organization. Make five copies of this letter, and put the original into your "permanent legal papers" file marked "Do not take." As a nonprofit corporation, you may qualify for exemption from local sales taxes. If so, you will want to give copies of the letter with your federal identification number to any volunteer who buys supplies for the organization.

FILLING OUT FORM SS-4

The questions on Form SS-4 are self-explanatory, with two exceptions. Question 13 asks for "Nature of Business," and this requires you to answer in the words recommended by the IRS. Say "charitable," "religious," "educational," or whichever IRS category describes you best. Choose one of the examples in the instructions on the back of the Form SS-4.

Fiscal Year

Question 5 asks for "ending month of accounting year." Answering this deceptively simple question will require you to decide on a fiscal, or accounting, year. The fiscal year is the year used by your financial accounts. It is twelve months long, but it does not have to run from January 1 to December 31. You may choose any twelve months you like, based on what will be best for your organization's annual work flow. Many nonprofit groups choose a fiscal year that ends June 30. This also may be best for your group. Ask other groups like yours, your accountant, or your lawyer what they recommend based on the following questions.

☆U.S. GOVERNMENT PRINTING OFFICE 1980.331.197

PF 440

▷

For clear copy on both parts, please typewrite or print with ball point pen and press firmly

(See Instructions on pages 2 and 4)

Form **SS–4** (Rev. 3–79)
Department of the Treasury
Internal Revenue Service

Application for Employer Identification Number

(For use by employers and others as explained in the Instructions)

1 Name (True name as distinguished from trade name. If partnership, see instructions on page 2.)

3 Social security number, if sole proprietor

2 Trade name, if any (Name under which business is operated, if different from item 1.)

5 Ending month of accounting year

4 Address of principal place of business (Number and street)

8 County of business location

6 City and State

7 ZIP code

9 Type of organization (See Instructions on page 4)
☐ Individual ☐ Trust ☐ Partnership ☐ Other (specify)
☐ Governmental ☐ Nonprofit organization (See instructions on page 4) ☐ Corporation

10 Date you acquired or started this business (Mo., day, year)

11 Reason for applying
☐ Started new business
☐ Purchased going business
☐ Other (specify)

12 First date you paid or will pay wages for this business (Mo., day, year)

13 Nature of business (See Instructions on page 4)

14 Do you operate more than one place of business? ☐ Yes ☐ No

15 Peak number of employees expected in next 12 months (if none, enter "0") ▲
☐ Nonagricultural ☐ Agricultural ☐ Household

16 If nature of business is manufacturing, state principal product and raw material used.

17 To whom do you sell most of your products or services?
☐ Business establishments ☐ General public ☐ Other (specify)

18 Have you ever applied for an identification number for this or any other business? ☐ Yes ☐ No

If "Yes," enter name and trade name (if any). Also enter the approximate date, city, and State where you first applied and previous number if known. ▲

Date

Signature and title

Telephone number

Please leave blank ▶	Geo.	Ind.	Class	Size	Reas. for appl.	**Part I**

FISCAL YEAR QUESTIONS

1. "What tax reports will we have to file, and when are they due?"

The federal government requires annual tax reports 5½ months after the close of your fiscal year. Your state also may require annual reports at a fixed point after the end of your fiscal year. Some states also require an audit for some groups. If your group is required to file annual financial reports, if you will have to get help filling them out, or if you will need to be audited, consider making June 30 the end of your fiscal year. Then most of the work requiring a CPA can be done in the summer, when your CPA is most likely to have time to give you. If you close your books on December 31, you will have to compete in spring with every private taxpayer for the CPA's time and for advice from the IRS. (See Chapter 21 for more information on audits.)

2. "When will most of our money come in, and when will most of it go out?"

Most organizations have fewer financial dealings in the summer, so the bookkeeper and treasurer have more time to prepare reports. If this is true of your group, choose June 30 as the end of your fiscal year. But if you are treasurer of the Little League, or raise most of your money from a booth at the state fair — that is, in the summer — choose a winter month for the end of your fiscal year.

3. "Where do we plan to go to ask for money? Where do other programs like ours get their money? What reports do these funding sources require from the organizations they fund?"

There are costs included in taking large sums of money from outside funding sources. One cost is complicated bookkeeping and reporting. Usually, the more money you receive, the longer and more detailed the reports you will be required to make on how you used the money.

If you know that you will want to ask for money from the United Way, a national church program, a big foundation, or any federal agency, ask the source now what reports it requires and what fiscal year it recommends. Then ask a few organizations who took that kind of money in the last year what bookkeeping, reporting, and audits were required, and when. If you decide that you will want to ask for this money, choose a fiscal year that will make it easiest for you to prepare their reports.

STEPS TO GETTING A FEDERAL IDENTIFICATION NUMBER AND FISCAL YEAR

THE PLANNING COMMITTEE WILL:

1. Choose to become a nonprofit corporation.
2. Get Form SS-4 from the IRS.
3. Answer questions.
4. Choose a fiscal year based on when you have to file tax reports, when you raise most of your money, and major funders' reporting requirements.
5. Fill out the form in duplicate.
6. Have the president sign and date the form.
7. Make three copies of the form. Mail the original to the IRS Center for your state listed on Form SS-4.
8. When you receive the letter giving you your number, file the original in your "permanent legal papers" file, and mark the file "Do not take."

STARTING IN THE MIDDLE—FISCAL YEAR

If you are a new treasurer of an old group, ask the last treasurer for the dates of the fiscal year. You may find that this fiscal year has been inconvenient for the group. If recent treasurers and the other current officers recommend changing the fiscal year, based on answers to the questions posed earlier, you have to file a form to tell the IRS you are changing your fiscal year. This is IRS Form 1128, "Application for Change in Accounting Period." You must tell the IRS before you change your accounting year so that there will not be any gaps in your reports.

If the last treasurer is not available, get a copy of the last IRS annual report Form 990 filed by the organization. The first line at the top of the first page should contain the fiscal year. See the sample below:

Form **990** Department of the Treasury Internal Revenue Service	**Return of Organization Exempt from Income Tax** Under section 501(c) (except black lung benefit trust or private foundation), 501(e) or (f) of the Internal Revenue Code	**1980**
For the calendar year 1980, or fiscal year beginning _____ , 1980, and ending _____		, 19__

If you cannot find a copy of the organization's IRS Form 990 and do not know the fiscal year, call the IRS Toll-Free number for your state listed in Chapter 23. Tell the person in "Exempt Organizations" that you need to get a copy of the organization's Form SS-4 and last Form 990. The IRS will tell you how to get copies or else tell you that the organization has never filed. In that case, follow the advice earlier to choose your fiscal year.

7

Steps to Incorporation
and Tax Exemption

"Success is achieved by those who try!"
— W. Clement Stone
The Success System That Never Fails

After you have planned your structure, written bylaws, and recruited experienced professionals to give you advice, it is time to tackle the legal work for the new organization. Unless you have done it before, this part of starting your new organization requires a good deal of reading, studying, and planning. Take your time and ask the advice of your lawyer and founders of other groups. This job may be new to you, but you can do it! This is *your* group, so learn right now how to make plans and handle the legal work in the best interests of the organization. Keep trying until you understand it all, have made the decisions, and have finished the applications. Then plan a celebration for the red-letter day when you will get the letter from the IRS saying it has approved your tax exemption!

Forms for the incorporation in your state and the tax exemption from the federal government are two different forms you have to file with two different agencies. But these forms should be filled out together, because the words you use in the incorporation will be used to decide if you qualify for tax exemption. Your work will be easier if you look at these forms at the same time and do them both right the first time.

STATE ARTICLES OF INCORPORATION

The Articles of Incorporation are the legal document you prepare for the state in order to become a nonprofit corporation. Every corporation becomes a legal entity by being chartered in one state. Every state has different laws about incorporation, but most states require a relatively simple one- or two-page application. Ask your secretary of state to send you the application and instructions for becoming a nonprofit corporation.

APPLICATION FOR FEDERAL TAX-EXEMPT STATUS

After the group becomes a nonprofit corporation, the board can ask the federal government to make it tax-exempt. This means that the corporation will not have to pay corporate income taxes as for-profit corporations do. Applications for tax-exempt status are explained in IRS Publication 557, *How to Apply for and Retain Exempt Status for Your Organization.* This free booklet introduces the twenty-four categories of tax-exempt organizations that are currently legal in the United States. Order it from the IRS, listed in most telephone books, or call the IRS Toll-Free number for your state listed in Chapter 23.

The largest tax-exempt category is called 501(c)(3) for its number in the tax code, and it covers organizations that are "organized and operated exclusively for one or more of the following purposes: charitable, religious, educational, scientific, literary, testing for public safety, fostering national or international amateur sports competition . . . or the prevention of cruelty to children or animals."[1]

The federal government gives tax breaks to nonprofit organizations and their donors because these groups can do good work cheaper and better than the government can do it. By promoting good nonprofit groups, the government accomplishes desirable goals and avoids having to do the work itself.

To find out if your organization will be eligible for a 501(c)(3) status, look in the back of Publication 557 at the "Organization Reference Chart." Find the type of organization you are starting, and see which section of the tax code covers your group. For example, you will find that a labor union is a 501(c)(5) group, a trade association is a 501(c)(6), a social club is a 501(c)(7), and a credit union is a 501(c)(14).

Unless your group obviously falls into another tax category, it probably will be in either category 501(c)(3) or 501(c)(4). Check the current Publication 557 for up-to-date information, and ask your lawyer and other experienced leaders to tell you which is best for you.

What Is the Difference Between a "c3" and a "c4"?

You may have heard people call their groups a c3 or c4. These are abbreviations of numbers in the IRS code and refer to two different types of nonprofit corporations. Both are chartered in their own state and legally exempt from paying corporate income taxes. They are different in how much lobbying they can do and in whether donors can deduct contributions from the income on which they pay taxes.

Basically, a 501(c)(3) group may spend up to 20 percent of its total budget on work to influence legislation. A 501(c)(4) may spend 100 percent of its budget on lobbying for legislation. Neither may work to elect or defeat politicians.

Only donations made to a 501(c)(3) organization are considered deductible from a contributor's taxable income. The 501(c)(3) organization is tax-exempt because it does not have to pay corporate income taxes, and tax deductible because its donors may deduct money given to the group from their taxable income. A 501(c)(4) group is also tax-exempt because it does not have to pay corporate income taxes. But it is *not* tax deductible. People who give to a 501(c)(4) group do not get to deduct that amount from their taxable income. For more information on lobbying and 501(c)(4) groups, see Chapter 9.

Getting a 501(c)(3) Tax Exemption

Once you decide which IRS tax category covers the type of organization you are starting, get the correct application form and apply for tax exemption. We will look at the form and procedure for organizations covered under Code 501(c)(3). Most new groups choose to apply for 501(c)(3) status, because the benefits of the tax laws for c3 groups make it easier to raise money. Ask the IRS for Form 1023, "Application for Recognition of Exemption."

HOW DO THE IRS RULES FOR A 501(C)(3) GROUP
AFFECT MY STATE ARTICLES OF INCORPORATION?

In order to benefit from the tax laws, you must write your state Articles of Incorporation and fill out the IRS Form 1023 so that your organization will qualify for tax exemption. When you read Publication 557 and Form 1023, you will see that the IRS expects you to make certain statements in the "purpose" section of your application for incorporation in your state. This is the longest section of the Articles of Incorporation, which covers your purpose, profits, lobbying, and assets. Publication 557 tells you what the IRS wants you to say on the state application. It must be in writing. The IRS emphasizes that "the organizational requirement is not satisfied by the fact that your actual operations are for exempt purposes."[2] You must do tax-exempt work and *tell* the IRS that you are doing it.

Incorporation is the first step toward getting your tax exemption. As long as all of your work is of the tax-exempt type, when the IRS grants your exemption it will be retroactive to the date of your incorporation. Thus, if you are incorporated in Vermont in April and receive your federal IRS ruling in December, your and your donors' tax advantages will be effective as of April. But do not wait too long. If the IRS receives your application fifteen months or more after your state incorporation, the exemption is not retroactive to the date of incorporation, but only to the date of receipt of the application at the IRS.

THE "PURPOSE" SECTION
OF THE ARTICLES OF INCORPORATION

When you wrote a statement of purpose in your first planning committee, you designed a clear written explanation of your goals for a specific audience. You wanted to tell new people what you wanted this organization to do and to encourage them to join. The "purpose" section of your Articles of Incorporation is designed for a different audience, the IRS. The Internal Revenue Service is *not* the people next door. So describe your activities as briefly as possible using the words and style the IRS recommends.

The IRS wants to know only *what* you intend to do, not *why* you are going to do it. This is not the time to draft a political statement. Your ideals and your reasons for creating this organization are important to everyone on the committee, but the state and the IRS do not need this information. They are not empowered to judge how you think—only what you plan to do, based on what you say you will do in the "purpose" part of your Articles of Incorporation. Make their job easy. Save the passionate rhetoric for your next rally, and limit your legal statement of purpose to planned activities explained in simple words.

WHAT DO WE NEED TO SAY?

The IRS wants to know about your purpose, profits, lobbying, and assets. It will judge these by what you say in the "purpose" section of your Articles of Incorporation. Let us look at them one at a time.

Purpose

According to the IRS, "Form 1023 and accompanying statements [this includes your Articles of Incorporation] must show that 1) The organization is organized exclusively for, and will be operated exclusively for, one or more of the purposes (charitable, religious, etc.) specified earlier."[3] Publication 557 explains this in detail and gives examples of statements that indicate that your organization meets this qualification. Publication 557 also points out that the word *charitable* has a legal meaning. Use that word or other words that the IRS itself uses, such as *scientific* or *educational*. On the other hand, the IRS says that "the terms philanthropic and benevolent have no generally accepted legal meaning."[4] So do not use these or other words not used by the IRS.

Profits

Your Articles of Incorporation also must include a statement about profits. You may think it ludicrous to assume that your organization would ever make a profit. But you must decide what would happen if you did make surplus money. Publication 557 says that your Form 1023 and your Articles of Incorporation should show that "No part of the net earnings of the corporation shall inure to the benefit of, or be distributable to its members, trustees, officers, or other private persons . . ."[5] The sample Articles of Incorporation included in Publication 557 show you how to say this. A nonprofit corporation can pay salaries, and it does not have to spend all of the money raised each year. But if you raise more money than you spend in one year, the money must be allocated for the work of the organization. If you believe that your organization will earn substantial profits, and you personally want to get that money in return for the work you have done, you should start a for-profit corporation. See the section on alternatives to non-profit corporations in Chapter 5.

Lobbying

The IRS limits the amount of lobbying that a 501(c)(3) group may do. You may not do any work to elect a politician, but you may do some work to influence legislation. A charitable corporation may now spend up to 20 percent of its expenditures on lobbying and keep its tax exemption if it files an IRS form called Form 5768. See Chapter 9 for more information on Form 5768. If your group can achieve its goals spending less than 20 percent of the expenditures on lobbying, use the language the IRS recommends in the sample Articles of Incorporation in Publication 557 to say how you will limit lobbying.

Assets

The IRS wants you to state in your Articles of Incorporation what will happen to assets of the group if the group goes out of business. This "dissolution provision" is designed to discourage people from setting up a 501(c)(3); collecting money, furniture, and equipment; and then converting the organization to a for-profit business. You should say that the assets will go to another 501(c)(3) group if this group dissolves. Most state laws make this a requirement for becoming a nonprofit corporation. The IRS says, "Your organization's application probably can be processed much more rapidly if its articles of organization include a provision insuring permanent dedication of assets for exempt purposes."[6] Publication 557 gives you an example of how to say this in the sample Articles of Incorporation.

ARTICLES OF INCORPORATION

Once you have decided how to word your statement of purpose to satisfy the IRS, and you have decided that you honestly can make the appropriate statements about lobbying, profits, and assets, then look at the rest of your Articles of Incorporation. The planning committee can fill in the rest according to your organizational needs. Get the form from your secretary of state, and ask your volunteer lawyer to sit in on the planning meeting in case you have any questions. In Illinois, the application is as follows.

Name

What is the name of your group? You probably have been calling your group something. If it has worked well, go on using it. On the other hand, if it has caused problems, try something else. Try to keep it short, simple, and easy to remember, like Alcoholics Anonymous or Gray Panthers. If you must have a longer name, try to make the first letters of the words spell a word. If your name is in Spanish, the first letters can spell an English word — for example, Movimiento Artistico Chicano (MARCH). Your name can also say what you do, such as Action for Children's Television (ACT); who you are, such as Women Involved in Farm Economics (WIFE); or where you work, such as Save Our Cumberland Mountains (SOCM). Some groups prefer a name with a positive sound but no specific meaning, such as Common Cause or People United to Save Humanity (PUSH). Find out if your state nonprofit incorporation laws put any restrictions on your name. Some states will not let you use "foreign" words in your name; others will not let you use the word *cooperative* in your name unless you are legally incorporated as a cooperative.

Duration

What is the "period of duration of the corporation"? If you plan to be a permanent organization, say "perpetual." If you are working on a project that will only take a few years, you probably should get adopted by an older group rather than do all this work.

Address

You have to give the address of the "initial registered office" in your state. This does not mean that you have to open an office. Choose the mailing address that will be most useful for you for the next few years. You may legally use a post office box only if you are in a rural area. Otherwise you must provide the state with a street address. If it is not convenient to have mail sent to someone's home, ask another group to let you use their address for your mail and registered office address. That way your official address will remain the same even if your officers change.

Registered Agent

This sounds like a spy, but a registered agent is just the person who is legally designated to receive official mail for the group. You can choose any officer to be the registered agent. There is no advantage or disadvantage attached to the title. Choose someone who is committed to staying in your area and with the organization, because you have to file a form to notify the state every time you change your registered agent or registered office address.

Board of Directors

You have to choose a board of directors in order to obtain your Articles of Incorporation. You also have to list the people who are the "incorporators" filling out this form. They may be the same people as are on the first board. In Illinois you must have at least three incorporators, who must be at least twenty-one years old and citizens of the United States. The planning committee can list themselves as the incorporators, but the board must be chosen by the method established in your bylaws.

How to Complete the Application

Leave the "board of directors" section blank until you have held your first annual meeting. At that meeting, you can take the legal steps necessary to finish this form. First, ratify the bylaws. This creates the rules by which you can elect a board of directors. After you elect the board, put their names on the form; then they approve the contents of the Articles of Incorporation. (See Chapter 8 for more advice on your first annual meeting.) The incorporators then sign both copies of the form, have them notarized, and send them in with the filing fee. The secretary of state will send back an impressive certificate and one copy of the form to the registered agent.

Send the certificate and the copy of the application form to the county recorder of deeds. This office will copy them on microfilm and send the originals back to you. Now make two photocopies, and put the originals in a "permanent legal papers" file marked "Do not take." Or frame the certificate and put it on your wall.

Every state has different rules, forms, fees, and procedures. Check with your own state to be sure you are doing everything according to the law. If you want more help, ask your lawyer, other founders of nonprofit corporations, your state representative, or your state senator. In most states, a nonprofit corporation will be required to register with the attorney general or another state agency. See Chapter 21 for more on state regulation of nonprofit organizations.

SAMPLE

The following is a sample of the Illinois form for incorporating a nonprofit organization. Include information on your purpose, profits, lobbying, and assets in the "purpose" section at the end of the page. You can type this information on a separate page if you prefer.

File in Duplicate

FORM NP-29

ARTICLES OF INCORPORATION
UNDER THE
GENERAL NOT FOR PROFIT CORPORATION ACT

(Please type or print using black ink)

(Do Not Write in This Space)

Date Paid

Filing Fee $50.00

Clerk _____

Secretary of State, Springfield, Illinois.

We, the Incorporators

(Not less than three)

Incorporator's Names	Number	Street	Address City	State

being natural persons of the age of twenty-one years or more and citizens of the United States, for the purpose of forming a corporation under the "General Not For Profit Corporation Act" of the State of Illinois, do hereby adopt the following Articles of Incorporation:

1. The name of the corporation is:

2. The duration of the corporation is ☐ perpetual OR _____ years.
* 3. The name and address of the initial registered agent and registered office are:

Registered Agent _____

Registered Office _____

City, Zip Code, County _____
(Do Not Use P. O. Box)

4. The first Board of Directors shall be _____ in number, their names and addresses being as follows:
(Not less than three)

Directors' Names	Number	Street	Address City	State

5. The purposes for which the corporation is organized are:

(over)

File #_____

Form NP-29

ARTICLES OF INCORPORATION

under the

GENERAL NOT FOR PROFIT

CORPORATION ACT

of

_____

SECRETARY OF STATE
CORPORATION DEPARTMENT
SPRINGFIELD, ILLINOIS 62756
TELEPHONE (217) 782-7880

(These Articles Must Be Executed and Filed in Duplicate)

Filing Fee $50.00

_____

C-157.1

(NOTE: Any special provision authorized or permitted by statute to be contained in the Articles of Incorporation, may be inserted above.)

(INCORPORATORS MUST SIGN BELOW)

(Both copies must contain original signatures)

_____

_____

_____   } Incorporators

_____

_____

As the incorporators, we declare that this document has been examined and is, to the best of our knowledge and belief, true, correct and complete.

* The registered agent cannot be the corporation itself.
The registered agent may be an individual, resident in this State, or a domestic or foreign corporation, authorized to act as a registered agent.
The registered office may be, but need not be, the same as its principal office.

STARTING IN THE MIDDLE—INCORPORATION

If your organization never has applied for incorporation, follow the steps listed earlier. You may have to amend your bylaws to conform with the requirements of your state and the IRS. Follow the advice in Chapter 3 to revise your bylaws.

If the organization has already been incorporated in your state, get a copy of your Articles of Incorporation to see if they meet the IRS requirements before you apply for your tax exemption. If you cannot find the Articles in your files, contact the county recorder of deeds or the secretary of state to get a copy. If you want to amend the Articles of Incorporation, write or call the secretary of state and ask for the form for amending the Articles. The form will tell you how to change your Articles. For example, in Illinois, Articles may be amended if the changes are approved by two-thirds of the voting members at a meeting, by consent in writing from all members, or at a meeting of the directors. In Illinois, amendments are filed on a two-page form for a fee of twenty-five dollars. As when you filed the original Articles, the secretary of state will mail you a certificate, which you must file with the county recorder of deeds. Once your bylaws and Articles of Incorporation are complete, you can proceed to the "Application for Recognition of Exemption" to make the corporation exempt from federal taxes.

HOW TO APPLY FOR TAX EXEMPTION

Once the group has applied for its federal employer identification number and is incorporated in the state, the board can tackle the last major piece of legal work, which is applying for a federal tax exemption. Fortunately, you have already done the lion's share of the work by making the decisions necessary to write bylaws and incorporate.

Get and read IRS Form 1023, "Application for Recognition of Exemption," and Publication 557, *How to Apply for and Retain Exempt Status for Your Organization*. They can be ordered from the Internal Revenue Service office listed in most telephone directories or call the IRS Toll-Free number listed in Chapter 23. These may be new to you, but if you apply yourself, you can get through it all. When you have questions, check with someone who has successfully filled out a Form 1023 in the past, your lawyer, or the IRS.

Your job is strictly to answer the questions. Most of them are pretty straightforward, so answer the questions in simple, clear words. You may tell the Ford Foundation that you plan to do capacity building in literacy skills, but tell the IRS that you plan to teach children to read.

Tell Them What You Are

Parts I, II, and III of Form 1023 ask who you are, what you have done, and what you plan to do. If you already have done some activities and fund raising, say what you have done. If you only have planned future activities, write down your program, fund-raising, and budget plans. Part V asks for data on what money you have raised, what you have spent, what you have, and what you owe, Part VI asks if you do "special activities," and if so, refers you to other forms for special groups, such as schools, public interest law firms, or homes for the aged.

Tell Them What You Are Not

NONPRIVATE FOUNDATION STATUS

This leaves Part IV, "Statement as to Private Foundation Status," and Part VII, "Nonprivate Foundation Status (Definitive ruling only)." These parts may seem confusing at first, but they will make sense in the end.

While the other parts ask who you are and what you do, this part asks who you are *not*. This strange approach comes from Congress's desire to regulate private foundations, which belong in a unique tax category. The IRS considers any organization applying for a 501(c)(3) to be a private foundation until it proves that it is *not* a private foundation. For the IRS, a private foundation gets its funds from a few private sources, whereas a public charity is supported by money from the public or the government. Do not think that this is obvious or that the IRS will judge you by what you do. The IRS will judge you by what you put on the form.

WHY NOT BE A PRIVATE FOUNDATION?

Most community organizations do not want to be considered private foundations by the IRS. It is usually better to be considered a "public charity," which means that you get money from the public. With this status you will receive all the benefits offered by the current tax laws.

The advantages of being a public charity instead of a private foundation are that the organization will have fewer and simpler reports to the government, it will not have to pay an excise tax on income from investments, and its contributors may remain anonymous. A public charity can offer its wealthy contributors advantages on their income tax deductions. Even if you do not now have or want big donors, it is smart to give the organization this option for the future. For these reasons, you are likely to want the IRS to take the organization out of the "private foundations" category and instead consider the group a public charity. (If your group *does* want to be a private foundation, get more advice from the books listed in Chapter 24, Bibliography and Resources, under "Getting Started — Foundations.")

You can start to fill out Form 1023 as soon as you send in your Articles of Incorporation. Then send in Form 1023 as soon as you get your certificate of incorporation from the state. If you send in Form 1023 within eight months of incorporation, ask the IRS for an "advance ruling" on Part IV. This asks the IRS to give you a temporary ruling as a tax-exempt public charity, based on your planned budgets. When you can show the IRS two years of financial data, the IRS will give you a "definitive ruling" if you qualify. If it has been more than eight months since the group was incorporated by the state, also complete Part VIII of Form 1023, which asks for a definitive ruling right away.

To complete Part IV to be considered a public charity, make a plan of where you hope to get your money. Write down each source of money and the amount you plan to get. Be realistic. Use this planned budget to work through the simple arithmetic tests in Chapter 4 of Publication 557. These measure the amount of income you are getting or will get from various sources. Then read Publication 557 to decide which section of the law will cover your organization. Ask your lawyer or the founder of a group like yours which section is best for this group. As a grass roots organization, you benefit from getting many donations from many people. A broad base of funding will make you financially secure in the future, and it makes you a public charity today.

How to Complete the Application

Once you have completed the entire "Application for Recognition of Exemption," Form 1023, review the checklist on page 5 of Form 1023 and collect copies of supporting documents. *Do not send originals.* The IRS warns, "None of the documents submitted in support of this application, including organizational documents, will be returned."[7]

Ask your lawyer to check that all the information is clear and accurate. Choose one officer who can receive telephone calls during the day to be the contact person for the IRS. This person's name and telephone number goes on Form 1023. Give one copy of Form 1023 to the contact person along with Publication 557 and all correspondence. Have the president sign and date the other application; then send the complete package to the director at the IRS Key District for your state listed in Form 1023. The Key District director can make a decision for most cases. If the type of organization asking for exemption is unprecedented or unusual, the Key District Office will ask the National Office for more advice.

If the IRS has any questions, the Service usually will send the questions in writing. Write out your answers, review them with your lawyer, then send them in. Although the IRS says it can process Form 1023 in eight weeks, the processing may take longer if the IRS has questions. Be patient and cooperative. Remember, the ruling is retroactive to the date of your incorporation. So, if you see no reason for the IRS to turn down the organization, you can go ahead and pursue donations from individuals.

Most foundations will not accept a proposal from your group until you have received your advance ruling letter from the IRS. But if you decide that you want to apply for foundation grants, you can research foundations and write a proposal so you will be ready to roll as soon as you get the letter from the IRS.

When you receive your advance ruling determination letter from the IRS, make five copies of it, then put the original in your "permanent legal papers" file marked "Do not take." You will need the copies to send with applications for exemption from other taxes, nonprofit bulk mail rates, and foundation grants. Some groups frame their important legal documents and hang them on a wall. Especially if a lot of volunteers use your files, this will protect your legal documents from an unfortunate disappearance.

WHAT IF THE IRS SAYS NO?

What can you do if the IRS turns down the organization's request? If the IRS decides that the organization does not meet the legal requirements to be a 501(c)(3) tax-exempt organization, it will send you a proposed adverse determination letter denying your exemption. The board then has thirty days to appeal to the regional director of appeals. If you do not appeal in thirty days, the adverse determination becomes final. If you think that you have been denied a 501(c)(3) tax-exempt status you legally deserve, read the section on appeal procedures in Publication 557, discuss it with your lawyer, and decide quickly how you plan to appeal.

MAKING IT FINAL

Your advance ruling is good for two or three years. About one month before this time runs out, the IRS will send you a form letter stating that you have ninety days from the date on the letter in which to provide more information. Because your advance ruling was based only on projected budgets, the board now must give the IRS numbers to prove that the organization has been supported by the public and should be considered a public charity.

After the treasurer has compiled the information and written out the answers to the IRS letter, he or she should review this with your lawyer. The IRS says it takes ninety days to process the information, unless the Service has to ask more questions. Once approved, the IRS will send the definitive ruling determination letter, which should be copied and framed for protection as was your advance ruling.

EFFECT ON THE STATE LAWS
AND ORGANIZATION RECORDS

Check with your state attorney general for the effect of 501(c)(3) status on your state taxes. According to the Illinois attorney general, "Once the organization receives an exemption from the Internal Revenue Service, it also automatically exempts the organization from paying State Income Tax."[8]

Being a tax-exempt organization means that your corporation is exempt from paying corporate income taxes. However, you are still legally responsible for reporting every year to the IRS. Most states also require an annual report from nonprofit corporations. Read Chapter 21 for advice on how to set up your books and records to collect all of the information you will need for your tax reports. Read Chapter 9 for advice on how to report money spent on lobbying each year.

EXCEPTIONS

There are some organizations that are not required to file Form 1023 but can still be considered tax-exempt. These include "churches, interchurch organizations of local units of a church, conventions or associations of churches, or integrated auxiliaries of a church, such as a men's or women's organization, religious school, mission society, or youth group."[9] If you are starting a church or a church group, the organization should be considered tax-exempt, and donations to it are tax deductible.

Second, if you are starting a local group that will be part of a larger organization, you do not need to file Form 1023 for a tax exemption if the parent group already has a 501(c)(3) status that covers its state and local units. The IRS says, "If your organization is one chapter or unit in a large organization controlled by a central organization (for example, a church, the Boy Scouts, or a fraternal organization), you should check with the central organization to see if it has been issued a group exemption letter. If the central organization has been issued a group exemption letter that covers your organization, you will not be required to file a separate application unless your organization no longer wishes to be included in the group exemption letter."[10]

The third exception is a very small organization that is not a private foundation and every year has a total income of less than five thousand dollars. If you know you are starting a group that will always be very small, such as a block club, then you do not need to file Form 1023. However, if you want to grow in the future, it would be very smart to file Form 1023 this year to give your organization the option of pursuing large donations or foundation grants next year.

STARTING IN THE MIDDLE—TAX EXEMPTION

You may be the new president of an older nonprofit organization that was incorporated in the state, but never filed for federal tax exemption. Ask earlier officers and your lawyer if they remember filing for tax exemption, and try to find a copy of the organization's IRS Form 1023. If you cannot find a copy of the Form 1023, call the Internal Revenue Service listed in most telephone books or call the IRS Toll-Free number for your state listed in Chapter 23. Ask for "Exempt Organizations," tell them your federal employer identification number, and tell them you need a copy of the organization's Form 1023. They will direct you to your IRS Key District Office which will either send you a copy of the Form 1023 or tell you that it was never filed.

If your nonprofit corporation has never applied for tax-exempt status, it should do so immediately in order to avoid paying corporate income taxes and penalties. Unless you have asked to be tax-exempt, the IRS will consider you a for-profit corporation, which must pay taxes. The instructions for Form 1023 and Publication 557 tell you what to do depending on how long you have been operating and your current status. Before you fill out Form 1023, check your Articles of Incorporation and bylaws to make sure they are written the way the IRS wants them written. If the Articles of Incorporation are not complete or correct, file amendments to add the missing information.

CELEBRATE!

Your organization is now a tax-exempt nonprofit corporation! Your hard work has paid off! When you get the ruling from the IRS, plan a party to celebrate. Invite everyone who gave you advice, such as other community leaders, your lawyer, your accountant, and any government workers from the county, state, or IRS who gave you help. This is a milestone in the life of your organization. It is now officially recognized as a legal entity in the county, state, and nation. You have made the decisions and set the standards that will guide all future leaders of the organization. You should be very proud of yourselves!

STEPS TO INCORPORATION AND TAX EXEMPTION

THE PLANNING COMMITTEE WILL:

1. Choose to become a tax-exempt nonprofit corporation.
2. Choose a structure for the organization. Test it.
3. Write the bylaws.
4. File for a federal employer identification number (Form SS-4). See Chapter 6.
5. Get the application and instructions for incorporation as a nonprofit corporation from the secretary of state.
6. Get the application (Form 1023) and instructions (Publication 557) for tax exemption from the IRS.
7. Recruit an experienced lawyer to give advice.
8. Choose answers for forms.
9. Hold the first annual meeting. Ratify the bylaws, elect the first board of directors, approve the content of the Articles of Incorporation. See Chapter 8.

THE BOARD OF DIRECTORS WILL:

1. Send the application for nonprofit incorporation to the secretary of state.

2. Receive the certificate from the secretary of state. File with the county recorder of deeds.
3. Send the application for tax exemption to the IRS.
4. Answer any questions from the IRS.
5. Receive approval from the IRS.
6. Celebrate!

8

First Annual Meeting

> *"We are the bridge generation between the desert and the promised land."*
> —Rita Mae Brown
> *Plain Brown Wrapper*

The first annual meeting is the first official business meeting of what will be the permanent organization. At this meeting you will make several very important decisions. All of them are steps toward getting your state incorporation and your federal tax exemption. The immediate value to your own members it that the decisions will be made publicly, so everyone will know and follow the same rules.

The decisions you will have to make include:

1. Approving the bylaws, which are permanent rules for running the organization.
2. Nominating and electing the officers and the first board. They will take over all responsibilities from the planning committee.
3. Choosing to become a tax-exempt nonprofit corporation. Approving the content of the applications for incorporation and tax exemption.
4. Choosing a bank.
5. Collecting money to open a checking account.

As discussed earlier, the planning committee has already made decisions concerning the structure of the board, writing bylaws, and getting incorporated. You will now legally ratify the bylaws, elect the board, and approve the Articles of Incorporation. Then you will choose a bank and collect money to open the corporate checking account.

HOW TO PLAN THE MEETING

The people at your first annual meeting make a series of legal and financial business decisions. The meeting will work best if you limit the attendance at the first annual meeting to people who have served on the planning committee, the chairs of any other working committees, and nominees for the board. Legally, in some states you can have as few as three people at this meeting. Functionally, between ten and twenty seems to be best. The person who has chaired the planning committee meetings can chair this meeting, too. If he or she is a candidate for the board, the chair of the nominating committee should take over the chair during the election.

To plan the annual meeting, the planning committee can create two subcommittees: the nominating committee to get good candidates to run for the board, and the arrangements committee to organize the first meeting. Because the planning committee goes out of existence with the election of the first board, an easy way to divide the work is for those people who want to serve on the new board to serve on the arrangements committee. People who do not want to be nominated for a term on the board can serve on the nominating committee.

The Nominating Committee

In the beginning the nominating committee is made up of members of the planning committee and any other members of working committees who do not want to run for the board. The committee also may recruit outside advisers who know about the talent in the community to help recruit good candidates. The nominating committee can consist of only four to eight people, who elect one chair at their first meeting.

When you are just starting, you will have to choose hardworking people to serve on the board, based on work they have done for other organizations and on their expressed desire to do the job. You want people who are committed to your mission, enthusiastic about your goals, and eager to serve. You need people with the energy, idealism, and integrity to lead your organization during these important early years. The character of the first board will be reflected in the programs planned and the staff hired, so aim high and ask the best people you know.

HOW TO GET CANDIDATES FOR THE FIRST BOARD

First, ask the entire planning committee to schedule one meeting to talk about the kind of people the committee wants as officers and board. If the members have specific people in mind, they should say so, especially if one or two people are obvious favorites for first president or co-chairs.

Next, the nominating committee should make up a slate. Start at the top, with the president or co-chairs. In person, ask the people you want to run for president or co-chair, vice-president, treasurer, and secretary. When you have these jobs slated, ask them whom they recommend for the board. If one of the original candidates for the top offices says no to the office, ask whether he or she will serve as a member of the board. If you only can find good candidates for the top offices and part of the board, leave the rest of the slate open with a plan to elect additional board members in six months, or fill out the board in the second year.

At the first annual meeting the nominating committee should present one good, uncontested slate, that is, one name for each office. When you are just starting, contested elections probably create more problems than benefits. Unless you find that you have more good candidates than you have positions to fill, do not run a contested election. Find the best person for each job.

It is also the nominating committee's job to make sure that each candidate understands *exactly* how the organization works and what the committee expects. No one should agree to run thinking that the job is something other than what it is. The nominating committee must find good people who will work hard for a long time. Do not say, "It won't take much of your time," or "We only want your ideas," just to get someone to run for the board. Do not think, "Well, once we've got them, they will see how great we are and want to do a lot of work and raise a lot of money." If you trick people into being on the board and *then* ask them to work, they will be justified in saying no. Then you have wasted that position for an entire year. Honesty is the best policy for the nominating committee. Say, "We want you to serve on the board. We meet every Tuesday, the meetings are long, we have to raise thirty thousand dollars, and we expect the board to raise it. This is the most exciting organization doing the best work on the most urgent issue in town. It will be hard work, but you will see results and together we will make a big difference!"

See Chapter 14 for details on how to run the election. The arrangements committee can read Chapter 14 to learn how to plan the meeting. Also ask your volunteer lawyer and experienced volunteers for advice on running the first annual meeting and elections.

Once elections are over, the new president or co-chairs will take office officially and chair the rest of the meeting. Now that you have legally elected a board of directors, it can complete the Articles of Incorporation to make the group a nonprofit corporation in your state.

CHOOSING A BANK

The next item of business at the first annual meeting is choosing a bank. The temporary treasurer can research the local banks before the first annual meeting. He or she can ask the treasurers of other nonprofit organizations, the lawyer, and the CPA for an introduction to a good banker at a good bank. Based on answers to the following questions, the board can choose one bank for checking and savings accounts.

Questions for Choosing a Bank

1. Is there a person at the bank who respects our members, understands our program, and wants to see us succeed? Doing the banking and record keeping for a nonprofit corporaton is different from and more complicated than doing it for yourself. A new

treasurer will need good advice from a sympathetic banker. Ask veteran treasurers from other groups how they are treated at various banks, and talk to bankers they recommend.

2. What services will we need next year? What services will we need in five years? Right now you may need only a good local bank to handle cash deposits. In five years you may need a mortgage for your building program and advice on investments. Ask your banker what he or she can do for you right now—for example, waive the service charge on your accounts—and what he or she can do in the future.

3. Does the bank give mortgages and loans in our neighborhood or to the kind of people who will be our members? It is important to choose a bank that supports your community. You are asking your community to trust you with its money. It is wrong for you to put that money into an institution that does not trust your donors enough to give them mortgages or loans. Ask the bank for their current lending data, and double-check with people who use the bank.

Once the board selects a bank, the officers will have to fill out the applications and adopt a system for signing checks. See Chapter 19 for advice on the mechanics of banking.

COLLECTING MONEY

Now collect money to put in the bank. Functionally, this makes it possible to pay the filing fee for the Articles of Incorporation. Organizationally, it is important to collect the money from the group as a whole, so that each founder literally shares the ownership of the organization. The best way to get on the right track as a successful organization is to believe that your work is important, say that it matters, and then contribute some of your own money. Do it at the first annual meeting.

AFTER THE MEETING

Celebrate! You have *earned* it. Congratulate yourselves on a job well done. Since you launched the planning committee, you have planned your structure, written bylaws, elected officers and a board, held your first annual meeting, chosen a bank, and begun your fund raising. This is terrific, and you should say so! You are also halfway through the legal paperwork. You have made your decisions to get your state nonprofit incorporation and your federal identification number. Once this is done, all you have left to do is to apply for your tax exemption from the IRS.

Plan a party to follow the first annual meeting. Invite the friends and families of the planners to help you celebrate your birthday. This will be the first of many celebrations for yourselves as the group grows and changes.

The next day, the new officers can meet to plan their work for the next year. All of this book shares advice to help the officers, especially the president or co-chairs, do their work. The secretary can read Chapter 18 for advice on setting up the lists, files, and records. The treasurer can read Chapter 19 for advice on setting up the financial records and handling the money.

All of the new board can read Chapter 22 for advice on how to plan your work for the first year. Good work does not come from good luck, but from good planning. Annual calendars will help you do first things first and divide the work so that each person works best.

The first job of the first president is to write and send personal thank-you notes to everyone who served on the nominating committee, the arrangements committee, and the party committee. Thank-you notes are the most important tool of a successful president. Use them immediately after the first annual meeting, and every other opportunity, to create a happy, hardworking organization.

The president also should promptly meet with the treasurer and your insurance agent to purchase a bond for the treasurer, which will protect the organization against any misdealings by the treasurer. See "Bonding the Treasurer" in Chapter 19.

STEPS TO HOLDING THE FIRST ANNUAL MEETING

THE PLANNING COMMITTEE WILL:

1. Create an arrangements committee to plan the meeting.

2. Create a nominating committee to get good candidates to run for the board.
3. At the meeting, approve the bylaws.
4. Elect the officers and the first board.

THE BOARD OF DIRECTORS WILL:

1. Approve the content of the application for incorporation in your state.
2. Choose a bank.
3. Collect money to open the corporate checking account.
4. Celebrate!

Choosing a Method to Report Lobbying Expenses

"Citizen participation is the animating spirit and force in a society predicated on voluntarism."

—Saul Alinsky
Rules for Radicals

Once you have obtained your 501(c)(3) tax-exempt ruling from the IRS, you must decide how you want the IRS to measure your lobbying. The government requires every 501(c)(3) organization to report the money it spends to influence legislation every year. Your board will want to discuss what lobbying is, what kind of lobbying they will want to do, and how they want to report the lobbying to the IRS.

What is Lobbying?

Even if the board does not now plan to do any lobbying, it is generally advisable for it to send in IRS Form 5768. This will select how the IRS will measure any future work. Sending in the form does not mean that the organization *must* lobby now or in the future. Do this now while you are handling the other government forms to help future officers and to protect the organization's 501(c)(3) tax status. Because a "government of the people, by the people, for the people" requires citizens to participate actively in making good legislation, filing your Form 5768 makes it easier for your group to be a good citizen and a tax-exempt organization at the same time.

The word *lobbying* originally meant trying to convince a legislator to write a law according to your wishes. Traditionally, only elected legislators are allowed on the floor of the city council, state legislature, or Congress. Thus, if a private citizen wants to speak to his or her senator about a bill, he or she must have the guard at the door take in a note, then wait in the *lobby* until the senator comes out to talk.

As the IRS uses the word, "lobbying" is not limited to elected legislators. You also can lobby other government officials and employees. The IRS calls any money spent to persuade legislators, government officials, or government employees to do what you want, "direct lobbying." If you spend money to persuade the general public to agree with your group and thus influence legislation, that is considered "grass roots lobbying" by the IRS.

The IRS gives this example: "The Committee to Save Our Seashores spent $5,000 on grass roots lobbying in the form of newspaper advertisements to influence public opinion in favor of proposed legislation to control the disposal of industrial waste. In addition it paid a lobbyist $10,000 to present its views to members of the State Legislature. . . ."[1] The first five thousand dollars was spent for grass roots lobbying; the second ten thousand dollars was spent for direct lobbying.

The board can think about your goals and discuss whether you will want to spend any money for lobbying. If you know that it will be important for you to influence politicians and the voters, plan lobbying into your budget and yearly work plan. In order to make your job easier and to protect your 501(c)(3) tax exemption, file IRS Form 5768, which affects the way the IRS will measure the lobbying you do. Get Form 5768 from the Internal Revenue Service listed in most telephone directories or call the IRS Toll-Free number for your state listed in Chapter 23.

What is Form 5768?

Before 1976, many charitable organizations were afraid to lobby because such activities could result in the loss of their tax exemption. The IRS worked under a law that said that "no substantial part of an organization's activities [may consist of] carrying on propaganda, or otherwise attempting, to influence legislation." Any group that violated this vague standard would endanger its tax exemption.

Fortunately, the law has been changed to protect most public charities and at the same time make the job of the IRS easier. The new law states that most public charities may elect to replace the "substantial part of activities" test with a limit defined in terms of expenditure made for influencing legislation. If an organization makes the election, it is permitted to spend a specified amount of its expenditures—20% of the first $500,000 of total expenditures for charitable purposes—without being subject to a tax on the lobbying expenditures or jeopardizing its tax exempt status. Under this safe harbor rule, 5% of the first $500,000 of total expenditures may be spent on grass roots lobbying and 15% on direct lobbying. If the organization's lobbying expenses exceed the amount allowable under the safe harbor rule, the excess expenditures are subject to a 25% excise tax. It is only where an organization's lobbying expenditures exceed 150% of the limitations over a four-year period that the organization will lose its exempt status under 501(c)(3).

It is generally preferable for an organization to elect to have its lobbying expenditures measured under the objective test of the new law, rather than the vague "substantial part of activities" standard. If the board decides to elect to have its lobbying activities treated under the new law it makes an election on Form 5768, "Election/ Revocation of Election by an Eligible Section 501(c)(3) Organization to Make Expenditures to Influence Legislation." This Form, which is easy to complete, must be signed and postmarked within the first taxable year to which it applies.

GET ADVICE

Lobbying is complicated. Congress has written vague laws about lobbying which are left up to the interpretation of the IRS and the courts. Lobbying is further complicated by state and local laws, which will proliferate as local governments want more control. There are many exceptions and many other issues raised by lobbying by nonprofit groups.*

The best way for your group to proceed is to discuss what you want to do, how lobbying will relate to that, and how to do it under the current laws. Do not be afraid of lobbying. Our form of government requires you to make your wishes known to your representatives; our tax laws require you to do this according to the rules in order to remain tax-exempt. In order to lobby legally, get the advice of other groups that now lobby, of your lawyer, and of the IRS. See Chapter 24 for recommended reading and resources for more advice on lobbying.

CAUTION

Lobbying is legal, according to the IRS, only for work you do to pass or defeat legislation. It is *not* legal to work for or against a politician. The 501(c)(3) organization may work to pass Congresswoman Lacey Davenport's bill to stop the B-1 bomber. But it may not work to elect Lacey Davenport. If your members want to elect her, they can join her party or her campaign effort as individuals, but a tax-exempt organization may not work for her. The IRS says, "If any of the activities of your organization consist in participating in, or intervening in, any political campaign on behalf of any candidate for public office, your organization will not qualify

---

* The provisions of the tax law relating to lobbying expenses exclude amounts spent for three categories of activities. These are (1) making available the result of nonpartisan analysis, study or research; (2) providing technical advice or assistance to a government body in response to a written request by such body; and (3) so-called "self-defense direct lobbying"—that its appearances before, or communications to, a legislative body with respect to a possible decision of that body which might affect the existence of the organization, its powers and duties, its tax-exempt status, or the deduction of contributions to it. In addition, an exception is provided for communications between the organization and its members unless the communication encourages the members to lobby or to urge non-members to lobby.

for tax-exempt status under section 501(c)(3) of the code. Such participation or intervention includes the publishing or distributing of statements."[2]

STARTING IN THE MIDDLE—FORM 5768

If you cannot find a copy of the organization's Form 5768, contact the IRS Center where it would have filed the form. The addresses of the IRS Centers are listed in the bottom right corner of the Form 5768. Tell them the organization's federal employer identification number and ask if they have a copy of your Form 5768 on file. If they say no, file the form now.

AN ALTERNATIVE FOR ORGANIZATIONS THAT WANT TO LOBBY MORE—501(c)(4)

There is an alternative for the nonprofit organization that wants to lobby aggressively every year and still be a tax-exempt corporation. In that case, the board would ask the IRS to make the organization tax-exempt under section 501(c)(4) of the law rather than section 501(c)(3).

If the board decides that you will want to devote more than 20 percent of your budget to lobbying, or more than 5 percent of your budget to grass roots lobbying, you should ask the IRS for a tax exemption under a different section of the law. The organization still would incorporate in the state as a nonprofit corporation, but it would ask the IRS for a tax exemption under section 501(c)(4), "Civic Leagues and Social Welfare Organizations." These are described in the IRS Publication 557. Examples include community associations, homeowners' associations, and civic leagues. The IRS says, "If you submit proof that your organization is organized exclusively for the promotion of social welfare, its chances for obtaining exemption will not be lessened by evidence that its social welfare objectives require legislation and that it will attempt to bring about such legislation."[3]

This means that the organization may lobby all it likes as long as it is lobbying about its social welfare issues. It still will qualify for an exemption, so it will not have to pay corporate income taxes on its money. But when individuals give money to a 501(c)(4) organization, they may not deduct that donation from their taxable income.* A 501(c)(4) is tax-exempt as a corporation, but donations to it are not tax deductible as they are when made to a 501(c)(3) organization. A 501(c)(4) organization gains the freedom to lobby all it likes and loses the opportunity to offer donors a tax break.

The work of a 501(c)(4), like a 501(c)(3), may not "include direct or indirect participation or intervention in political campaigns on behalf of or in opposition to any candidate for public office."[4]

STEPS TO CHOOSING A METHOD
TO REPORT LOBBYING EXPENSES

THE BOARD OF DIRECTORS WILL:

1. Decide what the organization wants to do; choose a program.
2. Decide how it will do this; choose your tactics.
3. Make a budget for how much money the organization will spend:
    a. Total.
    b. For grass roots lobbying, that is, influencing voters.
    c. For direct lobbying, that is, influencing politicians.
4. Read the instructions for Schedule A of Form 990 from the IRS. This explains the arithmetic for figuring the legal amount you may spend on lobbying. Calculate the percentage of your budget you will spend on lobbying next year. Most grass roots organizations have a wide variety of activities and expenditures, so they easily meet the legal limits on expenditures. If your budget will go over the legal limit, revise your plan and your budget.
5. Get Form 5768 from the IRS.
6. If you want the IRS to measure your lobbying based on a specific percentage of your expenditures, file Form 5768.

---

* The only exception is a volunteer fire company, which is legally a 501(c)(4), but donors may take an income tax deduction if the money is spent for public purposes.

Part II
Getting Results

10

Members, Committees, and the Board of Directors

"Make it more fun to be on the inside participating than on the outside looking in."
— Richard Steckel
The Children's Museum of Denver

Community organizations give people the chance to discover that they are natural leaders. When most people join, they are content to be "just volunteers." But the next thing they know, they suggest good ideas and others say, "Great! Do it!" Then they are in charge of committees. They find that they like the work and watching their committees grow. The next thing they know, they are on boards and are learning about budgets, planning, and evaluation. After they succeed, they have the confidence and the skills to run for office and win! Even the most successful leaders often remark, "I never dreamed three years ago I would be able to do this! I am the president of an organization that matters, I am good at it, and I love it!"

You cannot learn that you are a leader until you have something to lead. Even if your first job is chairing the cleanup committee for the barbecue, you will be learning skills that you can use in every

105

future leadership job. Today the barbecue committee; tomorrow the presidency!

You can hire a great staff director from outside the organization, but you cannot recruit a great president from the outside. Great presidents are forged on the anvil of meetings, planning, participation, parties, fund raising, selling, listening, evaluating, sharing, and caring about organizations. The organization can recruit three hundred great members, encourage them to be active in committees, inspire twenty of them to chair committees, and challenge twelve of them to serve on the board. Out of these twelve, you will find a great president! So start now!

GETTING MEMBERS

What is a Member?

A member is actively involved in the organization. The key is *action*. These are the people you can count on to show up and take part when you need them. Some organizations call any person who sends money a member. For clarity I call people who give money but not time "subscribers." Subscribers send money each year and receive the publications of the organization. They are a valuable source of income and should be treated as such. Selling subscriptions is discussed in Chapter 15. For this chapter we are interested in describing how you get warm-blooded, lively members to come to your meetings, fall in love with your organization, want to become officers some day, and work hard to get there.

What Does the Membership Committee Do?

Every volunteer organization needs a special team of people to find and keep good members. This committee may be called the membership committee, the outreach committee, or the newcomers' committee. These people encourage new people to join the organization and then find a place for them in which they will be happy and productive.

The membership committee starts with two people who say, "We will do it." They recruit from four to twelve people for the committee; review the current list of members; and set a goal, such as a 50 or 100 percent membership increase in the first year, followed by 25 to 50 percent increases in succeeding years.

SETTING A GOAL

In setting membership goals, keep in mind the goals of the organization. If your goal is sharing and conversation, from twenty to thirty people may be plenty. On the other hand, if your goal is to influence legislation, and you know that a single congressional district has about 463,000 people in it, you will set high goals for the number of members you want per district. Never sell yourself short. Before the successful lawsuit to permit girls into the Little League, many adults said, "No girls are interested in Little League." Two years after the suit, sixty thousand girls were playing baseball! If you offer something people want, the sky is the limit for your recruitment. Whether you want to be large or small, set your goal and reach it!

The Annual Membership Drive

Although members can be signed up all year long at meetings and other events, the most productive way to get new members is to make a short, well-organized push once a year.

The best time to recruit adults is in early fall, after school starts, and in January, when they plan the new year. Recruit students in October, after they have settled into their school routines, and in May, when they are planning their summer schedules. Many churches run membership campaigns in the fall, just before they ask for yearly pledges. Some community organizations tie their membership campaigns to annual conventions. Rural communities hold their membership drives during the month the farmers or ranchers sell their produce.

In 1978, the Institute for American Church Growth asked people why they came to a particular parish. Seventy to 80 percent answered, "Invited by a relative or a friend." Only 6 to 8 percent answered, "Wandered in on their own." This holds true for other community organizations, too. So focus your work on getting your current members to *ask* for new members in a short, fun, competitive campaign once a year. Then you can also design a system to get the "walk-in" trade during the rest of the year.

If the annual membership drive is to fit into one month, it must be planned carefully and well in advance. The chairs of the membership committee will recruit and organize teams and prepare all membership material. Ask a top-notch salesperson or sales manager to give your teams a practice session and pep talk before they go out the first time. Before the campaign starts, the members of the board, the officers, and the chairs of the membership committee all can sell memberships to test sales pitches and show that the work is important.

Before you send the members out to sell memberships, ask them to think about why they joined this organization. How did he or she join? Who asked him or her? What does the organization mean to him or her today? What could it mean to newcomers? How does it help all of the community? Of course, you should practice what you preach. Pay your own dues first. Then you can say to the newcomers, "Join me in this terrific organization!"

DURING THE CAMPAIGN

The teams will turn in money and names each week. Build in some friendly competition to keep the ball rolling. Use your imagination and make up some prizes to give each week: for most sales per team; most valuable player; most improved team; best rookie for newcomers; best story; or most new members from the same family, club, or business. Ask a local celebrity to award prizes. Make it fun and exciting. Take photos of all teams, and put them on the front page of the newsletter. Have a final celebration, and *end on time!* Keep it short, fun, and successful this year, and it will be easy to get volunteers next year.

Brainstorm on busy locations where you could find people to buy memberships. Then ask each person to make a list of prospects. Their list could include:

1. Family. Ask your family—you may be surprised. Even if they say no, at least they will have a better idea of what you are doing.

2. Friends. Give your friends a chance to join this wonderful group! If you do not want to ask your friends (or family), give them gift memberships; most of them will pay to renew next year. Or trade friends with another team member. You sell to his or her friends, and he or she sells to your friends.

3. Co-workers. This depends on your boss, but you always can approach people before and after work and during lunch hours. Payday and the day after payday are best. Before payday, ask people to think about joining; then close the sale on payday.

4. Professional contacts. Ask your dentist, veterinarian, pharmacist, dry cleaner, or anywhere else you spend money.

5. Members of other organizations, such as your bowling team, political party, or book club.

6. Church members. Sell after services and at meetings such as choir, Sunday school, seniors' club, and young adults and singles' groups. If you want to recruit new members who are already experienced volunteers, the best place to look is the local church or synagogue. Especially if you are working in a low-income community, this is where most people learn volunteer skills. According to a federal survey, "Americans Volunteer, 1974," religion is the only category that shows an *increase* in volunteering as income goes down.

Year-Round Recruitment

In addition to the one-month membership drive, the membership committee can also make a plan to recruit members all year long. Every meeting, action, and special event offers an opportunity to sign up new members. The best people to ask to join your group are the people who have already seen your work and come to a meeting or benefit. As sales expert Barbara Pierce says, "Seeing is believing, but trying is buying."

Every time the organization holds a meeting or special event, two people from the committee can set up a table equipped with membership forms, receipts, and encouraging smiles. Officers are reminded to introduce themselves to newcomers, and escort them to the membership table. The chair or master of ceremonies can introduce the committee members and ask newcomers to join.

Table 10-1 presents a sample plan for one neighborhood organization to sell memberships during the year.

TABLE 10-1
One Year Membership Sales Plan

Action	New Members
Sign-up table at 10 monthly program meetings (10 meetings x two sales per month).	20
Sign-up table at spring and fall benefits (two benefits x five sales per benefit.)	10
Membership blank included in newsletter, circulation one thousand. Project one percent return.	10
Encourage members to give gift memberships as birthday and anniversary presents. Push sales for Valentine's Day (February), Mother's Day (May), Father's Day (June), graduation (June), Christmas (December), and Hanukkah (December). Project four sales per holiday.	24
TOTAL:	64

How to Welcome New Members

Each person who pays his or her dues should get a thank-you note and a receipt. You also can give a membership card or a button. Consider these promotional expenses, and include them in the budget of the membership committee. If members receive a newsletter, be sure you give the correct mailing address of the new member to the person who keeps the newsletter list. If you have other merchandise for members, such as T-shirts or books, let new members buy it.

The most important thing you can give a new member is the chance to participate in an organization that gets results. Invite the new members to a meeting and introduce them to the officers. Many groups print a simple brochure containing a short history of the group; how the organization works; how the new member can get involved; and the date, time, and place of meetings. You also can use a "Time and Talent Sheet" that tells new members the names and phone numbers of committee chairs and who to call for more advice.

COMMITTEES: THE WAY TO KEEP MEMBERS

Once you have members signed up, how do you keep them? As with fund raising, the figure that matters in a membership drive is the *net* — what is left at the end of the year. Every organization will lose some people each year because they die, move away, or lose interest. There is little you can do about the first two, but you can prevent the last. After you get members into the organization, keep them by giving them something worthwhile to do. This is where committees come in.

A committee is any group of members that has a specific job to do for the organization. Most committees are small enough so that each person can have a chance to participate, to speak, and to listen. People can work and gain confidence at the same time. Organizer Si Kahn's observation of the importance of small groups in poor people's organizations holds true for committees in all volunteer organizations. He says, "The process of membership education involves slow and patient work with groups small enough for people to interact and interrelate. This process will be of great value in convincing each member of the poor people's organization of his own individual importance to the organization, and will help give him a sense of his own dignity and worth. Members develop a sense of being part of the organization. They feel they are valued for who they are, and that their views are important."[1]

Most committees start spontaneously when one or two people say, "Let's do XYZ!" The president says, "Great! Start a committee." The committees that attract the most people will last the longest. Some committees may purposely be designed to have limited life spans, and others will work themselves out of jobs. Let us consider some of the committees that are common to many organizations.

Organization Committees

Some committees can be grouped under the title of "organization committees." These committees make the organization grow and run smoothly. Depending on the size and the goals of your organization they could include the following.

The fund-raising committee. This committee raises money each year. The chairs of the fund-raising committee are enthusiastic, high-energy salespeople who believe that this organization is the greatest investment in America. The committee usually has from ten to twenty members, but it can recruit up to one hundred for a special campaign or benefit.

The membership committee. Members *are* the organization. Like life insurance, memberships are *sold,* not bought. The membership committee is chaired by two people with "people" skills. They make new people feel welcome and old members feel important. The chairs believe that belonging to this organization has been the best experience in their lives and want every other person to have the same opportunity. Their committee usually consists of from four to twelve people, but may expand to fifty or one hundred for a one-month membership blitz.

The publicity committee. This committee tells the story of this organization to the community. The chairs combine razzle-dazzle ideas with hard work and attention to details. They believe that this organization, its leaders, its members, its work, and its dreams are the most exciting story in America. This committee may be relatively small, perhaps only two or three people for year-round liaison with the press. It can expand to twenty for special hoopla around the annual convention, membership drive, or special events.

The nominating committee. This committee is selected from among former board members and other current members who do not want to run for office. Their job is to find the best possible slate of candidates and encourage them to run for elected offices. The chairs believe that serving this organization is the most rewarding leadership opportunity in their community. They know this organization is so good that it will bring out the best in its people.

These four committees make up the typical work force of a small- or medium-sized organization, especially one without staff. Even organizations that employ staff will be stronger if fund raising, membership recruitment, publicity, and nominations are the responsibility of active committees.

Three other jobs are sometimes allocated to committees, but I believe they are better handled by the board. These are long-range planning; budget and financial management; and evaluation of programs, staff, and fund raising. All of these jobs should be done by the top decision-making group elected by the organization, because they all require long-range vision, value judgments, and action.

Other committees that organizations find useful are:

Foundation liaison committee. This committee researches local and national foundations, prepares and reviews proposals, visits foundation staff to sell the proposals, and maintains relationships with foundation staff. The committee makes sure that all reports, bookkeeping, and audits are correct.

Government liaison committee. Any organization that receives money from a government agency needs a full-time committee to work with government staff. Because the rules and the players change often, it takes constant attention to keep the organization in the game. The committee guarantees that reports, bookkeeping, and audits are correct, complete, and prepared on time.

Personnel committee. If the organization hires staff, it needs a personnel committee to set salaries and benefits, establish personnel policy, and hire the staff. Once the staff is hired, the committee reviews monthly work plans, recommends assignment changes, fires unproductive workers, and hires replacements. It also handles grievances.

Lobbying committee. This committee is often called legislative liaison, political education, or public affairs, but its job is lobbying. The committee makes sure that your point of view is expressed to local, state, or federal legislators. This may mean doing free research for legislators' staff, providing expert testimony, or organizing letter writing or in-person lobbying at your city hall or state capitol.

Ways and means committee. This committee does the long-range planning for the fund-raising committee. It does in-depth research on any money-making project that could (1) lose money, such as a concert; (2) change the makeup of the organization or the staff, such as door-to-door solicitation, or (3) cost money to start and run, such as a direct mail campaign or new business. The committee interviews people who have raised money successfully and prepares a five-year income projection for each proposed venture.

Office or buildings and grounds committee. If your organization rents an office, you need a committee to negotiate with the owner or manager, handle maintenance, and make the office a pleasant place to work. If your organization owns a building, you will need a committee to make sure that the decorating, maintenance, accounting, and insurance are handled properly.

Audit committee. An audit committee reviews each month's bookkeeping in detail and during the annual audit serves as the liaison with the independent accountant. This way a few experienced leaders are responsible for keeping a tight rein on expenses, while the whole board is free to focus on *making* money. An audit committee is valuable if you are an all-volunteer organization and indispensable if you hire staff to handle your money.

Program Committees

The program committees do the work of the organization. These committees may be defined by geographic area; by issues such as schools, zoning, or beautification; or by membership, such as senior citizens, young adults, or teens. How many program committees you have and what they work on is up to you and the enthusiasm of your leaders.

How Do I Get and Keep People on My Committee?

Whether the goal of the committee is to raise money or to start a community compost project, the mechanics of creating committees is the same. You get people on your committee by asking them, and you keep them by giving them a job that matters. First, find a partner to co-chair your committee; then make a plan to get the members you want.

You get people to join the committee by *asking* them to join it.

This is so obvious that it is easy to overlook. Many people waste time and money sending letters or putting pleas in the newsletter, when the most efficient way to get the people you want is to ask them. Asking in person is best.

Meet with your co-chair and make a list of people you want on your committee. Especially at the beginning, you will have to make a lot of visits because many of the people on your list will be committed to other projects or not interested. Here is a sample work plan for creating a committee:

WEEK ONE:

The two chairs each recruit four people for the first meeting. If you have a lot of experience recruiting people, you may get one out of two or one out of three people you invite, but novice chairs average about one out of five. If you have to make forty calls to get four people, do it! Keep a list of the people who say no or not now, so that you know whom you asked.

FIRST MEETING:

There are ten people—the two chairs and the eight people they asked—at the first meeting. Keep this meeting very short and upbeat. Introduce yourselves, emphasize the importance of the work, and paint a picture of the good times you will have. Then let the eight new people ask questions. Write down all suggestions. Be enthusiastic about their ideas. Propose the next step—to expand the committee. Ask each person to come back next week with one more volunteer. The chairs will each find two volunteers.

DAY AFTER THE FIRST MEETING:

The chairs call all eight people and thank them for coming. Tell them you will call back in two days to get the names of their new volunteers.

TWO DAYS AFTER THE FIRST MEETING:

The chairs recruit two new volunteers each.

THREE DAYS AFTER THE FIRST MEETING:

The chairs call new committee members and ask for the names of their recruits. To the few that do not yet have their recruits, suggest names or give tips on how to ask.

FOUR DAYS AFTER THE FIRST MEETING:

The chairs call people who have not reported the names of their recruits. If they still do not have volunteers, make an appointment to meet with them.

FIVE DAYS AFTER THE FIRST MEETING:

The chairs meet any committee member who still has to find a new committee member. Make a call and let the member listen to you do it. Then listen while the member calls someone. Give a lot of encouragement and a few suggestions. If the member has to call all the way through his or her phone book, stick with it until he or she has a recuit. Do *not* do it yourself! Your job is to make the other person succeed.

SIX DAYS AFTER THE FIRST MEETING:

The chairs call the entire list (now twenty people) to remind them about tomorrow's meeting.

SECOND MEETING:

The second meeting consists of twenty-two people: two chairs and their four recruits plus eight volunteers from the first meeting and their eight recruits. Now you have a committee! Use this meeting to get to know each other and begin to make a plan. Discuss your goals and how they relate to the organization as a whole. Schedule the next meeting for planning.

The recruiting system also can be repeated if you want or need a larger committee. Instead of doubling once, so that you go from ten to twenty-two members, you could double again, so you will have forty-four members, or eighty-eight members. This works well if you are recruiting for a short, intense campaign with an important deadline, such as an election. Just ask each person to bring one new person each week.

DAY AFTER THE SECOND MEETING:

The chairs call committee members and thank them for coming. A few will say, "This is not what I want. I was expecting something else." Thank them for their honesty, and find replacements.

DAY BEFORE THE THIRD MEETING:

The chairs call committee members and remind them about the meeting. If any more people have gotten cold feet, reassure them and encourage them to come to the meeting. If they back out, find substitutes.

THIRD MEETING:

Discuss plans. Set goals and a timetable. Pair up committee members. If you have twenty people on the committee, you have ten pairs.

Each chair will support five pairs. When they are serving as volunteers on committees, most people work better in pairs. People need some social rewards. Especially when working with new people, the job of the chairs is to make sure members take assignments they can do and enjoy. Ten pairs with support will do more than twenty-two individuals working alone.

Any activity of the committee should be done first by the chairs to show that it is important. The chairs will learn about the activity; then they can help their teams. They will call every day with advice and suggestions.

For example, in a membership sales campaign, the chairs may suggest better sales pitches, locations, days of the week, or times of the day. They may recommend taking along current newspaper clippings, newsletters, letters from local politicians or pastors, or lists of other members. They can listen to salespeople's war stories, assure them they are doing fine, find actions to applaud, and be sure they go out again tomorrow. Persistence is the key to sales! If your people believe they can sell, they will. The chair's job is to give them self-confidence and inspire them to keep trying.

This system will work regardless of the work of the committee. You may want your teams to collect signatures on a petition, call on church members to discuss their yearly pledges, or compile information on local taxes. The key to having a happy committee is high goals, hard work, campaigns and meetings that end on time, and lots of recognition. We all want to be told in front of other people that we did good jobs. Lots of praise and thank-you notes will keep your committee active and happy.

If this is the first time you have chaired a committee, think back on experiences you have had as a member of committees. What made you feel welcome and a part of the team? What made you work hard? What made you want to go to the meetings? How can you give your members these feelings? Then think about times when you joined committees and were disappointed. You may have joined with high hopes but felt frustrated and left out. What happened on that committee? What were you expecting that you did not get? How could the committee have been a rewarding experience? What mistakes should you be careful to avoid on your own committee? If you have little personal experience on committees, ask some veteran volunteers for their best and worst committee experiences. Make a list of do's and don'ts; then start the new committee.

THE BOARD

The board of directors is the ultimate committee. In interviews for this book, I asked hundreds of leaders in thriving community organizations to tell me what makes their group succeed. "Strong board of directors" was on every list. An effective board will be composed of people from your organization who are hardworking, enthusiastic, and committed to the goals of the group. Most of all, they must know what the job involves, and they must *want* to do it.*

---

* See Chapter 3 for advice on choosing a structure for the board, who you want on the board, and what the board should do.

I also asked leaders what would make an organization fail. Almost everybody answered, "Lack of dedicated leaders." The most experienced people say that dedication or the *desire* to do the job is the essential characteristic for successful community leaders.

Getting Good Candidates

Ideally, a candidate for the board should be an active member and serve on a committee. But even if the candidate is a veteran of the organization, the chair of the nominating committee must make sure that the candidate understands how much time and work are needed. The board as seen from the outside and the experience of current board members may be different. Be sure the candidate knows what this board does now and how he or she can fit in.

If you choose to nominate a nonmember to the board because of his or her experience, influence, or fund-raising abilities, begin your discussion with a history of the organization; its purpose, goals, officers, and staff; and the plan for the next term. This must be done before any candidate is slated.

Before agreeing to run for the board, each candidate should be given:

1. The bylaws.
2. The latest financial statements.
3. This year's and next year's budget.
4. The fund-raising strategy. How much is the board expected to raise?
5. Names and telephone numbers of the current officers.
6. Names and job descriptions of the current staff.
7. Newsletters, the annual report from last year, and copies of recent newspaper or magazine clippings about the organization.
8. A letter from the president to the prospective candidates. This is the president's chance to tell candidates what your organization wants from its board.

The president will ask each candidate to:

1. Make a commitment to the purpose of the organization.
2. Attend meetings.

3. Give time and money according to his or her means.
4. Plan the programs and budget, then raise the money to operate the programs.
5. Hire and supervise the best possible personnel, if work is delegated to paid staff.
6. Speak at public meetings on behalf of the organization.

The last job of the outgoing president is to guarantee that the candidates for the next board understand what they are getting into. Honesty is the best policy. Tell your candidates exactly what the board does now and what you want them to do. Especially if you want them to give and ask for money, say so before they agree to run for office.

Welcome the New Board

After elections and before the first meeting, the president sends a personal note welcoming the new board members. Then call or meet each new member to talk about what the board does, how it works, and what he or she hopes to add. Allow time to answer any questions. The president can pair each new member with an old member who will bring him or her to the first meeting and make introductions. The buddy system is corny, but it works.

If there is a staff director, he or she will then meet with the new board members to answer questions about what the staff can or cannot do. The director collects information for the new people about the organization, its programs, and goals.

The chair of the publicity committee will get a current résumé and photo of the new board members. A news release will be sent to the press and an article written on the new board members for the newsletter. Ask how each board member wants his or her name to be listed. Update the stationery, brochure, and any other material with the board names on them.

The First Board Meeting

The first meeting of the newly elected board is the president's opportunity to inspire the new members and invigorate the older members. Admit that being on the board will be hard work, but the reward is the satisfaction of running an organization that gets results.

Begin with the statement of purpose. What is our mission? Why does this organization exist? This may seem obvious to you, but it is important to emphasize that this is why the board and organization exist.

Second, what are our goals? New people especially need to know precisely what you want to do. If they have been involved in committees, they will know part of the picture. Now show them the big picture; point out how the board works to make all of the members and committees work. Ask the new and old members of the board for suggestions and dreams for the organization for the next year. They must have good ideas, or they would not be on the board! Schedule one meeting devoted exclusively to setting goals and making plans for this board to accomplish.

After you discuss the purpose and goals of the organization, go over the mechanics of how the board works. Many groups prepare a short, simple, "welcome to the board" fact sheet so that new members have the rules in writing. If you are part of a national organization, the national office may have brochures to help you orient new board members.

MECHANICS

For the benefit of all the board, tell the group the answers to the following questions. Who makes the agenda for board meetings? How can you put an item on the agenda? Who chairs the meeting? What rules are used?

What is confidential? Is anything covered at board meetings that should not be discussed outside of the meeting?

Who does what? Especially if your bylaws are out-of-date, it is important to discuss how to get the internal work done. For example, the treasurer may write checks and the president cosign them. The publicity chair may coordinate speaking engagements and booking of the slide show.

After you go over the nuts and bolts, go back to the beginning. Remind people of the importance of this job. Encourage them to participate fully and frankly in every meeting. *Ask* for their ideas. You probably will be pleasantly surprised to find what creative and caring people are on your board.

The day after the first meeting, the president calls new members to ask if they have questions. He or she asks, "Was anything perplexing about the meeting?" This will help the people who are thinking, "I wish I had asked . . ." or "I wish I knew . . ." Remind them of the procedure for adding something to the agenda.

Each veteran member of the board also calls his or her new "buddy" on the board to discuss the first meeting. Prime the discussion with a remark such as, "I remember when I first joined the board, I was confused about . . . until . . ." Answer questions and say you are glad he or she is now on the board.

Serving on the Board

The first year is really on-the-job training. Because most people are shy about speaking up until they have observed the group, new people probably will watch during the first few meetings. The president should make sure, however, that they do not spend their entire careers on the board as observers. As soon as possible, ask each new person to take an action for the group. Pair the new person with a veteran for a task, such as going with the fund-raising chair to sell a proposal to a local corporation or going with the chair of the jazz festival to a radio talk show. Let new people understudy with your most successful veterans for a while, then send them out on their own. When they succeed, be sure they have slots on the agenda in which to tell their stories. If they are disappointed by their early efforts, assign veterans to find better jobs for them.

Be sure there is opportunity both before and after the meetings for new people to meet and talk to the top officers of the organization. Plan to make the hospitality happen. Boards with twelve members can put a different person in charge of refreshments each month to get variety and a fair distribution of the work. Schedule a nonbusiness meeting two or three times a year, too, such as one day-long brainstorming session with an outside facilitator, one board picnic for families, and one board dinner with the paid staff.

It is a responsibility of the president to make sure that he or she has found the right job for each person. Meet quarterly, in person, with each board member until each has found a job he or she can feel good about. Create an atmosphere in which people are willing to propose new ideas and provide the leadership needed so that the money and people will be found to implement the ideas.

It is the responsibility of the president to handle, in person, any problems that may arise. If these are not eliminated immediately, they only will get worse. Decisions will begin to be made based on the personality of the person making the motion, rather than on the merit of the idea. If there are disputes to resolve, do it now!

Growing to the Role

The best part of serving on an active volunteer board is seeing the growth of the board members. People really *do* grow to the role. When they see that they can propose ideas, be listened to, get support, implement the ideas, involve other people, and expand the ideas next year, they will bring bigger and better plans to each meeting. Once new members feel confident in their jobs, it is time for the president to begin challenging them to chair committees, prepare reports, represent the group at a state or national meeting, testify for the group before government agencies, take bigger fund-raising responsibilities, or supervise the staff. Offer people serious responsibilities, rotate jobs, and give plenty of encouragement. You will be rewarded with a board that keeps getting better and better!

When You are the Veteran

When you have already served on the board a year or two and have a year or two left, your perspective changes. It now becomes your responsibility to become a talent scout, to find the best possible person to replace yourself. It is also your job to evaluate the work you laid out for yourself as a board member. Will it get done during your term? For example, will you finish renovation of the building or implementation of a new record-keeping system? Is it the wrong project for this group at this time? You may find that, although your group was enthusiastic about the park cleanup last year, they are now tired of spending Saturdays as unpaid scavengers. If it was *your* idea, it is *your* job either to give it away or to suggest stopping the program. Most people are too polite to propose we ax another member's program. Or possibly you had a good idea, which will continue after your term. Then it is your responsibility to make sure that a funding system is set up and working to pay for the program and that good people are eager to step into leadership jobs when you leave.

Your Term is Over—What Now?

Boards work best when upward mobility is built-in, when you can begin on the board and then become an officer. The officers serve one or two terms, then rotate off the board. If the group is part of a larger organization, the officers can go on to become leaders on the state, regional, or national levels. Very often, people use the skills and confidence they have learned in one group to launch new groups for new causes or to work for business or government.

If you choose to remain with the group, you can do several valuable jobs after being on the board. You can serve on the nominating committee. Because you know what the job entails, you can find new talent and persuade timid people to try the job. You also can serve on the audit committee, which reviews monthly expenses in detail, supervises the annual audit, and recommends improvements in the accounting system. You can serve as the confidential consultant to the current officers. Or you can simply be a loyal member and enjoy watching other people succeed in the work you enjoyed!

Transition Plan

The good part about rotating board members and committee chairs is that you get a continuous supply of new energy and fresh ideas. The hard part about rotating leaders is maintaining the momentum of the work and the quality of the leaders. When one set of officers gets ready to turn over their jobs to the next set of officers, the board should make a plan for the transition.

A transition plan must be written down. Good leaders are smart enough to keep a lot of information in their heads. This is fine until someone else has to do the job. Then the new person needs information in writing rather than information stored in someone else's brain. Before the transition, each leader should write down what he or she has done, how he or she did the work, what worked best, and what did not work. Add suggestions for the next person and thoughts on what you would have done if you had stayed another year. Most important of all, make sure that you include the name, address, and phone numbers of *everyone* you call for advice, help, supplies, work, or inspiration. List leaders of other groups, key committee people, merchants, politicians, state and national leaders, members of the press, advisers, and former leaders. (Also ask for this kind of information when any of the paid staff leaves.)

Board Development

Unlike a for-profit business, a nonprofit group cannot *hire* the leadership talent it needs. Instead, you have to learn how to take the people you already have — your members — make them into great committee chairs, and then make them into great board members. In business, you try to find the right person for the job. In a nonprofit group, you try to find the right job for the person, because people develop their leadership skills through work. This is called *board development*. Actually, this entire book is about board development.

The only way the board will get better at being the board is by tackling the big jobs, asking for the first donations, and doing the hard work. You have to do it first. Then you have to do it again and again until you master all the skills. The only way you will become a leader is by actually doing the work the organization needs done. When other people see that you can get results, they will follow your lead.

I realized this most vividly after comparing "I quit smoking" stories with a doctor. The doctor had gone through five different programs and finally kicked the habit at a special program for physicians offered by the Mayo Clinic. He described the rigors of withdrawal in gruesome detail. I finally had to ask, "That sounds terrible! Why not just keep smoking?" He answered, "Because I was killing my patients. I could say, 'You must quit smoking,' but as long as *I* smoked, they believed what they saw instead of what they heard. They heard, 'Smoking will kill you,' but they thought, 'If he *really* believed that smoking will kill you, he would not smoke.' The only way I could communicate was to do it myself."

There are lessons to be learned from this for board members who want to become better leaders. These lessons are:

1. People believe actions more than words. They believe what they see more than what they hear.

2. You have to practice what you preach. You cannot ask someone else to do something you will not do yourself.

3. The best person to help someone take a new action or overcome an old fear is someone who has done it himself or herself. If you have done it yourself, you can honestly say, "I was scared. Here's what I did to overcome my fear." You have to do it yourself first before you can help anyone else.

HOW TO BECOME A GREAT LEADER

When I asked people how they became great leaders, I was impressed over and over again by two things. First was the simplicity of the comments they made. Second was the universality of certain comments. Regardless of whether I was talking to a board member in Montana, a parish leader in Cleveland, a director in Chicago, a youth leader in Washington, D.C., a fund raiser in Mississippi, a publicity chair in California, the fresh vegetables chair of a barbecue committee in Tennessee, a newsletter editor in Oregon, or a volunteer coordinator in Montreal, I heard the same things. All had arrived at the same principles of how to make committees and boards succeed. Here are the tips from the best community leaders on how to be a great leader:

"Be there." Show up at all events. If corn has to be husked at 6:00 A.M. for the barbecue, signatures have to be collected on a petition in a downpour, or the hot line has to be answered on Christmas Eve, you do it first. Be there so that you know how it feels. Your presence makes the job important, and, because the job is important, you should be there.

"Pay attention to detail." The best leaders care about small details. They make sure that everything gets done so that people feel good. From giving the first greeting at the door to getting a ride home for the last senior citizen, a leader makes sure the job is done and done right.

"Listen." Listening can be learned and taught. A good leader will learn *from* the people in the organization. We all have seen a strong president take office after a weak president and make lions out of losers. When someone is asked "Why didn't you suggest that before?" they usually answer, "Nobody asked me." Give your people a chance to talk, work at listening to them, and teach them to listen to each other. Your reward will be the best organization with the best ideas in town.

"Work as a team." Even if you are inclined to go it alone, the strongest and most durable organizations are remarkable for how much they share work. Especially in strong community organizations without paid staff, it is essential to share leadership in order to cover the times when illness, divorce, transfers, or layoffs will deplete the leadership. The more people are involved, the broader your base will be and the harder it will be to collapse under strain.

"You are there to meet the needs of your members, not the other way around." Great leaders have one-track minds. They always ask, "How will this strengthen my organization? What will my people get? What will my board learn?"

"Do not do it for them." It is always tempting to sail into a crisis and be the hero by straightening out the mess. You will make better leaders and a more supple membership if you let them solve their own problems. They will learn to be resourceful, competent, and confident. They will make decisions and handle responsibility by themselves. But if you do the work for them, you will take away their independence and self-esteem. Leaders say, "You know that you have done a great job if you can leave and never be missed."

"Give a lot of reassurance." Work on their strengths. Say, "Look how well you are doing at . . ." If they think they are stars, they will act like stars.

"Keep your sense of humor!" Especially organizations that work with people under stress need to balance the work with humor. Humor keeps everything in perspective and keeps you going. Plan some fun, and enjoy celebrations as often as possible.

Ask your own board members to share tips for being a leader. Add to the list above, review the list often during your term of office, and then turn it over to the next group. Each board has the advantage of being able to build on the work of the last group, so it will accomplish even bigger and better things!

STEPS TO WORKING WITH MEMBERS, COMMITTEES, AND THE BOARD OF DIRECTORS

THE MEMBERSHIP COMMITTEE WILL:

1. Set a goal for the number of new members they will recruit in the next year.
2. Make a plan to sell memberships in a short membership drive and all year long.
3. Ask current members to ask new people to join the organization.
4. Match new members with a committee where they can be happy and get results.

THE BOARD OF DIRECTORS WILL:

1. Ask organization leaders to become candidates for the election to the board of directors.
2. Tell candidates exactly what is involved in serving on the board, especially concerning the responsibility to raise money.
3. Welcome and train new board members.
4. Use the committees and board work to improve the leaders' skills and encourage each one to tackle bold new programs.
5. Develop a transition plan to transfer important history and information as veteran members leave the board.

11

Program Planning and Evaluation

> ". . . it wasn't raining when Noah started
> building the ark."
> —Harold J. Seymour
> *Designs for Fundraising*

Planning is your chance to explore where the organization can go. Your only limit is your imagination. If the board can dream it up, you can find a way to do it! Planning is also your chance to find new ways for your organization to solve problems and get results. It is the tool you use to keep your organization young, fresh, supple, and powerful.

If you do *not* plan seriously, the organization will do "the same as last year," and the current officers will do what the last officers did. There will be no growth, no expansion, no innovation. Before you know it, you will have done the same program with the same people for ten years, with no new blood and no thrills.

Good planning will get you out of the doldrums into action! If the board takes time for serious, long-range planning, you will:

1. Know what to do next.
2. Agree on what to do next.
3. Get the results you want—not just run programs or have meetings.

4. Allocate your limited resources, money, staff, and time to doing what you want done.

5. Reduce burnout among board members and staff.

6. Raise money more easily — good planning makes the organization cost-effective, because you are doing the right thing. This appeals especially to business and corporate sponsors.

7. Know who you are, where you are, how you got there, and where you are going next. This will make it easy to orient new board members and staff.

The first challenge to the president is not the planning itself. The challenge is to persuade the members of the board that they ought to plan! Once they have tried it, they will be delighted at how planning improves their results and their understanding of the operation. Furthermore, planning gets easier, quicker, and more effective every year that you do it.

Board members are usually eager to do whatever the organization exists to do — feed hungry children, paint murals, or stop nuclear power plants. So the best way to get them to want to plan is to show them how good plans will help each of them achieve his or her goals more quickly.

WHEN TO PLAN

The best time to start planning is right after the election of new officers. Arrange a meeting during which the officers and chairs will discuss the goals of the organization. This will encourage people to express new ideas, set high goals, and inspire each officer to carry out the organization's mission. The president can review the present state of the organization. Then schedule one or more meetings to map out a plan for the organization.

BEFORE THE FIRST PLANNING MEETING

First, the president should decide what he or she wants to see happen in the organization during his or her term of office. Make a list of programs that should be kept, programs to be phased out, and programs to start. Challenge the board. This will be the president's own plan.

Then, the president should encourage board members, committee chairs, and other officers to make similar plans. Ask, "If you could wave a magic wand over the organization (or your committee), what would you make happen during the next three years?" This allows the leaders to think about their dreams for the organization, then make them come true.

WHO SHOULD PLAN?

Anything done is done because somebody decided to do it. If you want to make a plan that will work, those who will do the work should do the planning. Newly elected officers and committee chairs should plan for themselves, their committees, the organization. If you have paid staff, see the section on work plans and supervision in Chapter 16 for more information about how to make plans with your employees.

THE PLANNING MEETINGS

Break the planning into two sections. First, make the plan for next year. Second, make your plan for five years.

Have your best people attend the planning meetings. Do not take no for an answer. Remind them that the meetings will help them plan their own work. Even if they never have planned as part of a group before, they can plan well. All they need is curiosity about what makes the group work and a desire to do their best.

ONE-YEAR PLAN

Review Statement of Purpose

First, review the organization's statement of purpose. This is always the place to start when making plans. Why is the organization here? What is it for? What are we supposed to be doing? If your mission statement is current, you can move to setting goals. If your purpose has changed, bring it up-to-date.

Set Goals

The key to making great plans is to set clear goals. The goals do not have to be complicated or novel, but they should be clear to everyone on the board. Successful leaders I polled ranked clear goals as the most important factor in creating a successful organization.

Clear goals are the link between the philosophy of the organization as expressed in its statement of purpose and the activities of the organization, which make up the program. Without clear goals the group may be "all talk" without results, or it may be mired in repetitive activities. Setting goals is the single most important job of the board of directors.

Make a list of goals for the coming year. Ask, "What do we want to do?" Use numbers. For example, the statement of purpose of a group of ex-offenders may say, "Our purpose is to improve education for ex-offenders in Houston." This is still the group's purpose. The group then translates this into goals — with numbers — for the year:

1. Teach twenty ex-offenders how to teach reading. Help them set up and run a reading program for one hundred ex-offenders who want to learn to read.

2. Help fifty ex-offenders finish high school.

3. Increase the membership of the organization from two hundred to four hundred.

The first few times you set goals, you may choose numbers that are too high or too low. But you will get better with practice. Meanwhile, it still is essential that each goal be as specific as possible. If a goal does not have a number, it is not a goal; it is still a dream. Dreams are wonderful, but they are not part of serious, long-range planning.

As management expert Peter Drucker says, "Achievement is never possible except against specific, limited, clearly defined targets, in business as well as in a service institution. Only if targets are defined can resources be allocated to their attainment, priorities and deadlines be set, and somebody be held accountable for results."[1]

Inventory Current Programs

After the board agrees on goals for the next year, take an inventory of your current activities. Take inventory of what the organization did last year and, most important, who did it. What happened and who made it happen? New officers should talk to outgoing officers to get an idea of what their predecessors did the previous year. If you hire staff, ask each staff member to prepare a one-page report on what he or she accomplished the previous year, and hopes to do this year.

Now go through your current programs one at a time. List what is good about each one and the problems connected with each. Decide which programs to keep, to change, and to stop. If you choose to continue a program, find out what the program will cost and what it will accomplish. If you decide to change the program, the leaders in charge of this program will have to decide what changes are needed and who will make them.

HOW TO DISCONTINUE A PROGRAM

You may have programs that began years ago but no longer pay their own way and fail to attract volunteers. If a program cannot raise its own money, or does not attract new people, you should stop the program. It is a drain on the organization. This is very hard for new officers because they do not want to antagonize anyone.

Sometimes a feeble program is kept alive just for a few people who love to do the work. If the program can be run by this handful of loyal workers and does not cost anything, leave it alone. In 1971 I worked in a church that let five women use a meeting room every month. The women started their project, rolling bandages, during World War I. They liked rolling bandages and used the occasion socially as well as to do "good work." The bandages and space were free. They were not interfering with anything else. So they went on rolling bandages for decades.

But sometimes a few people keep up a "favorite" program that drains dollars away from the organization. The program may use office space, supplies, or even staff. If the program does not pay its own way by raising money, bringing in members, or producing leaders, stop subsidizing the program.

There are two simple ways to discontinue a program. The best is to give it away. Say you started a recycling center when everybody was enthusiastic about recycling, only to find that the center produces less income and requires more work than you projected. Only four people turn up on Saturday mornings to run it. After a little investigation, you will find that you can give the project to the local high school. Then the center will be run by high-energy teenagers; the apathy problem is solved by sharing responsibility among high school organizations. The four adults who like the program can serve as community sponsors if they like.

The second way is to put the project "on hold" for three months. Do not spend money on it, and transfer staff to something else. If, after three months, people are clamoring to get the program back, locate the two people who clamor most and put them in charge. If they can find a way to involve more people and make the program pay for itself, the program can survive. More likely you will find that after three months, no one misses the program.

Stopping out-of-date projects is most difficult for organizations whose boards are made up of the chairs of active committees. The advantage of this system is that members of the board know the organization's activities firsthand — what they are and what they cost. The disadvantage is that in order to keep their seats on the board, board members may want to keep their committees alive well past the end of their usefulness.

One way to solve this is to set a dollar figure or a new-member quota for each committee. For example, you could say that each committee must raise two hundred dollars more than its expenses or recruit twenty new members each year. If the committee misses its quota two years in a row, it is no longer considered a committee. The members may continue to meet for purely social or altruistic reasons, but they need not be allocated organizational resources or a seat on the board.

Before you can start new, exciting projects, you must stop unpopular older programs that are a drain on resources. So the first step in planning is to prune old projects that no longer are wanted.

Starting New Projects

New projects are the most enjoyable part of planning. Having stopped some projects and decided which projects will continue, the board can decide what money, staff time, and other resources you will need to continue the projects you want to keep.

Now evaluate what resources are available to invest in a new project. Decide what new programs you want to try. You can get plenty of good ideas if you give leaders a chance to say what they want to do. Then decide which program you want to try first. Here are some good reasons to start a new program:

1. The program will improve the quality of people's lives.

2. It will give your members a sense of power. It will give them the confidence they need so they can solve their problems and control their lives.

3. It will build the organization. It will bring in members and develop leaders.

4. It will produce dependable, renewable, internally controlled income.

5. It will be manageable. The program must not be so large or the outcome so uncertain that your members will get discouraged. The members must believe from the start that there is a good chance of reaching the goal.

6. It will matter. The members should care deeply about the program.

7. It will be clear. It must fit into people's experience and understanding of their community.

8. It will be urgent. It must be either a program that people are eager to try or a new tactic to solve an old problem. "What we did last year" is seldom urgent.

9. It will provide many opportunities for people to participate. There should be a place for every person who wants to help.

10. It will be fun.

11. It will make your members proud. It will appeal to their spirit. Your members will be eager to participate because they admire the leaders, respect the program, and look forward to working together.

For any direct-action or advocacy organization, a good program will have one more feature:

12. It will alter the relations of power. It will make the organization and its members a factor in future decision making by politicians, employers, or public officials.[2]

Here are some *bad* reasons to start a program:

1. We always have done it this way.
2. We can get a grant.
3. We can put someone we like on the payroll.
4. We can let the staff do it.
5. We can get a lot of publicity.
6. If we do not do it, no one else will.
7. If we do not do it, someone else will.

These might be results of doing a program, but they should not be *reasons* for starting it. Remember: you get what you ask for. If you choose a program in order to get a grant, you will get the grant. You will not necessarily get a good program. When the grant runs out, you will have nothing at all. If you choose a program in order to get publicity, all you will get is a scrapbook full of clippings. You will not necessarily get money, people, or power. But if you choose a program in order to get results, you can always raise money, hire pleasant employees, and generate publicity on the basis of the results you will get.

If you still are uncertain whether to launch a program, ask yourself, "What would happen if it were *not* done?" "What difference would the program make three months, six months, or one year from now?" If no one on the board can offer an urgent reason for this program, there is probably more to be lost than gained by starting it now.

It is much harder to stop a program than to start one. The two hardest jobs facing a good board are stopping obsolete programs and firing unproductive staff. Save yourself this unpleasant work by being *very* selective about what you start and whom you hire. A good program idea should make your spirits soar. If an idea does not do this, leave it until another time.

Planning a New Program

After you decide what new program ideas meet the criteria, write a plan for each one. Do as you did at the beginning, when you were planning the organization itself. Ask: Who, what, when, where, why, how, and how much? The most important question is, Who? Each member of the board who will lead a new project can make a plan for his or her project. At the planning meeting, the board can compare the plans and make a budget for each one. The enthusiasm of the board and amount of money available will determine how many programs you can do.

FIVE-YEAR PLAN

As soon as the board has completed the first-year plan it can take action on the plan. It is a psychological boost to get an early start and see tangible results early in your term of office. Later, the board should pull back and consider a long-range plan for the organization as a whole.

Really stretch your imagination and plan what the organization will do for the next five years. The planners should not only decide what they will accomplish during their terms of office, but also plan what the next person will do. By planning through two terms you anticipate what the next person will need, and you will help the organization avoid transition problems. Long-range planning will make people think of the organization as an entity that will continue after their terms of office are over.

Advance Work

After three months, the president should meet with each officer and review the annual plan. What is working well, and what unexpected problems have come up that you did not anticipate? It is usually in the first three months that officers begin to discover what previous officers *should* have done. They begin saying, "Boy, I wish that when Joe was the treasurer he had . . ." or "When Maria turned this over to me, she should have . . ." This is the president's opportunity to say, "OK, let's not make the same mistake twice. How can we plan our work to prepare for the long run?" Then set aside a day or two to consider seriously the long-range plans of the organization. It is very helpful to recruit or hire a person from outside the organization to chair this discussion.

How to Make Long-Range Plans

A five-year plan is hard to put together the first time you try because few of us make long-range plans. At most we plan one year at a time. But it can be done, and it is worth doing.

A long-range plan enables you to accomplish greater goals. If you know where you want to be five years from now, you also will know better how to plan your activities for this year. Start with this year's plan, then project what will happen over the next five years. If this year's program can have more than one possible outcome, plan what you will do in each case.

Here is an example of a five-year plan for a membership drive. The first version is a conservative plan, and the second version is a bolder plan. Once the board chooses which plan it wants, each person can set a personal goal to make the plan work. The board can plan a budget to provide enough money and put the work on the annual calendar to get all the work done at the best time.

MEMBERSHIP DRIVE

Say that the organization now has two hundred paid members. The board's goal for the coming year is to sign up another two hundred members. If you make a five-year plan, you will see that there are two ways to plan the membership campaign. You can copy what you did last year, in which case you can hope to get two hundred new members each year:

Last Year	This Year	Second Year	Third Year	Fourth Year	Fifth Year
200	400	600	800	1,000	1,200

Or you can be more ambitious. You could decide to double your membership each year. In that case your membership each year would look like this:

Last Year	This Year	Second Year	Third Year	Fourth Year	Fifth Year
200	400	800	1,600	3,200	6,400

Obviously there is a big difference between 6,400 members and 1,200. By planning your work over five years the board can — and should — decide now if you want to grow at a slow but steady rate or if you want to work harder to grow more quickly.

A five-year plan will make sure that *you* control the organization, rather than letting the organization control you. You can get the results you want rather than react to crisis. Long-range planning gives you strength and freedom. Most important, be sure that you have a five-year plan for your fund-raising strategy, so that you do not live from budget to budget, or even worse, from grant to grant. This is *your* organization. You can make the plans to accomplish your goals today and five years from today.

EVALUATION

"At the end of a concert at Carnegie Hall, Walter Damrosch asked the composer Rachmaninoff what sublime thoughts had passed through his head as he stared out at the audience during the playing of his concerto. 'I was counting the house,' said Rachmaninoff."

David Ogilvy,
— *Confessions of an Advertising Man.*

"Don't expect what you don't inspect."

W. Clement Stone,
— *The Success System That Never Fails.*

Evaluation is an essential part of planning. It is the last step in this year's plan and the first step in next year's plan. The board inspects the year's work in order to see whether it has produced results. Use evaluation to find out which of your programs are most valuable — hence the word *evaluation.*

An evaluation by the board makes it easier to create next year's plan. If your board is new at planning, the best way to improve is to determine once a year which plans worked and which did not. Evaluation tells you where to spend your money and assign your staff so that you reduce waste and staff burnout. It tells you where you are getting results and where you are just running programs or holding meetings.

Fortunately, you need only two qualities in order to be a great evaluator: curiosity and courage. You must want to know what works and does not work. You will have disappointments if you are at all bold in your planning, but you need curiosity to ask, "What went wrong? Where did our plan fail? What did we miss? How can we do better next time?" And you need courage to use the answers to make better plans next year.

How to Evaluate Your Program Plans

The key to making competent evaluations, like the key to effective planning, is to set clear goals. Begin by reviewing your goals. Will they accomplish the purpose of the organization? Can you measure whether you have achieved them? If the answer to those questions is yes, collect the data you need to measure the results. If possible, try to collect the information you need throughout the year.

Collecting information never should be allowed to become an end in itself. The facts are the raw material the board uses to decide what it wants to do next. After you collect the numbers you need for each program, the board must evaluate — make value judgments.

Consider the value of the program to the organization. In each case you have three options: stop the program, increase the program, or decrease the program. There should be no such thing as "doing the same thing as last year." If the program is working well, you should expand it. If it is not working well, it must be stopped. If a program works well, but will be less successful because of circumstances beyond your control, you should decrease it. For example, your voters' registration drive may be very effective in an election year. You decided to register 2,000 people and registered 2,300. But there is no election next year, so there will be less demand for this program. You reduce your organization's work in this area.

OUTSIDE EVALUATION — FOR YOU

If you are part of a local coalition or a state or national network, you can help other organizations and be helped if you evaluate one another. In this way you each get an outsider with experience in the same field to inspect your work. At the same time, you can pick up new ideas to improve your own group.

OUTSIDE EVALUATION — FOR THE FUNDER

If you get large grants from foundations or government agencies, they may ask you to have the funded program evaluated by someone outside the organization. The funder will tell you if you should include a fee to be paid to an outside evaluator in your proposal, or if the funder will hire someone to evaluate your program. A professional outside evaluation is supposed to make your program accountable to the foundation board and to the taxpayers.

You may be given little or no choice about the style or substance of the evaluation. In that case, be polite and helpful, but do not expect to get an evaluation that will be very useful to you. But if you can, try to take this opportunity to obtain a top-notch evaluation that will help you do a better job.

When you begin the program, try to meet the funder's staff and set goals. What, exactly, does the funder want to know, and what, exactly, do you want to know? Then discuss who could best do this evaluation. Do you need someone with personal experience, work experience, academic credentials, or expertise in your field? Will you need more than one person? Get the best people available to give you the benefit of their experience and ideas. Be sure that both you and the funder know what the evaluator will do, how long the evaluation will take, and what is expected of you during the evaluation.

Allow enough time to interview and hire the best possible person to do the evaluation. You may have to fight to get the kind of person you want. Do not be intimidated by credentials or complicated language. You know your organization. It is right for you to insist on an evaluator who understands your needs, respects your members, and appreciates your mission. It is fair to ask for someone who can speak and write in words you understand.

Once the evaluator is hired, your board members and staff who have worked on the funded program, the funder's staff, and the person or persons doing the evaluation must meet and write goals for the evaluation. Without clear goals, groups sometimes feel the outside evaluator is working on a hidden agenda. He or she is treated like an inquisitor, the results are ignored or denied, and the effort is wasted. It is much more to your advantage to make one of the goals an evaluation that will *improve* your program. This goal should be stated in writing, too. Then the work of the evaluator will pay off for you as well as for the funder.

Tell the evaluator the questions you would like answered and problems you would like solved. Each member of the board and staff can be asked, "What do you need to know to do a better job?" If the evaluator knows that you *want* answers to your questions, he or she will work harder to produce information you can use. Then, you can use the results immediately and with gratitude. If you establish mutual respect, you will both be able to enjoy and benefit from the evaluation experience.

THINK BIG!

Great leaders make great plans. As with all the other skills you need to run your organization, your planning will get better and better the more often you do it. After the first few years, you will look forward to the planning sessions because they will allow you to stretch your imaginations and shake up the organization. Be bold — make a great plan, and then make the plan work! Remember the words of Daniel Burnham: "Make no little plans. They have no magic to stir men's blood and probably themselves will not be realized. Make big plans; aim high in hope and work, remembering that a noble, logical diagram once recorded will never die, but long after we are gone will be a living thing, asserting itself with ever-growing insistency. Remember that our sons and grandsons are going to do things that would stagger us. Let your watch-word be order and your beacon beauty. Think big!"[3]

STEPS TO PROGRAM PLANNING
BY THE BOARD OF DIRECTORS

THE PRESIDENT WILL:

1. Make a personal plan for next year.
2. Ask new officers and committee chairs to make personal plans for next year.
3. Ask leaders to attend a planning meeting to review each person's plan of action and the organization's plan.

THE BOARD OF DIRECTORS WILL:

1. Review and reaffirm or revise the statement of purpose.
2. Set goals for the organization for next year. Clear goals are written down, described with numbers, and approved by the board; for example: sign up two hundred new members.
3. Plan programs to accomplish these goals.
4. Have one or two people take responsibility for each program. They set it up and keep it going.
5. Have people responsible for each program create a method for collecting data to measure whether the program meets the goal.
6. Prepare a five-year plan of action for the organization.
7. Evaluate the programs. Collect final data — such as total number of new members per program — then decide which programs to keep and which to stop.
8. Turn the evaluation over to new officers to prepare next year's plan.

STEPS TO EVALUATION

The board of directors can use the same steps to evaluate their programs, fund raising, structure, or staff.

THE BOARD OF DIRECTORS WILL:

1. Recruit key leaders for evaluation meetings.
2. Collect information.
3. Make value judgments.
4. Design additions, subtractions, and changes.
5. Make changes.
6. Establish a method of collecting data for the next evaluation.
7. Choose a date for the next evaluation. Write it on next year's calendar.

EVALUATION CALENDAR

Because evaluations are so important, they should be treated as special opportunities and given priority on your calendar. The evaluations and other activities can be scheduled on next year's calendar in this order:

THE BOARD OF DIRECTORS WILL:

1. Evaluate bylaws. Revise if necessary. Approve at board meeting before annual meeting.
2. Hold annual meeting. Delegates approve changes in bylaws and elect new board of directors.
3. Outgoing board evaluates their program work. Gives evaluation to new officers.
4. New board makes program plans for next year.
5. If it hires staff, board evaluates last year's staff work. Reassign to accomplish this year's program plans.
6. Prepare budget for next year.
7. Evaluate last year's fund-raising strategy.
8. Design strategy to guarantee income for this year's programs.

12

Strategy for Self-Sufficiency

> *"I go fishing up in Maine every summer.*
> *Personally, I am very fond of strawberries*
> *and cream; but I find that for some strange*
> *reason fish prefer worms. So when I go fish-*
> *ing, I don't think about what I want. I think*
> *about what they want. I don't bait the hook*
> *with strawberries and cream. Rather, I*
> *dangle a worm or a grasshopper in front of*
> *the fish and say: 'Wouldn't you like to have*
> *that?' Why not use the same common sense*
> *when fishing for men?"*
> —Dale Carnegie
> *How to Win Friends and Influence People*

Fund raising for a nonprofit organization is a great opportunity for leadership. You get to use all of the skills of the for-profit world and all of the art of the nonprofit. You can sell tangible results like clean air, healthy children, and safe streets and also the intangibles like justice, equality, and dignity. You get to offer people what *they* want and make them feel good about themselves and their community. What more could you want?

An organization's fund-raising strategy is like a for-profit company's sales plan. It is a carefully designed campaign to get more people to give you more money every year. As in any sales effort, you are looking for renewable money—people who will give to you every year, year after year. You want to find ways to get a dependable income in the least time, expending the least energy and money to get it.

An organization that can raise all of its budget is called *self-sufficient.* This chapter will show you how the board can develop a strategy to make the organization self-sufficient. You *can* raise all of the money you want to achieve your goals. Decide that you want to be self-sufficient; then plan a strategy to make the money.

FUND-RAISING GOALS

The board can set goals so you raise money and strengthen the organization at the same time. Then you can conduct your fund raising so that the people involved all feel good about the campaign, themselves, and the organization.

First, list the organization's sales goals. This will help you divide the work into steps. For example, the board can say that its sales goals are:

1. Identify what you have to sell.
2. Identify who will sell.
3. Identify the market for your program. Who will buy? Who needs it and who wants it?

Second, set goals for the impact of the fund-raising campaign on the members and leaders. You can say you want to:

1. Reflect the strengths and values of the organization.
2. Give many people an opportunity to learn new skills.
3. Identify new leaders.
4. Challenge the existing leaders.
5. Make people feel more competent and confident as individuals and as a group.

If your organization is new, it can prepare a one-year fund-raising plan and a five-year self-sufficiency plan at the same time. If the organization has been in existence for a year or more, it already will have funding sources. If these are dependable, renewable sources, your organization is already on the right track. If they are sources that you do not control and cannot depend on for the next five years, then the board needs to consider two plans. First is the fund-raising plan to raise the money for your programs for next year. Second is a five-year plan to move your fund-raising efforts to sources that can produce dependable, internally controlled funds.

WHAT CAN WE SELL?

Fund raising is just selling your organization to the public. The first step in your fund-raising plan is to identify what the group has to sell. What do you do that other people need? What do you have that someone else may want? It is often helpful to bring in someone from outside the board to help you brainstorm about the best points of the organization. You may be so close to the group that "you can't see the forest for the trees." The help of an enthusiastic consultant or experienced fund raiser from another group will help you see all of the advantages of your organization in a fresh way. Make a list of the benefits of your group, such as:

Personal benefits. Why do you belong to this group? Why did you join, and why did you stay in? What is your payoff? The answers may be material or emotional or both. If you are a member of a community group, you may get tangible benefits: I helped open the health clinic, or I helped stop the expressway. If you are a member of a self-help group, you may get personal benefits: every meeting makes me more confident of my ability to solve my problems, or belonging to this group has given me joy and strength.

Whatever type of group you belong to, you are getting many benefits. You may learn new skills, such as how to chair meetings or make supper for two hundred people. It could be that you were able to get results in a group that you were not able to get as an individual. You can get access to the press or to politicians who would not listen to you if you were alone. It simply may be that you get to make and keep new friends.

Community benefits. What does the community gain from our work? Make a list of your accomplishments and who will benefit from them today and in the future. For example, if you launch the first adult literacy program in your county, you immediately benefit everyone who learns to read and teaches people to read. In the long run, the program will benefit local employers who want to hire skilled workers, the insurance companies that pay out claims because injured workers could not read instructions, the taxpayers who have to pay for unemployment and welfare programs, the citizens concerned about crime (the highest rate of illiteracy is among the incarcerated), the public libraries whose budgets are based on the volume of books checked out, the advertising agencies and direct mail marketers who sell through the written word, the companies that publish or sell books, magazines, or newspapers, and writers.

Dreams. These are the intangibles that you can sell as well as you can sell tangible results. For example, the members may love your group because you saved the historic railroad station from demolition and made it a tourist center. People outside the group may like the *idea* that people in the town were able to preserve American culture or that respect for the past triumphed over greed. Donors often are more responsive to the ideals symbolized by a victory than to the tangible results.

Think about what your program represents in terms of human values. Tug people's heartstrings. As salespeople say, "You have to sell the sizzle as well as the steak." Especially if you do not have the steak yet — just plans for one — you have to sell your dreams along with the plans. Richard Steckel of the Children's Museum of Denver has used this technique successfully. He says, "By its nature, the Children's Museum projects and can market a number of intangibles that individuals and businesses want to buy. Some of these are creativity, wonder, learning, discovery, fun, enthusiasm, resourcefulness, and self-esteem." What are the qualities represented by your organization? What are the dreams of the members?

WHO CAN SELL?

Great fund raisers are made, not born. You get to be a good fund raiser by asking people for money. You get to be a *great* fund raiser by getting *other* people to do it. When you believe in the organization's mission, you will teach yourself and others the sales skills you need.

First consider the best fund raisers you know. Think of the people who ask you for money and make you glad to give it. What is so outstanding about these people? Make a list of the qualities you see. Your list may include:

1. Passion for the cause.
2. Sense of humor.
3. Patience and persistence.
4. Enjoyment in working with others.
5. Appreciation of others—for example, always sends thank-you notes.

Now consider some names of people who might be willing to give you advice on how to raise money. These would include successful fund raisers for other nonprofit organizations and successful salespeople for for-profit businesses. They can tell you how to choose prospects, practice and test a sales pitch, use teamwork and quotas, and do prompt follow-up to assure repeat sales. Then recruit salespeople.

Leaders as Sellers

Anyone who cares about the organization can sell. The more someone wants this organization, the more he or she will sell. In order to guarantee a dependable income every year, as many members as possible should ask for money from as many sources as possible. But although everyone can sell, the elected officers are the "pace cars" for the fund-raising effort. They set the standards in both time and money. They ask for the largest donations, and they ask first. They also give first. In order for all of the members to believe that this is worth doing, worth doing well, and worth doing *now*, the leaders must set the example!

The elected leaders should set the pace in raising money, because people believe what they see more than what they hear. The president may say, "We really need to raise money." But if the president does not ask for contributions, no one else will believe that asking for money is important. The president should say, "I want to see this program take place now, so I have raised one thousand dollars. I know that our neighbors and local businesses want this program, too, because I got donations from twenty families and five local businesses. Only one business said no, and even they said I should come back in October to ask again. I know that this program will work, and that our community will 'buy it.' "

Giving and asking go together for the leaders of a community organization. Giving first makes it easier for them to ask others for money. Nothing is more convincing to a leader than investing his or her own money in a worthwhile organization. Ironically, people who persuade others to give also persuade themselves to give more at the same time. It is not unusual for the board to give their donations, ask others to give, and then give again.

Asking others to give to the organization will make the leaders put into words what the organization means to them. When they ask others to give, the leaders will learn how the group is perceived by others. You may be delighted to learn that the community thinks you are wonderful and wonders why you did not ask for money sooner! It is usually easier to ask for money than you thought it would be.

Most of all, when board members ask for money, it is *their* victory when the money is raised. They know they have the ability to plan a program and raise the money. Because all money raising is "people giving to people," when your board members ask for money, they will create lasting relationships that will raise money year after year.

Should Staff Sell?

If you have paid staff, should the staff raise money? There are several disadvantages to this. The most serious is that the staff become self-employed if they raise their own salaries. They no longer work *for* the board or the organization; they work for themselves. Secondly, if the staff develop good relationships with funders (people give to people) and then are hired away by another organization, or get mad and quit, they take those relationships with them. Letting the staff raise money makes for very fragile funding.

The staff are your employees. You hire them because they have special skills—secretarial, counseling, organizing, bookkeeping, teaching. You pay them because you want talented people to do those jobs full-time. Why ask someone with special skills to ask for money? You can do that yourself, and you can train any member of your group to do it.

If the staff does not ask for money, what can they do? They can prepare the necessary papers and sales packages. They can do the reporting and record keeping for the campaign. Best of all, they can serve as trainers. They can teach new people how to sell the organization. As the organization grows, they can teach the more experienced fund raisers how to train the newcomers.

Any leader can be taught to raise money if he or she cares about the organization and is willing to practice. Persistence is the key to sales and the key to teaching leaders to sell. The job of the staff is to encourage the leaders to keep trying with a positive attitude until they succeed. Sue Gould, president of Chimera Self Defense for Women, proved this works teaching women to kick. The same principles will work when the staff teaches the leadership to sell the organization. Gould says, "We demand that women be positive about themselves. Women who say 'I can't kick!' after two attempts are not being fair with themselves. Women who have practiced a kick forty times never tell us they can't do it. Practice always works, and improvement comes with repetition."[1]

Professionals

If you do not have your own staff, you may be tempted to hire a professional fund-raising firm to "do it for us." If you are planning a short-term campaign to raise a very large amount of money (at least $100,000), it may be a good investment for you to hire an outside consultant. A fund-raising consultant can help you plan your campaign, choose prospects, set up the committees, and make a calendar. But he or she will *not* "do it for you." You still will have to do the asking yourselves.

According to the ethics of the fund-raising profession, a professional never will ask for a percentage of the amount raised. Instead, the professional will ask for a fee based on the time spent and the cost of the staff provided. Professional fund raisers consider taking a percentage unethical because this would tempt the fund raiser to organize a hard sell in order to increase his or her share. But the following year *you* could discover that a heavy-handed campaign created a burned-out market. If you want to hire a reputable firm to design a campaign for you, ask the largest nonprofit organizations in your town, such as the university or the hospital, whom they have employed. Then ask for bids on your job, and interview the person who will be assigned to work with your group. In the long run, most groups are better off doing the work to raise money themselves. See Chapter 24, "Bibliography and Resources," for advice on books and resources to help the board improve their fund-raising skills.

MARKETS: WHO WILL BUY?

After you decide what to sell and who will sell it, the board can discuss whom to sell it to. This is your "market," the people who will buy all the wonderful activities of your group. You can sell to anyone who will need or want your organization. In general terms, the sources of money available to your nonprofit organization will be churches, corporations, foundations, government agencies, individuals, and United Ways.

Independence comes from diversity in fund raising. The more sources of money you can count on, the stronger your organization will be. A clear understanding of the advantages and disadvantages attached to each source of money will help the board plan to produce the money the organization needs now and in the future.

Plan one meeting to discuss the pros and cons of each source of money. Here is an introduction to some of the advantages and disadvantages of your options. Depending on your community, some may be much better or worse than others. Planning will get easier every year, as the leaders get more experience working with funding sources. In the beginning, you will have to check with successful organizations in your own field and in your own community for recommendations on the most reliable funding for your group.

All Sources

Six things are true for all sources of money. These are:

1. You are good people doing good work to improve your community. You *deserve* the money!

2. The only way to get money is to ask for it.

3. You are never the only one asking. There is competition for every source of money.

4. People give to people. Even in the largest government agency, you have to find the right person to ask if you want to get the money.

5. It is there. The money is there to be had if you ask.

6. There are strings attached. There is always a string on the money. Be sure that you can accept the money and the string in good faith.

Church Money

Church money may be in the form of small donations from a local church or large grants from a national program such as the Roman Catholic Church's Campaign for Human Development (CHD), which gave away six million dollars in 1979. The largest national church programs run like foundations. They require written proposals, give grants for only one to three years, are based in New York or Washington, and tend to fund more traditional programs.

On the local level, churches and synagogues always have supported local community activities through their funds, staff, communications networks, buildings, and examples. They will continue to be excellent resources for new organizations. Almost any organization can ask for support from local churches or synagogues. The advantages of money from a local church or synagogue follow:

The donation may be big or small, depending on the size of the church.

Churches also can give you in-kind donations such as office space, use of audiovisual and office equipment, and facilities with kitchens and child care rooms for fund-raising benefits or meetings.

Their leaders can teach you how to raise money. Churches raise all of their own money every year. They get no government money (other than a break on their property taxes) and virtually no foundation grants. In 1980, churches received 46.3 percent of all charitable contributions—more than twenty-two billion dollars.[2] Church leaders can teach you how to raise money from your own members because they do it best.

Receiving money from a church can legitimize your organization.

A church may fund a wider variety of projects than would either the foundations or the corporations. The church's *purpose* is to help the poor, the homeless, the oppressed, the prisoners, the widows, and the orphans (Matt. 25). Unlike foundations, churches are not required to report their contributions to the IRS, and they do not have to limit their gifts to 501(c)(3) organizations.

Like local corporations, churches have an investment in the community. Many churches have a large physical plant and many members in the community. They are more likely to give you ongoing donations because they have a stake in the future of their congregation.

There are a few problems associated with asking for money from churches and synagogues in your community, and you must consider them before you ask. The disadvantages follow:

Many churches have their own programs and projects, which come first. They may do very little outside funding unless the program will benefit or involve members of the church.

Most churches require organizations to conform to their moral views.

Because churches are not required to report their giving to the IRS, there is no central collection of church giving records. The only way to find out where a church gives its money is through leaders of the church.

Corporate Money

Corporations are for-profit businesses. The money they give to charity comes out of their profits before taxes. Legally, American corporations may give away up to 5 percent of their pretax net income, but the national average is around 1 percent. In 1980, corporations gave $2.4 billion—5.3 percent of all philanthrophic dollars to nonprofit organizations.[3] This was the second year that corporate giving exceeded foundation giving in the United States. Approximately one-half of the money was given to United Way drives and then redistributed through the United Way to local agencies. In recent years, corporations have been the fastest-growing source of funds for nonprofit groups. This source probably will continue to grow as community organizations get better at asking.

The advantages of taking corporation and business funds follow:

The donation can be large or small.

They can keep giving you money every year.

Business people succeed because they are able to make good decisions quickly. Thus you may be able to get a donation from a corporation in a matter of weeks, as opposed to months for a foundation grant or years for a government grant.

They can give you more than money. In addition to grants, gifts, and loans, the corporations in your community can make in-kind donations such as supplies, equipment, or printing. If you make any sort of product, from crafts to cookbooks, businesses can purchase your products in bulk to use as premiums or employee gifts. Best of all, corporations can share their expertise with you. Larger companies already employ people with the skills you need — secretaries, artists, salespeople. Ask for their help. For example, the Lambs farm offers retarded young people a chance to do productive work. When they began a mail-order business from their bakery, the experts at the Kitchens of Sara Lee invented a kind of brownie that can be prepared by the retarded young people at the farm and that also will freeze and mail well.

It is easy to find out what a corporation will like. Grant expert Tim Saasta says, "The corporate apple never falls very far from the corporate tree." If you read the business section of your newspaper, ask a stockbroker, or simply ask employees, you can find out what the company does. Then match your program with the company's products. Bottle and can companies sponsor recycling centers. A shoe company paid for booklets describing walking tours of historic cities. A camera company promoted high school photojournalism. A paper company gave $5,000 and advice from their forestry specialists to a historic property in Virginia to replace and restore the trees killed and hurt during a freak storm. Ask yourself, "What do they do, what do we do, and how can we do it together?" Or start with your own program and ask, "Who benefits? Who *makes* money from this program?" Every company that will sell more of its product because of your work is a likely partner.

Like foundations, few corporate giving programs have full-time staff, but most of those that have staff are excellent. Find one good corporate giving person, and he or she can introduce you to others.

The disadvantages of taking corporate and business funds follow:

It can be difficult to find out where corporations have given money in the past. Unlike foundations, they are not required to report their contributions to the IRS. Most of your research will have to be from word of mouth, by talking to the corporation's employees and to organizations the corporation has funded in the past.

Corporations traditionally have funded older, more conservative institutions and United Ways. But corporations are exploring new ways to get their money's worth out of their philanthropic dollar, so with creativity you can tap into this source.

Corporate money does not build the organization.

The project is accountable to the corporation, not to your own members.

Foundation Money

A foundation is "a nongovernmental, non-profit organization, with funds (usually from a single source, either an individual, a family, or a corporation) and program managed by its own trustees or directors, established to maintain or aid social, educational, charitable, religious, or other activities serving the common welfare, primarily through the making of grants."[4] A grant is a gift of money; some foundations also make loans. A foundation also may be called a fund, trust, or endowment. On the other hand, some charitable organizations include the word *foundation* in their names, but if their *primary* purpose is not to give money, they are not considered foundations. There are 21,500 active foundations in the United States that give grants to worthy nonprofit organizations. In 1980, U.S. foundations gave away $2.4 billion, representing 5 percent of all philanthropic dollars.[5]

The advantages of asking for foundation money follow:

Ordinarily you ask for a grant in a written request called a proposal. Writing a grant proposal will help you clarify and organize your plans. If you follow the example for proposals in Chapter 13, your board will consider the entire project from beginning to end as it writes the proposal.

The donation may be larger. The larger the foundation's assets, the larger its grants will be. In 1978, foundations with assets of more than $100 million gave average grants of $54,000; foundations with assets from $25 million to $100 million gave average grants of $20,000. Nearly one-half of all foundation grants come from foundations with assets of less than $25 million. They make more grants than the bigger foundations do, and their grants average from $3,000 to $11,000.".

Foundations can give seed money. This is money to fund a new project as a demonstration that such a project will work. Grants can support a new effort until it involves enough people so that it can pay for itself.

Foundations can give you more than money. Many also give in-kind contributions such as supplies or printing. Some also give helpful advice through their staff or consultants.

Although only about 5 percent of foundations have any paid staff, those that do often hire very helpful people. The staff can give you introductions to other foundations, funding sources, and names of organizations working on the same issues.

It is easy to find out about foundations. Your public library probably will have a copy of the eighth edition of *The Foundation Directory,* which contains information about the 3,363 largest foundations. In addition, every state plus Canada, Mexico, Puerto Rico, and the Virgin Islands have regional collections of the Foundation Center. These are 90 free libraries staffed by professional librarians who can help you find out everything you need to know about foundations and writing proposals. See the list in Chapter 13.

Most foundations require reports on what you did with their grants. These range from simple letters to complete audits. In either case, the reports will help you learn how to keep track of funds restricted for a special purpose.

Getting foundation money can give you credibility and legitimacy in your community or field of interest. Especially if you get funds from local foundations, this will act as an endorsement to other funders.

Some foundations will give you a matching grant or a challenge grant as an incentive to your fund-raising efforts. If you raise a certain amount of money, the foundation will give you an equal amount of money. Matching grants can help you launch a new project or jump your grass roots fund raising to a higher level.

The disadvantages of taking foundation grants follow:

Foundation grants almost always run out after two or three years. Although there are exceptions, a foundation usually considers its grant to be seed money. The grant will not be renewed forever.

Foundation funding is subject to fashions. One-year houses for runaways are the fashion; solar power is fashionable the next year. Also, foundation funding is subject to economic cycles. The funds most foundations give come from investments, so the amount available to give is affected by the economy.

Foundation guidelines can work against you if you are selling a project that is new, controversial, or remote. Most foundations give most of their money to organizations and places familiar to them. According to *The Foundation Grants Index,* in 1979 organizations in New York received 3,413 grants worth $207,516,000, while organizations in Idaho received 17 grants worth $262,000.[7] On the other hand, if you are a pioneer, you could use this to your advantage. If you are the first to ask, or the only one from your area, you will have less competition.

The project is accountable to the foundation, not the people served.

It is difficult to involve more than two or three people in seeking the money. Although this could be considered an advantage if you are very shorthanded, it is a disadvantage if you want democracy in your organization.

Foundation grants will not build the organization.

Government Money

Government money includes an estimated $200 billion in grants, contracts, and salaries. You have so many choices that the best way to proceed is to interview the leaders of groups that are in your federal district or doing the same kind of work to find out what

works best. In many cases, you will have to work with several levels
of government. For example, Title XX funds for social services
need state approval in order to get federal money. In general, start
at the local level and then work your way up to federal programs.
Spend as much time as possible learning about local government
policies and standards.

The advantages of taking government money follow:

It is *our* money! To most taxpayers, this is my money taken out of
my taxes. Getting government money is like getting my own money
back rather than like asking someone else for money.

The donation can be large.

You may be able to ask the same agency for funding year after
year.

Government money can make your program seem legitimate.

The government may require bookkeeping that will be valuable
to the organization. Unfortunately, in some cases the paperwork required is so great that it becomes a problem instead of a benefit.

Seeking government money can give the leadership firsthand experience in working with several levels of government.

The disadvantages of taking government money follow:

It is political. It is vulnerable to changes in elected politicians and
party platforms. Remember, people give you money because they
will get what *they* want. What politicians want is to get elected and
to stay elected. They will fund those projects that are the most
popular and the least controversial.

It may require a great deal of expensive reporting, accounting,
and auditing that has no benefit for the organization itself.

It may cost you money to take a government grant. Some government programs cover only part of the organization's expenses.

In other programs you will have to negotiate an indirect cost rate
based on your previous financial statements and audits.

Unless you have a very sophisticated bookkeeping system and the
advice of a very talented CPA, the government may give you a rate
which is too low to cover your costs.

Because the money is "public money," some government agencies
can require you to make public the names of your members. One
self-help group of epileptics had to turn down Title XX funds

because the government demanded a list of members. The organization chose to keep their membership list confidential because of job discrimination against people with epilepsy.

It can make it more difficult to raise grass roots money. Because people perceive government grants as "our money," they are reluctant to give "again." They believe that they already have "given" — in their taxes.

It does not build the organization.

The program is accountable to the government agency, not to the people involved in the program.

You may get *too much* money. Many experienced leaders can tell stories of large government grants starting fights that put the group out of business within two years. Although a big grant is tempting, consider how fast you want to grow, how to maintain the feeling the group has now, and how to be sure that the people involved keep control of decisions. If too much money will change the style and the purpose of the group more than you want it to, stay away from government grants.

Grass Roots Money

Grass roots money includes all the funds you raise for your organization by having your own members ask for it. Individuals ask individuals, which produces most of the money Americans give. In 1980, individuals gave $39.93 billion to their favorite charitable groups and another $2.86 billion in bequests. Individual donations and bequests together represented 89.7 percent of all philanthropic support for nonprofit institutions.[8]

Grass roots fund raising also includes any donation solicited in person from a local business. Ninety-four percent of American corporations reported that their charitable contributions were less than five hundred dollars per year to nonprofit groups.[9] Most of these donations probably were solicited by local people for local causes in person. There is plenty of money to be had by those who ask for it. There always has been, and there always will be.

The advantages of grass roots fund raising follow:

The organization is directly accountable to the people who pay for it.

It is democratic. Anyone involved in the organization can ask for and can give money.

It is dependable, renewable, and internally controlled.

It is quick. You can get money the same day you begin asking for money.

It encourages the growth of the organization. The more people you have, the more asking they can do.

Grass roots fund raising is fun.

It serves as an ongoing form of board development. The people who ask for money will be recognized as leaders.

It identifies the most popular issues, because these are easiest to "sell."

It gives you freedom. If you are confident that you can raise your core budget from grass roots money, you will have greater independence in negotiating for other funds.

It can be used as a "match" for other government or foundation funds. It proves that your community wants this organization, so the outside funders know they are making a safe investment.

The volume of transactions requires rigorous record keeping. You can design and keep records for your own benefit.

Grass roots fund raising can publicize the program and the organization.

It serves as an ongoing form of evaluation. If people pay for the program, they want it. If they do not pay, they do not want it.

It deepens the commitment of the people involved. If they pay in, they stay in.

It builds the organization. Grass roots money is the only money that produces more members and stronger leaders.

The disadvantages of grass roots fund raising follow:

It is very labor intensive. It requires many people if it is to succeed. (This also can be considered an advantage.)

The money comes in small amounts. This requires many transactions, more bookkeeping, and more money handling.

It is hard work.

It takes a lot of time. If not well planned, it could take time away from other program activities. But if it is well planned it will promote and provide for other activities at the same time.

Most people do not like asking for money until they try it and succeed. It may be difficult to get fund raising started until the members taste success and want the independence and power their own money brings.

United Ways

Federated fund raising was tried first in Denver in 1887, when twenty-two agencies formed the Charity Organization Society to coordinate their services and fund raising. Their fund raising arm, the Associated Charities, distributed $17,880.03 in 1888. Although the Denver organization went under in the silver panic in 1893, the idea that social service agencies could join together to deliver services and collect money was copied. The first "modern" United Way was formed in Cleveland in 1913, and United Way drives have been a part of American giving ever since. The 2,095 United Ways in the United States distributed $1.4 billion in 1979.[10] Most of this was collected by corporations from their employees through payroll deductions.

Today, the United Ways are criticized for the way they collect and distribute their funds. Because of this debate locally and nationally, there may be great changes made in United Way operations in the next decade. For now, United Ways remain among the most dependable funding sources for agencies that qualify for their funds.

The advantages of taking United Way funding are:

The donation can be big.

It can legitimize your work in the community.

It requires thorough reports and accounting.

It can be ongoing. Some United Way recipients have been funded for decades.

Some United Ways offer their recipients advice, consultants, executives, or workshops.

The disadvantages of taking United Way funds are:

In some locations, the reporting is considered to be too much work for the amount of money you get.

United Way funding is vulnerable to economic swings. If the local economy is down, the collection will be lower and the amount available to be distributed will be less.

Most United Way programs restrict the fund raising the recipients are allowed to do for themselves. You may find that you could make more money from your own campaign than by taking the United Way grant and restricting your own fund-raising program.

It does not build the organization.

The program is accountable to the United Way, not its own members.

PLAN TO GET RENEWABLE MONEY

There is plenty of money out there for you to get. You are limited only by the amount of time the board is willing to spend asking for money. To insure an ongoing plan to get the most money in the least time, focus most of your efforts on getting money that will be renewed each year. Then you will not have to start over each year. Once you plan where to ask for money, research each person, foundation, corporation, or agency. Ask the following questions to complete your research on your markets. Then begin asking for money.

What do we want to do? How much will it cost?

Who will benefit? Who needs it? Who wants it?

Who will ask for money?

What kind of paperwork will we need in advance?

How can we research this source of money? Who else has received money from this source?

How long will it take to ask for money? How long will it take to get the money? How dependable is the payment schedule?

What can this source of money give us in addition to money?

What will the source want if we take their money?

Are there any restrictions on our activities if we take this money? Are those restrictions acceptable to the board?

Can this money be renewed? Can we get more from the same source?

If this is a one-year donation, do we have a plan to replace the money from other sources? Or are we willing to run the project for only one year?

What is the cost of asking for the money? Will we have any extra expenses if we take this money?

If they turn us down, can we do the program anyway? Will we?

Do we have the skills and the financial system ready to handle this much money in the way both we and the donor want? Are we confident that we will have complete control of this money? Will we need to hire paid staff to do the bookkeeping or accounting?

ACHIEVING SELF-SUFFICIENCY

In your organization's first few years, a low budget and high enthusiasm may keep you going. As the organization matures, you may want to hire paid staff or expand to a bolder program. Or the board may be satisfied with the size of the current program but be tired of riding a funding roller coaster with highs of too much money and lows of not enough. Either way, the time has come for you to develop more dependable income. If you want to guarantee that the group always will have enough money to do what it wants to do, you should plan for financial self-sufficiency. This requires money that is:

1. From a variety of sources. Independence comes from diversity.

2. Internally controlled. You know how and when it comes in and goes out. This requires sound business management and rigorous record keeping.

3. Renewable. It comes from sources that can produce income year after year. It is not vulnerable to fads, politics, or economic fluctuations.

4. Democratic. It is produced by the work of the membership and the value of the organization, not by the skills or relationships of a few people. Most important, it is not dependent upon the relationships of any paid staff, because they can easily work somewhere else tomorrow.

5. Dependable. It will not produce peaks and valleys of money. It will not require exhausting efforts to raise emergency funds (the "rent party" syndrome) and lulls during which eager volunteers are rejected because "there is nothing for you to do." A dependable self-sufficiency plan gives people control of their time and the satisfaction of getting the best dollar return for time expended.

6. Honest. It answers the old question, "If you're so smart, why aren't you rich?" If you raise your own budget, you can be sure of being around for the next twenty years. Your members and others will respect your organization and know they can count on it. Especially if the *purpose* of the organization is to teach self-

reliance—to either individuals or organizations—it is essential that you practice what you preach. Who is going to listen to, or apply advice from, an organization that depends on grants and is always six months away from extinction?

The board can use these standards to put together a plan to move the organization toward self-sufficiency within five years. This will free the board and staff to focus on the programs rather than on the danger of running out of money. Especially if you hire paid staff (or want to), self-sufficient finances will guarantee that you can hire and keep a staff of the caliber you want.

REPLACING NONRENEWABLE FUNDS

How do you put together a funding plan that will give you the amount of money you want now and at the same time move the group toward self-sufficiency? The first step is to get a clear picture of the money you have now and its future. Make a graph with money on the vertical axis and time on the horizontal. If you know your twenty-thousand-dollar grant will run out in two years, graph it this way:

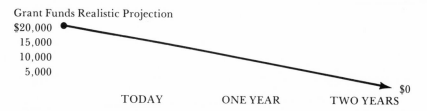

Grant Funds Realistic Projection
$20,000
 15,000
 10,000
  5,000
                                                                    $0
          TODAY   ONE YEAR   TWO YEARS

Because we are all wishful thinkers, we hope that the money we have now will go on forever. So we mentally picture our money like this:

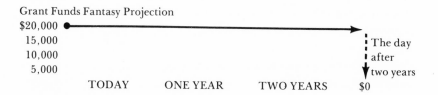

Grant Funds Fantasy Projection
$20,000
 15,000   The day
 10,000   after
  5,000   two years
          TODAY   ONE YEAR   TWO YEARS $0

When the money runs out, we plunge from twenty thousand

dollars to zero dollars, instead of having anticipated the decline and planned for it. Planning is the step you have to take. If you know that your grant will run out in two years, you have to start *today* to find dependable, renewable funds to replace that grant. Picture these funds increasing as below:

This tells you that to replace the grant, you eventually will have to raise five thousand dollars every six months, or ten thousand dollars every year. You may not be able to reach this goal the first year. However, if you start to work toward it immediately you *will* be able to reach the goal by the third year, when you will need it. Your grant money will have bought you two years in which to perfect your fund-raising tactics. As your seed money runs out, your self-generated funds will increase.

Why not simply write another foundation proposal? If you do, you will be back where you started. This is still fragile money, and it still will run out. You only have bought a little time. In addition, the longer you postpone asking your own people to give and raise most of your budget money, the harder it will be to do it. Ask any group that gave its board a free ride on seed grants for a few years and *then* had to raise its own money.

Furthermore, with a self-sufficiency plan you can (1) plan a program, (2) make a budget, and (3) make the money to pay for it. If you now depend on grants, your organization probably (1) finds out where the money is, (2) finds out what it is for, and (3) plans a program to do that. Thus your funding sources, not you, control your programs and the work of your staff. If you have been coasting along on grants, you will need hard work and determination to raise your own money. But the payoff is that you can then make your own decisions and run your own organization.

An excellent example of a group that always has raised all its own money is Alcoholics Anonymous. A.A. runs on "Twelve Traditions." Number seven is, "Every A.A. group ought to be fully self-supporting, declining outside contributions." A.A. was started in 1939 by two alcoholics, a doctor and a broker. At the end of the year it had one hundred members. By 1955 it had 6,000 groups and 150,000 members. In 1980, it had 33,000 groups and more than one million members in ninety countries.[11] The group has been so successful at giving its own members what they want — their lives as sober persons — that it has to put a *limit* on the amount a person can give. No one is allowed to give more than three hundred dollars in one year. Alcoholics Anonymous has had this success because it delivers what its people want. If your organization also is delivering what people want, you will be assured of the income you need.

Take an inventory of the work you are doing now. For each program, ask yourselves, "Who benefits from this program? Who needs it? Who wants it?" These are the people who can and will pay for the program if asked. According to a national study, only 4 percent of the people surveyed ever had contributed to a political candidate, but 89 percent said they would give *if asked.*[12] If your own people have not given in the past, do not assume they cannot give now. If no one asked them, it was impossible for them to give. You probably will be delighted at the response once you start asking.

What if you ask the people in your community and they say no? You just have received a free, current, accurate evaluation of your program. Either change your program, or stop it and start something new.

What are some of the more dependable ways to raise money?

1. Membership dues. See Chapter 3 for more on dues.
2. Subscriptions and advertising revenue from publications. See Chapter 15 for more on selling subscriptions.
3. Sales.
4. Services.
5. Businesses such as thrift shops.
6. Contributions from individuals and local businesses.
7. Payroll deduction plans.
8. Contributions from local churches.

9. Deferred giving plans — insurance, annuities, bequests, pooled income funds. Ask your insurance agent and the trust officer at your bank about these.

10. Canvassing, also known as door-to-door solicitation. Direct mail.

11. Training programs and speakers' bureaus.

For more information on dependable money-making ideas, ask the most successful local organizations and businesspeople. For more advice, read *The Grass Roots Fundraising Book,* by Joan Flanagan, available from the Youth Project, 1555 Connecticut Ave., NW, Washington, DC 20036. 1977. 224 pp. $5.25.

STEPS TO SELF-SUFFICIENCY

THE BOARD OF DIRECTORS WILL:

1. Commit itself to the purpose of the organization. Review the statement of purpose, the goals for the year, and the programs the organization will do to reach its goals. Begin with the mission.

2. Make a budget or "shopping list" of what will be needed to accomplish the programs. Find out how much money is needed to buy the necessary items and staff. Set a dollar goal for the fund-raising strategy.

3. Commit itself to raise this money. Each member of the board must set a personal, specific goal to raise his or her fair share of the budget.

4. Be the first to give and ask for money.

5. Plan to raise the money needed. Evaluate the benefits and restrictions attached to each source of money available. Consider both the long-term and short-term results of taking the money.

6. Plan to develop and expand sources of ongoing, dependable, renewable, internally controlled income. Assign specific leaders to pursue renewable money sources.

7. Plan to collect seed money for new programs. Assign specific leaders to pursue them.

8. Establish an accurate record-keeping and reporting system.

9. Evaluate the strategy once a year. Emphasize the most reliable money sources; eliminate undependable money sources.

13

Fund Raising:
How to Ask for Money

> *"Imagine what success looks like. Say the amount you want, tell the donor why you want it, then repeat the amount. Then be quiet and wait for them to say, 'Yes!'"*
> — Kim Klein
> *Coalition for the Medical Rights of Women*

Every source of money has one thing in common: you only get money if you ask for it. With rare exceptions (and you cannot run a strong organization on exceptions), the sources of money will not *ask you* to take money. So your board has to learn how to ask for money with courage and confidence. It has to learn how to "sell" this organization.

Thousands of Americans have mastered these skills, and you can, too. You do so by deciding:

This organization is vital to our community. It does important work that no one else can do.

I want to see this organization succeed. In order to succeed, it needs money. I pledge myself to raise the money it needs.

We have a bold program for today and a grand vision for tomorrow. This organization's need for financial support is more than I myself can meet. Therefore, I will find others who believe in this organization and train them to join me in asking for support from the rest of our community.

I will do it now!

169

TAKE THE NON OUT OF NONPROFIT

American businesses are the best in the world at making money. The best thing you can do for your organization is to copy their money-making ideas. Ask a local business leader to help you make a one-year marketing plan and a long-range plan for self-sufficiency. Successful community businesses already have mastered most of the skills needed by new nonprofit community organizations — such as planning; record keeping; finding, training, and keeping good staff; working with government agencies and financial institutions; and, most of all, making a profit from limited resources. Learn the principles of successful selling. Make your motto: Take the *non* out of *nonprofit!*

Instead of thinking of your organization as a charity that must depend on welfare from foundations or government agencies, think of yourself as a worthwhile business providing valuable products and services to the community. Thinking of your fund raising as selling helps everyone involved think of it as a positive effort to sell something valuable — your program — to people who want it and need it. Before you can sell anything to anyone else, you have to believe that it is valuable. Believe: We are worth it! We will give our own money to this; we will ask the people who benefit to support it; and we will ask others who want it to pay!

Ask the experts to give you advice on how to sell the program of your organization. Practice with different sales pitches, then ask the experts for suggestions. Get and read some good books on selling. You can apply sales principles to your fund-raising campaign and see your people succeed as never before.

Here is the best advice I have found on asking for money. These are the "people" rules of fund raising. Follow them and you will be solvent forever!

THE SEVEN PEOPLE RULES
FOR FUND-RAISING SUCCESS

1. People give to people. Ask in person.
2. The best people you can ask for money are people who already have given money. Keep complete records of your donors.

3. People cannot respond unless you tell them what you want. Always ask for a specific amount or item. Be enthusiastic, optimistic, and bold. You get what you ask for!

4. People who ask for money become better givers. People who give money become better askers.

5. People want to back a winner. Be proud of your organization, what you do, and how you do it. Success breeds success!

6. More people means more money and more fun. Find a job for every volunteer. Make it more fun to be on the inside and participating than on the outside and looking in.

7. People want recognition. Send thank-you notes!

In addition to these general rules, what follows is the best advice I have found on how to ask for money from corporations, foundations, government agencies, and your community.

HOW TO ASK FOR CORPORATE MONEY

Corporations are businesses. They exist to make a profit. So speak to them in their language. Tell them why you are a good investment—what you do right and what the benefits *in dollars* are from your work. The more you can measure the benefits of the work you do in dollars, the easier it will be for you to raise money from business people.

One excellent example is the following brochure, used by the Rehabilitation Institute of Chicago in 1972. It includes four short profiles of former patients who are now back on their jobs as editor, research analyst, student, and homemaker. Then the Institute explains that every dollar spent on rehabilitation returned eight dollars to the economy. This kind of "cost-effective" sales pitch has helped the Institute raise millions for its work. See how it makes its program attractive to executives who are concerned about "the bottom line." The left side is the outside cover; the right side is an inside page. Reprinted with permission from The Rehabilitation Institute of Chicago, 345 E. Superior St., Chicago, IL 60611.

For more advice on asking for money from corporations and businesses, order *Special Events Fundraising,* listed in Chapter 24, "Bibliography and Resources." Expert Sally Berger tells you how to get introductions to corporate executives, how to prepare for the appointment, and how to make the sale. Berger's system was used by volunteers to raise $1.4 million in one year for a medical research program. It will work for your group, too.

FIGURE 13-1
Rehabilitation Pays Off

Sample of effective brochure to raise money from corporations and businesses. Written in 1972. Left: Outside cover. Right: Inside page. Reprinted with permission from The Rehabilitation Institute of Chicago, 345 E. Superior St., Chicago, IL 60611.

HOW TO ASK FOR GOVERNMENT MONEY

The best advice on how to ask for government money is included in *The Bucks Start Here: How to Fund Social Service Projects,* by Kathleen Fojtik. Even if your organization does not consider itself a social service project, it can use this advice to ask for government money from local or federal agencies. It is so good because the author has worked both sides of the desk. In Michigan she was elected Washtenaw County Commissioner and has served as chair of the county's Ways and Means Committee; she was also the founder and fund raiser of the NOW Domestic Violence and Spouse Assault Fund in Ann Arbor. Listen to the voice of experience on how to ask for money from your local government:

> When a meeting date is scheduled and your proposal is on the agenda, bring many people with you to the meeting. Stack the meeting with supporters of your proposal: battered women, professionals, law enforcement officials and others. . . . Be sure to say exactly, in very specific terms, what you want from them. Don't let them decide what you need; you tell them what you need.
>
> Attend all meetings prepared to answer questions. Have a script and a dynamic, knowledgeable spokesperson or two. Keep your goals and objectives in your mind at all times. Do not allow yourself to be sidetracked. Keep bringing the discussion back to the specific thing — hotline, shelter, funds for a director, local match money — you are asking for. Don't sell yourself short, but be prepared to compromise. Don't underestimate the importance of your program, and the urgent

FIGURE 13-1

Rehabilitation Pays Off

It's good for the individual
It's good for the family
It's good for the economy
It's good for society
It's an investment that's
good for
YOU

REHABILITATION   INSTITUTE   OF   CHICAGO

REHABILITATION PAYS OFF!

Last year . . . . . .

- RIC successfully placed 53% spinal cord injured persons in jobs

- A total of 65 patients went back to work. . . earning combined annual salaries of $ 370,000

- They paid $ 78,000 in TAXES

- The same patients had previously received $ 104,000 in benefits from private and public agencies or insurance companies

- This was EXCLUSIVE OF TREATMENT COSTS

- Society's GAIN?

    $ 78,000 (taxes)
     104,000 (benefits)
    ─────────
    $ 182,000 (total)

- For every $ 1 spent on Rehabilitation $ 8 return to the economy as the patient goes off benefits and becomes a tax-paying consumer

REHABILITATION <u>DOES</u> PAY OFF

- SOCIALLY

- VOCATIONALLY

- ECONOMICALLY

need within the specific community. Don't allow yourself to be intimidated, but don't be defensive. This is your government and your tax
dollars.

One request for funds from a local unit of government may take as
many as 10 meetings before the final funding is made. This is a long
and time consuming process, and that is why you need others to help
you. But one person should be coordinating all the phone calls, letters, informal meetings, and formal presentations. One person needs
to be in charge: a proposal director, project director, fundraiser,
president of your board, or a dedicated staff person. A dedicated,
knowledgeable volunteer willing to make a large time commitment
can also be the Project Person.

Whether it is for General Revenue Sharing Funds, CETA Funds, or
locally generated tax revenues, your job is to ask assertively, project a
positive image, and convince others that you are a good risk. If you
are convinced that your program deserves to be funded, then others
will perceive this confidence and will trust you with the funds. Be
positive. Don't apologize for anything. Failure is impossible, even if it
takes two or three tries.[1]

You can extend the same zeal to state and federal sources. Fojtik's
tips on asking for federal grants follow.

Start where the bucks are. Plan to work hard to get the funds and
plan to work even harder after you get them.
Make sure the funding source funds programs like yours.
Ask questions and get answers.
Look into and evaluate all possibilities.
Write a clear, concise proposal.
Keep narrative simple and use little or no professional jargon.
Keep the budget very specific, giving detailed explanations and
examples.
Submit proposal within the time limit.
Lobby appropriate persons; send additional information.
Receive the award graciously. Begin fulfilling reporting require-
ments immediately.
Account for all funds carefully.[2]

For more help in tracking down government funds, ask the nonprofit groups in your community which agencies and officials they recommend. The office of your member of Congress or U.S. senator can also give you help.

You also can look in a huge book called the *Catalog of Federal Domestic Assistance.* This is a five-inch-thick book listing every federal program giving grants, loans, and other assistance. The last four pages of the book give the addresses and phone numbers of federal information centers from which you can get free advice. This catalog is sent free to every member of Congress and to all state and local governments with populations down to 250. It is available at all public libraries that are federal depositories (usually the largest public libraries and university libraries).

Your first dip into the catalog can be a heady experience. The 1980 edition is 1,025 pages long. Fortunately, the text is cross-indexed in six different ways in a 140-page index. The subject index is the most detailed. For example, there are twenty-one entries under the heading "Community Health Services," ranging from "ambulatory health care" and "Appalachian health demonstrations" to "Upper Great Lakes Region" and "urban rat control." Like the Sears catalog, the *Catalog of Federal Domestic Assistance* makes you want to try everything. Ask a veteran fund raiser to show you how to use the catalog and how to decide where to apply for funds.

HOW TO ASK FOR FOUNDATION MONEY

There are four steps to asking for foundation money. First, decide what you want to do. Second, write an irresistible proposal describing this program. Third, find the right foundation to ask. Fourth, sell the proposal to the foundation.

Begin by deciding what the board wants to do and writing a case statement. This is a brief description of your work, which "makes the case" that you are a good investment for a foundation. Take one board meeting to brainstorm on everything good about your group. Discuss and write down everyone's ideas about the job your organization is doing, why your services are valuable, what opportunities you have to provide additional services, why your program should be supported, and why this program is needed *now*. After the entire board has agreed on the case statement, you can ask two board members to start writing the proposal. A proposal is a written request for funding from a foundation for a specific part of your work. Although all the board should approve the final draft, it will be easier and faster if only two people actually plan and write the early drafts.

Here is some good advice about how to write a grant proposal, written by Jessye G. Payne, the resource services coordinator at the W. Clement & Jessie V. Stone Foundation.

How to Write an Irresistible Proposal

"A grant proposal is a written expression of a proposed solution to a problem. It must present a persuasive argument for your program. Here are some techniques that might help:

"*Style:* A good grant proposal should be written in down-to-earth language. Keep the proposal short and clear. Write it as you would say it. Each section of the proposal should be specific and follow logically from what went before.

"*Contents:* Every well-written proposal should contain the following: (1) cover letter, (2) title page, (3) table of contents, (4) introduction, (5) statement of the need for the program, (6) objectives, (7) methods, (8) evaluation, (9) future funding, (10) budget, (11) appendixes.

"The cover letter is a condensation of the total proposal. It should be a one-page statement written to the funding executive and typed on your organization's letterhead. State the major feature of your program, such as the need for it, how you will meet the need, your group's qualifications, and the amount of money being requested. Use words the funder will understand and highlight the best features of your program. Often, this letter is the only part of the proposal that is read slowly and completely.

"The introduction tells who you are, so use it to establish your credibility. State your organization's interest in the issue and how you got started, what is unique about how you got started, how long you have been around, some outstanding accomplishments, and what support you have received from other organizations.

"The need for the program must be genuine. This problem or

need must be documented. Do not assume that "everybody knows this is a problem." They do not! Explain how the need relates to the interests of the foundation. Then describe how your innovative plan will meet the need either by extending your services to a new area or by introducing a new program. Tell what you expect to accomplish within a given time.

"In the next section explain what you hope to achieve as a result of your project. List objectives that will meet the need you listed in the section above. Objectives are what the proposal is all about. They tell what is going to be done, who is going to do it, when it is going to be done, and who will receive the service. A common mistake in stating objectives is to say you will try to do more than can be done with the available time, money, and personnel. As a general rule, when preparing objectives, think small.

"By now you have told who you are, the problem you want to work on, and your objectives. Now you must describe the methods you will use to bring about these results. The methods section usually is read more closely than any other section, because it tells *how* you plan to achieve your objectives. Describe what you plan to do, how you plan to do it, and your projected time schedule. Include a plan for meeting each objective.

"Now explain how the foundation will know that your program has accomplished its objectives. An evaluation is essential because it shows how well you understand and have planned your project. Include here the type of information to be collected, how it will be analyzed, who will analyze it, and what you will do with the information. A built-in evaluation process will help you determine the strengths and weaknesses of your total program. It also can serve as a tool in making changes and adjustments in your program.

"Now say how you will continue your program when the grant runs out. If this is a request for a one-time grant for the purchase of equipment, future funding is irrelevant. But if you are seeking program money, how will you keep the program going when the foundation stops supporting it? Describe your efforts to establish permanent funding and indicate any firm commitment you may have from other funding sources.

"Realistically project what your program will cost and present this information in an accepted accounting style. Expenses such as salaries, employee benefits, travel, office supplies and equipment, rent, and telephone should be itemized. If your program has been in operation for more than a year, include a copy of your most recent financial statement. Also, report any in-kind donations or donated services you receive. Preparing your budget is valuable for you because it helps clarify the plan. You will be judged not on how small or how large your budget is, but on how sound it is. Professional help in preparing this section might be useful, and local accounting firms frequently will donate the time of a staff member to a nonprofit program as a community service.

"The following materials should accompany your grant proposal as appendices:

"Documentation of statements made in the body of the proposal. The documents might include maps, charts, and newspaper accounts.

"A copy of your IRS 501(c)(3) ruling granting your federal tax exemption.

"A list of the members of the board of directors.

"A list of staff members, if any, and the credentials of each.

"A copy of your last annual report, if any.

"Supportive materials such as letters of endorsement.

"When you have finished your first draft and have all of the supplementary materials assembled, see if your proposal contains Rudyard Kipling's "six honest men": why, what, when, who, how, and where.

"Why has the proposal been written? Is the purpose of your proposal clear? Why is your organization the most logical one to conduct your proposed program?

"What does your group hope to achieve as a result of carrying out the program?

"When will you achieve your objectives? Are they measurable and attainable?

"Who are you? Have you established the credibility of your agency? What is unique about your program? What are some of your outstanding accomplishments?

"How do you plan on achieving your objectives? Are the methods for their achievement realistic and stated clearly? How will your proposed program help to achieve the larger mission of your organization?

"Where will your program be conducted? Are the evaluation techniques practical?

"Good luck!

"Researching and writing a grant proposal that will bring in dollars to correct a social ill takes time, hard work, and patience. If you feel your patience ebbing, remember the words of Ted Key: 'Every job is a self-portrait of the person who did it. Autograph your work with excellence.' Then, in the words of Jessye Payne, "'Mail your proposal with pride and confidence!'"[3]

You can use this method of writing a proposal to organize your plan for any new program. The same kind of information will be required if you ask for a grant from a national church program or a government agency. Even if the funding source says no, the process of planning and writing the proposal will help the board clarify its ideas before it begins any new activities.

Find the Right Foundation

Once you know what you want to do, you can begin to look for a foundation that funds that sort of work in your community. The best way to find the right foundation is by asking other groups in your community which one they recommend. They will be able to suggest the best staff at the best foundations. Once you get to know one or two members of the staff of a foundation and prove that your organization is a good investment, they will introduce you to others.

If you cannot get any introductions, you will have to introduce yourself. In this case, ask two members of the board to find out which foundations are most likely to fund your project. They can start by using reference books, especially *The Foundation Directory,* available in most public libraries. The directory gives information about the 3,363 largest foundations in the United States. The listings are arranged by state in alphabetical order. Each entry in *The Foundation Directory* includes the foundation's name, address, officers, purpose, activities, and financial data.

There are many other reference books and magazines about foundations and where they give their money. Most foundations give most of their money to universities, colleges, and hospitals, so ask for help from the directors of development at large institutions. They probably already own basic reference books and magazines and can show you how to use them.

The most complete collection of published information on foundations is available at the ninety regional collections of the Foundation Center. See the list in this chapter for the collection nearest you. The Foundation Center is a national service organization established and supported by foundations to provide a single, authoritative source of information on foundation giving. The regional collections are free libraries operated by professional librarians, who can show you how to use all the information. Each library has a roomful of material on how to find the right foundation and write the best proposal.

Every foundation has to file two annual reports to the IRS every year, a 990-AR (for "annual report") and a 990-PF (for "private foundations"). You can see copies of these reports at the regional collections. The foundations' annual reports will tell you the names of the organizations to which they gave contributions, gifts, and grants, and the amounts of the grants.

The best book to teach you how to find the right foundation is *Foundation Fundamentals: A Guide for Grantseekers.* Written by Carol Kurzig of the Foundation Center, this book is easy to read and easy to use. It will tell you exactly what to do to find every possible foundation that makes grants in your field of interest and in your geographic area. Order the book for $4.95 from The Foundation Center, 888 Seventh Ave., New York, NY 10106.

Foundation Fundamentals will tell you how to use the information in the regional collections. Each collection has several books that index foundations according to where they give their money, the kinds of programs they fund, and the amounts of the grants. For example, by using the indexes, you can list all of the foundations that gave grants of more than five thousand dollars to mental health programs in Indiana. By checking the IRS annual report for this list of foundations, you can find the names of the organizations that received those grants. Ask the groups that received grants for advice on which staff people to contact and what information to put in or leave out of your proposals.

FIGURE 13-1   The Foundation Center

The Foundation Center has a nationwide network of foundation reference collections for free public use. These collections fall within three basic categories. The four reference libraries operated by the Center offer the widest variety of user services and the most comprehensive collections of foundation materials, including all of the Center's publications; books, services and periodicals on foundations and philanthropy; and foundation annual reports, newsletters, and press clippings. The New York and Washington, D.C. libraries contain the IRS returns for all currently active private foundations in the U.S. The Cleveland and San Francisco libraries contain the IRS records for those foundations in the midwestern and western states, respectively. The cooperating collections generally contain IRS records for only those foundations within their state, although they may request information or copies of other records from the New York library.

• This symbol identifies reference collections operated by foundations or area associations of foundations. They are often able to offer special materials or provide extra services, such as seminars or orientations for users, because of their close relationship to the local philanthropic community.

All other collections are operated by cooperating libraries. Generally they are located within public institutions and are open to the public during a longer schedule of hours and also offer visitors access to a well-developed general library research collection.

Please telephone individual libraries for more information about their holdings or hours. To check on new locations call toll free 800-424-9836 for current information.

Where to Go for Information on Foundation Funding

Reference Collections Operated by The Foundation Center

The Foundation Center
888 Seventh Avenue
New York, New York 10106
212-975-1120

The Foundation Center
1001 Connecticut Avenue, NW
Washington, D.C. 20036
202-331-1400

The Foundation Center
Kent H. Smith Library
739 National City Bank Bldg.
629 Euclid
Cleveland, Ohio 44114
216-861-1933

The Foundation Center
312 Sutter Street
San Francisco, Calif. 94108
415-397-0902

Cooperating Collections

Alabama
Birmingham Public Library
2020 Park Place
Birmingham 35203
205-254-2541

Auburn University at Montgomery Library
Montgomery 36193
205-279-9110

Alaska
University of Alaska,
Anchorage Library
3211 Providence Drive
Anchorage 99504
907-263-1848

Arizona
Phoenix Public Library
Social Sciences Subject
Department
12 East McDowell Road
Phoenix 85004
602-262-4782

Tucson Public Library
Main Library
200 South Sixth Avenue
Tucson 85701
602-791-4393

Arkansas
Westark Community College
Library
Grand Avenue at Waldron Rd.
Fort Smith 72913
501-785-4241

Little Rock Public Library
Reference Department
700 Louisiana Street
Little Rock 72201
501-374-7546

California
California Community
Foundation
1644 Wilshire Boulevard
Los Angeles 90017
213-413-4042

San Diego Public Library
820 E Street
San Diego 92101
714-236-5816

Santa Barbara Public Library
Reference Section
40 East Anapamu
P. O. Box 1019
Santa Barbara 93102
805-962-7653

Colorado
Denver Public Library
Sociology Division
1357 Broadway
Denver 80203
303-573-5152

Connecticut
Hartford Public Library
Reference Department
500 Main Street
Hartford 06103
203-525-9121

Delaware
Hugh Morris Library
University of Delaware
Newark 19711
302-738-2965

Florida
Jacksonville Public Library
Business, Science, and Industry Department
122 North Ocean Street
Jacksonville 32202
904-633-3926

Cooperating Collections (continued)

Miami — Dade Public Library
Florida Collection
One Biscayne Boulevard
Miami 33132
305-579-5001

Georgia
Atlanta Public Library
1 Margaret Mitchell Square at
   Forsyth and Carnegie Way
Atlanta 30303
404-688-4636

Hawaii
Thomas Hale Hamilton Library
University of Hawaii
Humanities and Social
   Sciences Division
2550 The Mall
Honolulu 96822
808-948-7214

Idaho
Caldwell Public Library
1010 Dearborn Street
Caldwell 83605
208-459-3242

Illinois
• Donors Forum of Chicago
208 South LaSalle Street
Chicago 60604
312-726-4882

Sangamon State University
   Library
Shepherd Road
Springfield 62708
217-786-6633

Indiana
Indianapolis — Marion County
   Public Library
40 East St. Clair Street
Indianapolis 46204
317-269-1733

Iowa
Public Library of Des Moines
100 Locust Street
Des Moines 50309
515-283-4259

Kansas
Topeka Public Library
Adult Services Department
1515 West Tenth Street
Topeka 66604
913-233-2040

Kentucky
Louisville Free Public Library
Fourth and York Streets
Louisville 40203
502-584-4154

Louisiana
East Baton Rouge Parish
   Library
Centroplex Library
120 St. Louis Street
Baton Rouge 70802
504-344-5291

New Orleans Public Library
Business and Science Division
219 Loyola Avenue
New Orleans 70140
504-586-4919

Maine
University of Southern Maine
Center for Research and
   Advanced Study
246 Deering Avenue
Portland 04102
207-780-4411

Maryland
Enoch Pratt Free Library
Social Science and History
   Department
400 Cathedral Street
Baltimore 21201
301-396-5320

Cooperating Collections (continued)

Massachusetts
- Associated Grantmakers of
  Massachusetts
  294 Washington Street
  Suite 501
  Boston 02108
  617-426-2608

Boston Public Library
Copley Square
Boston 02117
617-536-5400

Michigan
Alpena County Library
211 North First Avenue
Alpena 49707
517-356-6188

Henry Ford Centennial Library
16301 Michigan Avenue
Dearborn 48216
313-943-2337

Purdy Library
Wayne State University
Detroit 48202
313-577-4040

Michigan State University
  Libraries
Reference Library
East Lansing 48824
517-353-8816

University of Michigan — Flint
UM — F Library
Reference Department
Flint 48503
313-762-3408

Grand Rapids Public Library
Sociology and Education Dept.
Library Plaza
Grand Rapids 49502
616-456-4411

Michigan Technological
  University Library
Highway U.S. 41
Houghton 49931
906-487-2507

Minnesota
Minneapolis Public Library
Sociology Department
300 Nicollett Mall
Minneapolis 55401
612-372-6555

Mississippi
Jackson Metropolitan Library
301 North State Street
Jackson 39201
601-944-1120

Missouri
- Clearinghouse for Mid-
  continent Foundations
  Univ. of Missouri, Kansas City
  Law School, Suite 1-300
  52nd Street and Oak
  Kansas City 64113
  816-276-1176

Kansas City Public Library
311 East 12th Street
Kansas City 64106
816-221-2685

- Metropolitan Association for
  Philanthropy, Inc.
  5600 Oakland, G-324
  St. Louis 63110
  314-647-2290

Springfield — Greene County
  Library
397 East Central Street
Springfield 65801
417-869-4621

Cooperating Collections (continued)

Montana
Eastern Montana College
   Library
Reference Department
Billings 59101
406-657-2337

Nebraska
W. Dale Clark Library
Social Sciences Department
21 South 15th Street
Omaha 68102
402-444-4822

Nevada
Clark County Library
1401 East Flamingo Road
Las Vegas 89109
702-733-7810

Washoe County Library
301 South Center Street
Reno 89505
702-785-4190

New Hampshire
• The New Hampshire Chari-
   table Fund
One South Street
P. O. Box 1335
Concord 03301
603-225-6641

New Jersey
New Jersey State Library
Governmental Reference
185 West State Street
P. O. Box 1898
Trenton 08625
609-292-6220

New Mexico
New Mexico State Library
300 Don Gaspar Street
Santa Fe 87501
505-827-2033

New York
New York State Library
Cultural Education Center
Humanities Section
Empire State Plaza
Albany 12230
518-474-7645

Buffalo and Erie County Public
   Library
Lafayette Square
Buffalo 14203
716-856-7525

Levittown Public Library
Reference Department
One Bluegrass Lane
Levittown 11756
516-731-5728

Plattsburgh Public Library
Reference Department
15 Oak Street
Plattsburgh 12901
518-563-0921

Rochester Public Library
Business and Social Sciences
   Division
115 South Avenue
Rochester 14604
716-428-7328

Onondaga County Public
   Library
335 Montgomery Street
Syracuse 13202
315-473-4491

North Carolina
North Carolina State Library
109 East Jones Street
Raleigh 27611
919-733-3270

Cooperating Collections (continued)

- The Winston-Salem Foundation
  229 First Union National Bank Building
  Winston-Salem 27101
  919-725-2382

North Dakota
The Library
North Dakota State University
Fargo 58105
701-237-8876

Ohio
Public Library of Cincinnati
  and Hamilton County
Education Department
800 Vine Street
Cincinnati 45202
513-369-6940

Toledo — Lucas County
  Public Library
Social Science Department
325 Michigan Street
Toledo 43624
419-255-7055 ext. 221

Oklahoma
- Oklahoma City Community
  Foundation
1300 North Broadway
Oklahoma City 73103
405-235-5621

Tulsa City-County Library
  System
400 Civic Center
Tulsa 74103
918-581-5144

Oregon
Library Association of Portland
Education and Documents Rm.
801 S.W. Tenth Avenue
Portland 97205
503-223-7201

Pennsylvania
The Free Library of
  Philadelphia
Logan Square
Philadelphia 19103
215-686-5423

Hillman Library
University of Pittsburgh
Pittsburgh 15260
412-624-4528

Rhode Island
Providence Public Library
Reference Department
150 Empire Street
Providence 02903
401-521-7722

South Carolina
South Carolina State Library
Reader Services Department
1500 Senate Street
Columbia 29211
803-758-3181

South Dakota
South Dakota State Library
State Library Building
322 South Fort Street
Pierre 57501
605-773-3131

Tennessee
Resources Center for Non-
  Profit Agencies, Inc.
502 Gay Street, Suite 201
P. O. Box 1606
Knoxville 37901
615-521-6034

Memphis Public Library
1850 Peabody Avenue
Memphis 38104
901-528-2957

Cooperating Collections (continued)

Texas

• The Hogg Foundation for
    Mental Health
  The University of Texas
  Austin 78712
  512-471-5041

  Corpus Christi State
      University Library
  6300 Ocean Drive
  Corpus Christi 78412
  512-991-6810

  Dallas Public Library
  Grants Information Service
  1954 Commerce Street
  Dallas 75201
  214-748-9071 ext. 332

• El Paso Community Foundation
  El Paso National Bank Building
  Suite 1616
  El Paso 79901
  915-533-4020

  Houston Public Library
  Bibliographic & Information
      Center
  500 McKinney Avenue
  Houston 77002
  713-224-5441 ext. 265

• Funding Information Library
  Minnie Stevens Piper
      Foundation
  201 North St. Mary's Street
  Suite 100
  San Antonio 78205
  512-227-8119

Utah

Salt Lake City Public Library
Information and Adult Services
209 East Fifth South
Salt Lake City 84111
801-363-5733

Vermont

State of Vermont Department
    of Libraries
Reference Services Unit
111 State Street
Montpelier 05602
802-828-3261

Virginia

Grants Resources Library
Ninth Floor
Hampton City Hall
Hampton 23669
804-727-6496

Richmond Public Library
Business, Science, & Tech-
    nology Department
101 East Franklin Street
Richmond 23219
804-780-8223

Washington

Seattle Public Library
1000 Fourth Avenue
Seattle 98104
206-625-4881

Spokane Public Library
Reference Department
West 906 Main Avenue
Spokane 99201
509-838-3361

West Virginia

Kanawha County Public
    Library
123 Capitol Street
Charleston 25301
304-343-4646

Wisconsin

Marquette University Memorial
    Library
1415 West Wisconsin Avenue
Milwaukee 53233
414-224-1515

Cooperating Collections (continued)

Wyoming
Laramie County Community
  College Library
1400 East College Drive
Cheyenne 82001
307-634-5853

Canada
• The Canadian Centre for
    Philanthropy
12 Sheppard Street, 3rd Floor
Toronto, Ontario M5H 3A1
416-364-4875

Mexico
Biblioteca Benjamin Franklin
Londres 16
Mexico City 6, D.F.

Puerto Rico
Consumer Education and
  Service Center
Department of Consumer
  Affairs
Minillas Central Government
  Building North
Santurce 00904

Virgin Islands
College of the Virgin Islands
  Library
Saint Thomas
U.S. Virgin Islands 00801
809-774-1252

Sell the Proposal

After you get a list of foundations that may give money to your kind of program in your community, write each one and ask for current guidelines for giving, an application to apply for funds, the dates on which the foundation accepts proposals, the dates the foundation decides on grants, and the annual report. If the foundation publishes an annual report, it usually will tell you its current interests, who it has funded in the past, the size of grants it has given, and its philosophy. Each foundation has different requirements for the size, style, and content it wants in proposals. Tailor your proposal to fit the format the foundation wants. Send each proposal with a one-page cover letter; then call to make sure it was received.

About 5 percent of all foundations hire paid staff to screen proposals. For these, you have to sell the staff on the ideas in your proposal so they can persuade the board of trustees of the foundation to give you a grant. For most foundations, the trustees themselves decide which organizations they will support with grants.

After the proposal is received by the foundation, the staff or trustees have three choices. They can say no, yes, or tell us more. If the staff or trustees send you a letter saying no, without explanation, call immediately and find out why. Your proposal may be fine, but they may have allocated all their money for this year. Then you know that you can reapply. They may have changed their guidelines and stopped funding your sort of program. In that case, do not reapply, but ask for advice on other funders. They may not have been satisfied with the proposal itself. If so, find out why. They may think you are too small now to do this project; then you might reapply in two or three years. Or they may already fund some other project in your area. Perhaps you could work out a joint project or wait until the other grant runs out; then reapply. In any case, as salespeople say, "The sale begins when the customer says no." Use a rejection to find out how to improve your proposal and what to do next.

The staff or trustees may say, "Tell us more." They may ask for more material; they may check your references to see if others in the field believe you can accomplish this project; or they may ask to see you. In that case, two or three of your officers can arrange to meet the foundation people, probably at their office during business hours. Practice before you go so that you feel confident. Ask how many foundation people will be at the meeting, and be sure you have enough clear copies of all written materials.

At the interview, make a good impression. Your job is to raise the money for your organization. So dress conservatively, be there early, have all your papers in order, and enjoy the meeting. After you are introduced, the president can tell the foundation staff who you are, what your organization is, what the proposal is for, and how much money you want. Try to do this in three minutes or less. Do not assume that they have read or will remember your proposal. This is your opportunity to tell them why you are a better investment than all the other proposals they have sitting on their desks. Make their jobs easy. Tell them, simply, who you are and what you want. Then let them ask you questions. Be patient and polite. Use their questions as an opportunity to say what you want to say. If you have questions of your own, ask those at this time. Anecdotes that are easy to remember will make your proposal come alive for the staff. Impress upon the foundation staff that, dollar for dollar, you are the best investment they can make.

After the interview, send a note thanking them for the meeting. Send favorable press as it comes up, but do not bother the staff once you know that your proposal will be considered at a coming meeting—even if the meeting is three months away. If they need new material before the meeting, they will ask for it.

The foundation staff or trustees also may say yes. You will get the grant you want! Send a thank-you note from the president immediately. If there are any questions about how to handle the money, the treasurer and bookkeeper should ask to meet with the foundation staff before you get the first check. Make sure that your bookkeeping system will provide the data they want and you need.

Keep in touch all year long. Invite the foundation people to your benefits, annual meeting, convention, installation of officers, or other important meetings. Send them your newsletter. Send them monthly or quarterly updates with copies of your favorable press. Mention the grant in your newsletter and on any printed material paid for by those funds. If your leaders will be on radio or television shows, alert the foundation. You want this to be the beginning of a good relationship. Even if you only get a one-year grant, the staff can recommend you to other foundations if you act professionally and graciously.

HOW TO ASK FOR GRASS ROOTS MONEY

For more than two centuries, observers have commented that Americans are the most generous people in the world. Benjamin Franklin figured this out early and became the most successful fund raiser in the American colonies. In his *Autobiography,* written between 1771 and 1788, he gives an account of one successful campaign. He writes:

"In 1751, Dr. Thomas Bond, a particular friend of mine, conceived the idea of establishing a hospital in Philadelphia . . . for the reception and cure of poor sick persons, whether inhabitants of the province or strangers. He was zealous and active in endeavoring to procure subscriptions for it, but the proposal being a novelty in

America, and at first not well understood, he met with but small success.

"At length he came to me with the compliment that he found there was no such thing as carrying a public spirited project through without my being concern'd in it. For, says he, I am often ask'd by those to whom I propose subscribing, have you consulted Franklin upon this business? And what does he think of it? And when I tell them that I have not (supposing it rather out of your line), they do not subscribe, but say they will consider of it. I inquired into the nature and probable utility of his scheme, and receiving from him a very satisfactory explanation, I not only subscrib'd to it myself, but engag'd heartily in the design of procuring subscriptions from others. Previously, however, to the solicitation, I endeavored to prepare the minds of the people by writing on the subject in the newspapers, which was my usual custom in such cases, but which he had omitted."

Franklin then relates how he lobbied the Pennsylvania Assembly to give the first matching grant: two thousand pounds for the hospital if Franklin could raise another two thousand pounds. The rural members of the assembly were opposed to allocating colony funds in the city, but they approved the matching grant. Franklin says the members of the assembly "now conceiv'd they might have the credit of being charitable without the expenses, . . . and then, in soliciting subscriptions among the people, we urg'd the conditional promise of the law as an additional motive to give, since every man's donation would be doubled; thus the clause worked both ways. The subscriptions accordingly soon exceeded the requisite sum, and we claim'd and receiv'd the public gift, which enabled us to carry the design into execution."[4]

What are the lessons to be learned from this account?

Be enthusiastic! Bond was "zealous and active"; Franklin was "heartily engaged."

Do not give up! Persistence is the key to sales. If you have difficulties, get more advice or try something new. When Bond got discouraged, he asked for and got help from Franklin; when Franklin got discouraged, he asked for and got help from the assembly.

Listen to the people you ask for money, and take their advice.

They are the experts. The people Bond asked for money told him, "Ask Franklin." He did it.

Enlist the help of community leaders. Once Franklin was involved, the campaign took off.

Leaders give first, then ask others.

Good publicity prepares people to give. Asking gets their donations.

Foundations or government matching grants can be used to challenge your fund raisers and increase local giving.

The next story Franklin tells can help you, too. Before long everyone with a fund-raising campaign asked Franklin to head it. Of course, he had to say no to most of them. Rev. Gilbert Tennant asked Franklin to help raise money to build a new meetinghouse. Franklin refused to help the campaign or share his list of prospects. Rev. Tennant "then desir'd I would at least give him my advice. That I will readily do, said I; and, in the first place, I advise you to apply to all those whom you know will give something; next, to those whom you are uncertain whether they will give anything or not, and show them the list of those who have given; and lastly, do not neglect those who you are sure will give nothing, for in some of those you will be mistaken. He laugh'd and thank'd me, and said he would take my advice. He did so, for he ask'd of *everybody,* and he obtained a much larger sum than he expected, with which he erected the capacious and very elegant meeting-house that stands in Arch-street."[5]

The lessons to be learned from this are:

1. If you cannot get the top community leaders to head your campaign, find out what they *would* have done, and then you do it!

2. Ask *everyone!* Do not let stereotypes, fears, or laziness stop you from asking everyone to give.

3. Start with the most likely givers first. Once they give, you will have a list of supporters to show the undecided. There is often a bandwagon effect in fund raising, so the indifferent people will give if they know the people they admire have given.

Fortunately, you can take advantage of the best of both worlds — for-profit and nonprofit — when you plan your fund-raising strategy for next year and the next five years. The best marketing and sales brains from a for-profit company can teach you how to sell and how to motivate others to sell. The best nonprofit fund-raising brains can show you the markets — the foundations, government agencies, corporations, and individuals who will be best to approach. Then your board members can put their expertise on *how* to sell together with *where* to sell to begin raising money and moving toward self-sufficiency.

CONTROVERSIAL MONEY

> *"There is nothing either good or bad but thinking makes it so."*
>
> *Hamlet* (act 2, scene 2)

There are many potential sources of money for your organization. How you choose to combine the sources will depend on the goals of the organization, the resources available in your community, and the enthusiasm of your leaders. After your board has made a fund-raising plan, it needs to consider one more question. Is there any money that the board specifically will *not* pursue or accept? Are there any specific donors, foundations, corporations, or government sources the board should officially rule out?

It is important to have this discussion *before* you launch your fund-raising campaign. First, the discussion will tell everyone involved that, although some specific sources of money may not be all right, the activity of fund raising itself *is* all right. It is important for you to believe that fund raising is a healthy, desirable activity, fundamental to the life of the organization.

Second, it is much worse to ask someone to return a donation than to forbid him or her to take it. Here is an example from Jane Addams:

> A trustee of Hull-House came to see us one day with the good news that a friend of his was ready to give $20,000 with which to build the desired new clubhouse. When, however, he divulged the name of his generous friend, it proved to be that of a man who was notorious for underpaying the girls in his establishment and concerning whom there were even darker stories. It seemed clearly impossible to erect a clubhouse for working girls with such money and we at once said that

we must decline the offer. The trustee of Hull-House was put in the most embarrassing situation; he had, of course, induced the man to give the money and had had no thought but that it would be eagerly received; he would now be obliged to return with the astonishing, not to say insulting, news that the money was considered unfit. . . . However the basic fact remained that we could not accept the money, and of this the trustee himself was fully convinced.[6]

This incident provoked several meetings about "tainted money," which created an official Hull House policy.

What you decide about money is entirely up to your leadership. You always will be able to sell your group to enough sources to raise the money you want. You *need* to have the courage of your convictions. You *never* need to take money from any source that does not live up to the values of your members. Massachusetts Fair Share will not let politicians buy memberships. They may observe meetings, but they may not vote until they are out of office. Women Employed will not accept money from employment agencies. The National Coalition Against Sexual Assault (NCASA) will not accept funds from the pornography industry. Use this discussion positively by saying, "Here is the 1 percent we will not ask for money. Now let's focus on the 99 percent whose money we *will* take."

You should try to avoid blanket indictments. Some groups have said, "We will never take government money," or "We will never take money from corporations." This is both foolish and poor planning. The "government" and "corporations" are only the people who work there, as is your organization. Some people are better than others. As a capable leader, your job is to find the people within the possible funding sources who are just as intelligent and caring as you are. Then find a way for your organizations to work together to benefit you both.

In the last analysis, money is just a means of exchange. It goes in and out of different pockets, but money does not "belong" to anyone. For this reason, many people say that it is all right to pursue money from all possible sources. As fund raiser Gail Fujioka puts it, "I look at fundraising as the liberation of money. I am going to get it, from any source, and use it to do good." Robert Therese of the Lambs farm for retarded young people says, "At the County Fair two years ago, Herb Lyon auctioned off a week's vacation at the Playboy Club in Lake Geneva, with the proceeds to go to the Lambs. Some of the local church people got a little worried by that; they said that anyone who dealt with Playboy could not be a Christian. Corinne's and my answer to that charge was that the devil has had the money long enough, and now it's our turn. Besides, we feel that anyone who helps and believes in us must be Christlike, no matter what his denomination."[7]

COMPLAINTS

Sometimes groups find themselves embroiled in arguments over sources of money, and these take their time and energy away from their programs. Unless your organization is so small that every member can participate in every decision, the elected leaders have to make decisions on behalf of the members. The board must try to make choices that satisfy most of the members. This gets more difficult as the membership gets larger. Sometimes you simply will have to accept that *someone* will complain regardless of what choices you make. Your task, then, becomes to create a fund-raising plan that the board can accept and plan to handle any complaints that arise from your choices.

Everyone on the board must agree about where to ask for money. So that they will feel confident about explaining their choices to the members, the board members can use one meeting to discuss all of the questions surrounding fund raising. Then the members can get all the money they need and feel good about it, too.

In order to honor your responsibility to the members *and* raise the budget, the board should discuss the following questions:

Is the basis of our budget dependable and renewable funds?

Do our funds come from a variety of sources so that we are not too dependent on any one source?

Has the board itself created the budget and fund-raising strategy, so that we can explain them to anyone who asks?

Does the board get monthly reports on all income and expenses so we all know exactly where our money comes from and where it goes? Can the officers handle any complaints about our income or expenses with courtesy and confidence?

Has the board discussed and made a public policy about which sources of money we will *not* pursue or accept?

Does the board understand and accept the strings that come with each source of money?

STEPS TO ASKING FOR MONEY

THE BOARD OF DIRECTORS WILL:

1. Decide to raise the money needed for the organization.
2. Set personal, specific goals for the amounts each board member will raise. If your budget is $24,000 and you have twelve people on your board, each board member is responsible for raising, or motivating others to raise, at least $2,000.
3. Think of your organization as a valuable resource that deserves the support of the community.
4. Ask for advice from successful salespeople and fund raisers.
5. Make a plan to "sell" the mission and the work of the organization.
6. Set a board policy about sources of money, if any, that board members may *not* ask.
7. Calculate the dollar value of the work of the organization.
8. Collect several stories that show the human value of the organization.
9. Practice your sales pitch.
10. Divide up the potential sources so that in one year you will ask everyone who needs or wants the organization.
11. Be enthusiastic! Ask with pride.
12. Thank everyone who gives you money or advice.

14

Making Meetings Fair
and Effective

> *"Common sense and experience are the biggest helps a chair can have in presiding at a meeting. She won't go far wrong if she remembers what the members want and develops an organized, agreeable meeting. Like Pavlov's dogs, people want to repeat a pleasant experience and to avoid repeating a disagreeable one."*
> —*Citizens Information Service Leader's Guide*

In a democratic organization, meetings are where decisions are made, actions are planned, and the future is shaped. They are the magnets that bring in new members and the showcases for new leaders. The best meetings are exciting, fun, and productive.

Any group from two to two thousand can have a meeting. When you sit down for a cup of coffee and discussion with your biggest donor or your newest staff person, this is a meeting. When the national political parties hold conventions with thousands of delegates, this is a meeting. In either case, the results depend on careful planning before the meeting and the cooperation of the people at the meeting. Here are some tested ideas for preparing for all of your meetings. Later in the chapter we will discuss minutes, elections, board meetings, and how to hold a large community meeting.

LEARNING HOW TO PLAN

No matter what the size or purpose of the meeting, it must be well planned in advance. The larger the meeting, the more planning you will need. If you are meeting a donor at lunch, you may plan the meeting the day before. If you are planning an annual convention, you may create a convention committee a year in advance. In either case, this meeting may be the only opportunity you will have to reach this audience. Whether the meeting involves one person with funds you want or two thousand members with energy you want, make the meeting work through planning.

The best way to learn about good meetings is to attend good meetings run by other organizations. Check the community calendar in the newspaper, or call other groups to ask when their next meetings will be. Get there early and stay late. See what a group does to make you feel welcome and want to participate. What is first? What gets the most time? What is skipped? Who chairs? Does the meeting start on time and end on time? Whom do you notice? Why? Are you comfortable? Why? Is some hospitality built-in? How? Does the group follow up (call you) the next day? How many people are involved in making the meeting work? Then use these ideas to plan your own meetings.

WHEN *NOT* TO PLAN A MEETING

Here are two good rules to prevent unnecessary meetings.

1. Respect your people's time. Time is the most valuable commodity anyone has to give. If you ever have organized a fund-raising campaign, you know it is easier to get money than time. Fund raiser Sally Berger tells a story about a bank president who asked fifty of his peers — other bankers, company presidents, chairs of the boards of big corporations — to help him raise money for his favorite cause. He offered to pick them up, give them lunch, and cover their expenses. All he wanted was for them to come to his office for one day and make calls for his favorite nonprofit organiza-

tion. All fifty of the executives said, "I don't have time. Let me send a check instead!" Time is *the* nonrenewable resource. If you want people to invest their valuable time in building your organization, you must treat it like *gold!*

If you ask twenty-four people to sit in a one-hour meeting, you have just used up an entire day — twenty-four hours — of their time. Will you get a day's worth of results from that meeting?

This leads to the second rule:

2. Do all work in the smallest possible group. If a task can be done by one or two people, that is the way to do it. The entire fifteen-member fund raising committee may plan a benefit, but they do not all have to write the invitation, design the centerpieces, or hire the band. A big meeting can be used to produce a plan that is democratically agreed upon to guide the people doing the work. Most of the actual work will take place after this meeting, however, based on the wishes of the group. Remember: people want to do worthwhile work for the group. Do not keep good workers tied up in meetings when they would rather be out getting results!

PLANNING A GREAT MEETING

If your people are all alike and have plenty of time, you will not need much planning for most of your meetings. Usually each person at a meeting can simply say what he or she wants to say; everyone will discuss it, and you will decide what to do next and move on to the next person or item. Especially in very new or very small groups, meetings are really just conversations about the organization. This is fine as long as your group is small enough for everyone to speak and your meetings are long enough for all decisions to be made.

Once your organization is established in the community, your reputation will attract people and your ambition will create more programs to discuss. People will come to the meetings because they are passionate about your cause and eager to get something done. It will quickly be clear to you that the conversation style of meeting will not work for larger groups. You will need a plan, usually made by the board members, to teach meeting skills and get decisions made. The three parts of your plan for fair and effective meetings are a written agenda, which is the list of items you will discuss; clear rules to guarantee the rights of everyone in the audience; and a fair chair to make sure that everyone understands what is going on and how to participate.

Written Agenda

The first part of your meeting plan is a written agenda. The agenda is the list of topics to be discussed. It tells everyone at the meeting what is happening now and what will happen next.

An ideal meeting runs about one or two hours. When you are starting out, your meetings may be longer, but as you get more experience and more confidence you can keep them shorter and get just as much accomplished. Because your meeting may run over the alloted time despite your best intentions, put the least important topics at the end of the agenda. Then, even if these have to be postponed or referred to committees, your most important work will have been done.

When you make the agenda, you have to decide what should be the most important topic and *who* you want to spotlight. Do first things first. Put your most important topic and the people you want to get attention at the beginning of the agenda. Go directly to the most important item of business.

Keep your purpose and your goals in mind at all times. If the goal of this meeting is to showcase a new leader, let him or her give the keynote address or lead the meeting. If the goal is to find new community leaders, provide many opportunities for people to speak from the floor. If the goal is to educate the audience, plan short, dramatic, memorable demonstrations. If the goal is to create unity in the group, plan many ways for the group to act together — they can stand for unanimous votes, sing an inspiring song, or come forward to pick up materials.

When planning the agenda, try to offer a balance between the work that needs to be covered in the business part of the meeting and enjoyable activities which will inspire or motivate your audience. Use your imagination to keep your meetings fresh and effective. Some techniques other groups use to add variety to their meetings include:

- Offer a door prize.
- Hold a raffle drawing at the meeting.

- Put on a skit; sing songs; or act out the next activity, such as selling advertisements for the newsletter or collecting signatures on a petition.
    - Show slides illustrating your history or your next project.
    - Show an inspiring movie, and then discuss it.
    - Offer a demonstration, such as self-defense for a women's group or cardiopulmonary resuscitation (CPR) for a neighborhood group.
    - Recruit or hire a celebrity, a speaker, an expert in your field, or the veteran leader of a similar successful organization to entertain, educate, or motivate your group.
    - Serve special refreshments—holiday specialties, ethnic favorites, or samples from your cookbook.

A well-planned agenda will help you to do first things first, focus on one item at a time, leave the least important items to the end, highlight certain leaders, and set a tone for the meeting. All of these will help your meeting get work done and get out on time so people will want to come to the next meeting!

Clear Rules

The second step of a meeting plan is the choice of clear rules. These rules will set the style for the meeting. Your rules will affect how much gets done, who likes the meeting and comes back, and who dislikes the meeting and does not come back. The purpose of the organization and the style of the majority of the members will decide which rules are best for you.

Many small groups and cooperatives choose to make decisions by *consensus*. "Consensus means reaching a unanimous decision through discussion and compromise. Consensus may require full discussion, but it assumes that members are prepared to cooperate."[1] When trying to achieve consensus, the people at the meeting discuss each topic until the chair (or clerk) believes that they are all in agreement. He or she states the sense of the meeting, and if there is no disagreement, consensus is reached. If the members have one purpose, plenty of time, and a shared goal of cooperation, consensus will work very well.

Groups that use consensus to make decisions believe that it gives them greater clarity on all the choices available and greater solidarity around the final choice. Although it may take more time to reach a decision, they believe that "earnestly laboring for moral clarity through the consensus process very often results in profound leaps of personal growth."[2] Consensus works best for small groups in which every member comes to the meetings with "an understanding of, and unity with, the ideals of the organization."[3]

Some groups — for example, a rape crisis center — may choose to use consensus all the time because it will reflect their political beliefs. The members want a feeling of mutual respect and support in the organization. They get it by making all decisions by consensus, as well as by rotating the jobs of chair and secretary.

However, if you want to include a large number of people in decisions, if the audience has strong opinions and varied interests, if you have a bold program with many issues, or if you want to involve busy people, you probably will find that you can get more done, involve more people, and have better meetings if you make decisions by voting. In that case you have a lot to gain by learning to use parliamentary procedure, which is completely explained in a book called *Robert's Rules of Order Newly Revised.*

Parliamentary procedure, developed in the British Parliament, is a system for conducting meetings and making group decisions. This system has been copied by American legislatures and small community organizations that have to make decisions as a group. In 1867, Gen. Henry M. Roberts was asked to preside over a meeting at his church. Unfortunately, he did not know how to chair a meeting. He later wrote, "My embarrassment was supreme. I plunged in, trusting to Providence that the assembly would behave itself. But with the plunge went the determination that I would never attend another meeting until I knew something of parliamentary law."[4] He became an expert and wrote *Robert's Rules of Order,* which became the authority on the parliamentary procedure. The book has been updated as better rules were invented.

Parliamentary procedure allows groups to make fair and effective decisions. Each item of business must be proposed by someone as a suggestion that the group do something. This is called a *motion.* The group can only consider a motion if it is *seconded,* which means that a second person also wants to discuss the piece of business. If only one person is interested in the motion, it will not get a second, and the group will not have to discuss it. If a motion is seconded, it will be discussed. The group may only discuss one motion at a time. A motion may pass, fail, be sent to a committee for more study, or be postponed until another meeting. But *something* happens! The group must handle each piece of business before it can move on to another piece of business.

Decisions are made by voting on each motion after discussion. The rules for voting guarantee that the will of the majority will be adopted and the rights of the minority will be protected. It is the right of the majority to end the debate and move to a vote, provided they have the support of two-thirds of the group. Why two-thirds? Because only one-half is needed to make a decision, so if two-thirds have made up their minds it is highly unlikely that talking any longer will change the outcome of the vote. The minority has the right to have their views heard as long as more than one-third of the group wants to hear them. You guarantee the majority that a decision will be made, and you also guarantee full opportunity for discussion as long as most people need and want new information. The minority, the "loyal opposition," can frankly state and keep their opinions. Using parliamentary procedure tells people that you want their convictions, not their conformity.

Making decisions by the parliamentary procedure system of voting has many advantages for your group. Voting enables you to accomplish the most business in the least amount of time. This tells people at the meeting that you think their time is important and will respect it. Busy people can participate.

Voting also gives you an accurate measure of the enthusiasm for an idea. With consensus, some people may go along with *every* decision just because it must be unanimous. But with voting, you can count how many people favored an idea — whether it passed eleven to one or seven to five. That way you learn what people want most.

Also, voting requires a proposal's real supporters to take responsibility for their idea. We all know from working in committees that "everybody" never does anything. One person has to make it happen. Once a proposal passes, someone on the winning side will have to take the responsibility of making the plan work.

Parliamentary procedure can be used by very large numbers of people. All three thousand people at your convention can use the system fairly and quickly.

Voting is how people with power in the real world make decisions. When reporters asked Chicago's Mayor Richard J. Daley why Hubert Humphrey did not carry Illinois in 1968, Daley said, "He did not get enough votes." Especially if the purpose of the organization is to get the city council or Congress to pass good legislation, your own members must understand voting. If you want your plan to win, you must have the votes. If the leaders relearn this lesson at every meeting, they will know what to do when they take on city hall.

Remember, the purpose of rules for a meeting is to make everyone feel good about the meeting and to get work done. You may choose different rules for different sorts of meetings. Many groups use parliamentary procedure for their board and large public meetings and use consensus for smaller committee meetings.

A Fair Chair

Legendary hostess Perle Mesta once said that the secret to having a successful party is that the hostess must have (or appear to have) a good time. If she is enjoying herself, so will the guests. In the same way, the secret of a successful meeting is a chair who can appear calm and confident at all times. The chair guides the discussion. He or she pays attention to the flow of the meeting rather than to the content of the talk. A well-planned agenda and clear rules will help, but a good chair will make the meeting work.

Good chairs combine grace, humor, and courtesy. They convey a sense of authority; you feel that they know what they are doing. They listen to speakers with the rapt attention of doting grandmothers. They clarify and simplify meetings for everyone. They make sure that majority opinions are adopted, that minority opinions are protected, that business is accomplished, that goals are achieved, and that people's feelings are protected. Most of all, they are fair—they do not favor one side or the other. A good chair makes people proud of what happens at a meeting and also of how it happens.

If you want to be a fair chair, before the meeting you will chair, go to other groups' meetings. Observe experienced chairs at work. Take notes and ask them for advice. Read the recommended materials on parliamentary procedure or consensus. Get and use a gavel and a watch. Memorize everybody's names and how to pronounce them. If the meeting is small, memorize the names of all the people who will be there; for larger meetings, memorize the names of everyone with a specific job to do.

Minutes

After you plan the agenda, choose the rules, and select a fair chair, you have virtually guaranteed the success of your meeting. There is only one more job to consider for any meeting you hold. One person must be responsible for making a record of the decisions and assignments made at the meeting. This record is called the *minutes.*

WHO SHOULD TAKE MINUTES?

Every meeting needs someone to take minutes. At a board meeting, this is usually one job of the secretary, who is elected for one year. At other meetings, choose someone as clerk or recorder, whose only job is to take minutes. Some organizations prefer to rotate the job so that everyone takes a turn. If you have twelve people on your board and the board meets monthly, during one year each person could chair the meeting once, take minutes once, and provide refreshments once. This divides the work equally and gives everyone a chance to learn new skills. At any meeting, both the chair and the person taking the minutes must have a complete knowledge of the rules used at the meeting. Because the minutes record decisions and create the history of the organization, it is important that an officer take the minutes. Do not delegate the job to paid staff. If the board is afraid that taking minutes will prevent one person from participating fully, streamline the system or rotate the job.

WHY TAKE MINUTES?

The minutes do four things for you. For the members who were at the meeting, they provide a short review of decisions, assignments, and deadlines. For the members who missed the meeting, they provide an accurate account of what happened. For future officers and staff, they create a history of the organization. They tell who went to meetings, who worked, when important decisions and changes were made, and how work was done. For everyone, they serve as the official legal record of important decisions. For example, Illinois law says, "Each corporation shall keep . . . minutes of the proceedings of its members, board of directors, and committees having any of the authority of the board of directors. . . ."[5] In addition, your auditor usually will check your minutes to verify the board's decisions regarding financial matters.

Check with your lawyer and accountant for other advice on minutes. Ask veteran secretaries from other organizations how they do the job and what they find is most helpful to their boards.

Include in the minutes:

1. Date, time, place, and purpose of the meeting.

2. Names of voting members present and absent.

3. Motions made and passed. The person who makes the motion must give the wording of the final version of the passed motion to the secretary. Record who made the motion, who seconded, and the vote count.

4. Assignments and deadlines. After a motion passes, the person who made the motion is responsible for seeing that the work is done on time. Record the person in charge, his or her assignment, and when he or she will report on progress or finish the job.

5. List of reports made. Attach copies of all written reports. List correspondence read aloud.

There is no reason to include motions that failed or any part of discussions. Record only decisions and assignments: "Benjamin Franklin moved and Abigail Adams seconded that the Sons and Daughters of Liberty supply copies of the new Declaration of Independence to all school libraries in the colonies. Passed 11-1. Adams will collect list of school librarians and form a committee to address envelopes by July 10, 1776. Franklin will prepare copies of the declaration by July 17, 1776. Board members are invited to join the committee at the mailing party at the Adams' farm on July 18, 1776."

MECHANICS

Before the first meeting of your board, the secretary will multiply the number of board members by the number of meetings in a year and bring that many envelopes to the meeting. For example, if there are fifteen people on your board and it meets eleven times a year, bring 165 envelopes to the first meeting. Ask each board member to address eleven envelopes to himself or herself. Collect them all. Then the day after a meeting, make copies of the minutes and send one to each member, using the preaddressed envelopes. Send one to yourself, too, so you will know when they arrive.

Each person should read the minutes of the last meeting before the next meeting. At that meeting, ask if everyone received the minutes and if there are any corrections. Because the people making motions gave the secretary final versions of their motions, you should not have made mistakes with this system; however, some slight change may be needed about twice a year. If a change is needed, revise the secretary's copy, then vote to approve the minutes as revised. The secretary should sign the official copy and put it in a notebook or file it for safekeeping. You do not have to read the minutes out loud at each meeting unless you want to.

Because the secretary sends out the minutes after each meeting, he or she also can mail other reports and the calendar of coming events to anyone who missed the meeting. The secretary should call the absent members three days later to make sure they received the materials and to ask if they have questions. Remind them of the date, time, and place of the next meeting. If the meeting was a board meeting, the president also should call to be sure the absent members are up-to-date on all decisions made at the meeting. This makes sure that nobody gets out of touch and that everyone is reminded of his or her responsibilities.

Running an Election

Frequently at meetings you will have to hold elections. At your annual meeting, the nominating committee must run an election to choose members for the board. At other meetings, the chairs may want to run elections to choose people for specific jobs, such as the delegates to your national convention or representatives to go to a new coalition meeting. Here are some tested suggestions on running an election. Because the choice of officers and representatives is so important, it should always be handled by the officers and never delegated to employees.

Running an election for officers at the annual meeting is the job of the nominating committee. Before the meeting, the committee already has made up a slate of qualified candidates and prepared copies of the rules for voting, ballots, tally sheets, and bylaws.

ELECTION RULES

Ask other organizations what rules they use when they run elections. The nominating committee can prepare a draft of the voting rules for approval by the board. They will include who can vote, who cannot vote, how to nominate someone from the floor, what the candidates may or may not do, and how the votes shall be cast and counted. Make enough copies of the rules to give out ahead of time and at the meeting.

BALLOTS, TALLY SHEETS, AND BYLAWS

The ballots list the offices up for election and the names of candidates for each office. Leave a space for the addition of names of people nominated from the floor during the meeting. Even if the slate is unopposed, make up printed ballots and use them.

Use tally sheets to count the votes. These list the candidates by name, and allow plenty of space in which you can mark the votes.

The bylaws tell what each officer is expected to do, who may run for office, and who may vote. Have on hand enough copies for all the voting members.

AT THE MEETING

Each candidate may choose one person to be his or her poll watcher. This person will watch the preparation, distribution, collection, and counting of the ballots.

The nominating committee members should give ballots to qualified voters, watch the voting, and then collect the ballots. The ballots are counted in groups of three. One person opens and reads the ballot out loud so that the poll watchers can see each ballot. Two people mark tally sheets with one stroke for each vote. Add up all the votes. If the two totals are different, go through the procedure again until the totals match. When all the votes are counted, the chair of the nominating committee should announce the results.

If a candidate is not present, the chair should tell that candidate as soon as possible whether he or she won or lost.

AFTER THE ELECTION

Keep the ballots and tally sheets until the next election, in case there is any question about the vote. The chair should send a thank-you note to each member of the nominating committee, then prepare a report containing suggestions for next year's committee. Give copies of the report to the president and the secretary, and keep one for yourself.

STEPS TO PREPARING FOR A GREAT MEETING

THE BOARD OF DIRECTORS OR CHAIRS OF THE MEETING WILL:

1. Decide to have a great meeting.
2. Pre-plan with key leaders.
3. Choose a purpose for the meeting. Set clear goals.
4. Ask people to attend the meeting.
5. Plan the agenda.
6. Select a fair chair.
7. Choose helpful rules.
8. Select a person to make a written record of the meeting.
9. Plan elections, if any.

HOW TO PLAN A BOARD MEETING

Before board meetings, the president and active committee chairs should write the agenda and discuss who will lead which parts. Each board member must be polled to find out who will be at the meeting. The person calling should tell each member the purpose of the meeting—for example, "We will be talking about the budget for next year. Bring your ideas." Some groups mail the agenda in advance, then ask for additions when the meeting starts.

For groups that want to be self-sufficent, the first important item on a business agenda is fund raising. The easiest and fastest way to spark your fund-raising campaign is to move it to the top of the agenda. If a topic is important, show this by putting the topic first on the agenda.

Agenda for a Board Meeting

A typical board meeting agenda can open with a welcome from the president and agreement on the agenda. The treasurer can distribute a report on where money was raised and spent in the previous month. The secretary can ask if everyone received the minutes from the last meeting and if there are any changes, and you can approve them. The first major item would ideally be a report from the chair of the fund-raising committee about fund raisers, special events, and income projections for the next month. Recognize any special accomplishments—for example, "Rob finally got the appointment to see the manager at Sears and got one thousand dollars!" Let others speak whenever you can: "Martha will tell how the membership committee set a new record last month, signing up 120 new members!"

If finances are a problem, devote the entire meeting to money until you have an adequate dependable income. Once you have a dependable income, you can add some other reports, but it is still important that the chair of the fund-raising committee report at the beginning of each board meeting. A treasurer's report tells you only what was spent last month. You need the fund raiser's report to tell you the income projections for next month. You want your board to think in a businesslike fashion, to look *forward,* and always to consider more ways to make more money in less time. The fund raiser's report at the beginning of every board meeting tells the group that fund raising is important, that ideas are welcome, and that this is what makes the rest of the work possible.

In the rest of the board meeting, you can have either many short reports (if you want to give everyone a chance to speak) or a few long reports. Sometimes you will want to set aside an entire board meeting to discuss one topic—such as program planning and evaluation, next year's budget, staff evaluation and assignments, buying a building, or other long-range goals. Other meetings may focus on one or two committees—on membership and beautification at one meeting, publicity and traffic the next.

HOW TO PLAN A LARGE COMMUNITY MEETING

Before a large community meeting, you should have a planning meeting with the key people. Ask about twelve to twenty people—

your own leaders and other local leaders to come to the planning meeting. Talk about the purpose of the meeting—for example, to confront the fire commissioner about the arson problem in Akron. Then set specific goals for the meeting.

Your goals could be as follows:

1. Introduce the chairs of the arson committee to the community. The president will chair the meeting so the chairs can take the lead in the meeting.

2. Find the leaders or potential leaders who are concerned about arson and respected in this neighborhood.

3. Educate the neighbors about their rights and resources.

4. Create a feeling of unity in the group.

5. Present a show of strength.

6. Get a reaction from the fire commissioner. If he or she says yes to your requests, this will show that the group can get results. If he or she says no, the group can take the requests to the mayor, in which case you will get approval for this action from everyone at the meeting.

How to Attract a Large Audience

People come to a meeting because somebody *asks* them to come to the meeting. Posters, fliers, and publicity will make them believe that they made the right choice, but publicity does not produce people. People produce people. To get people to a small meeting, you can use the doubling method described in Chapter 10. For a large meeting, use the squad sheet system.

A squad sheet is a list of people who say they will come to the meeting. At a planning meeting about three weeks before the community meeting, hand out squad sheets and talk about people who should be invited to the meeting—family, friends, co-workers, or members of other organizations. Have two people act out inviting someone to the meeting. Then ask each person to ask as many people as possible. On the squad sheets, they will list all the people who say they will come to the big meeting. Be sure that everyone also has plenty of simple, clear fliers giving the date, time, day of the week, and place of the meeting. These should include a map, information about parking and nearby bus or subway routes, the organization's name, and at least one phone number to call for more information.

At another planning meeting just before the big meeting, each person reports the total on his or her squad sheets. This gives you an approximate idea of how many chairs to set up and the quantity of refreshments to make. The actual turnout is usually smaller because of duplication of names and people who change their minds at the last minute.

Ask people to keep their lists. After the big meeting, you can compare the list of attendees — who sign in at the door — with the squad sheets to find out which "askers" really delivered people. Make this part fun; offer prizes for the people who bring the most people.

This squad sheet is also an excellent tool to use if you pay staff to recruit members for you. The sheets give you an accurate measure of how well staff are doing their jobs. Table 14-1 presents a sample squad sheet.

TABLE 14-1   Sample Squad Sheet

Akron Arson Committee Community Meeting
Tuesday, June 9, 1981

Your name _____ Phone _____

People coming to the meeting:

Name	Address	Phone	Special needs:	
			Ride to meeting	*Child care: number & ages*
1.				
2.				
3.				
4.				
5.				
6.				
7.				
8.				
9.				
10.				

Instructions:
Give each person a flier with information about the meeting. Point out the date, time, and place. Explain why you are going and what will happen. Ask him or her to come to the meeting. Say, "Can I count on you to be there?" When people say yes, get their names and phone numbers. On Monday, June 8, call everyone on your list to remind them of the meeting.

Recruiting Workers

After you write the agenda, recruit people to take part in the meeting. This is the most important part of planning. Everyone who has a job to do has a reason to come to the meeting. He or she also will believe the meeting is important and will tell friends. Let us look at how many people can be involved in a large community meeting:

TABLE 14-2   Tasks for a Large Community Meeting

Task	Number of People
Chair—the president	1
Chair's helpers	4
Co-chairs of the arson committee	2
Secretary	1
Greeters	3
Sign-in table	2
Refreshments	2
Child care	3
Membership table	2
Sales table	2
Photographer	1
Press and publicity	2
Prayer	1
Giving testimony (floor team)	6
Security and clean up	2
Transportation	2
	36

Thirty-six people will have a reason to come to this meeting and bring their friends. If each brings two people, you already have 108 people at your meeting!

Notice that nothing should be left to chance. Before the end of the planning meeting, someone should have taken responsibility for each job and have a plan and a time set for getting it done.

Design Floor Plan

Once you have assigned the jobs, design the floor plan for the meeting. Have one planning meeting at the location where you will hold the big meeting. Check the sound equipment. Count the available chairs and tables. Does the room have a flag, sound system, fire extinguishers, or coffee maker? Make a list of what it has and thus of what you need to get. Who has the key to let you in and out?

Make a traffic plan. More meetings start late because of a bottleneck at the door than for any other reason. Walk through as though you were a newcomer. Where will you need signs — the parking lot, the front door, the stairs? Where do you need to station young people to help with stairs or coats? Is there a special entrance for people in wheelchairs? Where will your greeters be? Where will people put their coats? Draw a floor plan and add people's names. Then you will know where the traffic will move and who will do what. Figure 14-1 on page 217 is a sample floor plan.

Mentally walk through the layout as though you were walking into the room. A new person will meet:

Greeters (three people) — Greet new people at the door and escort them to the . . .

Sign-in table (two people) — Ask people to write their names and addresses on a list, give members blue name tags, and give non-members red name tags and show them the membership table. Give everyone agendas and song sheets. If another organization wants to pass out fliers, put them on the . . .

Free literature table — Where you put fliers about the auditions for the community theater and the rally against draft registration, the sign-up sheet for the mayor's marathon race, the brochures about the new co-op nursery, and the cards offering free kittens to a good home. No one will have to interrupt the meeting with commercials or to pass out anything, but all the material is available to people on their way to the . . .

Coatracks — Have enough racks and plenty of space so that people can get to them.

The child care room (three people) — The door to the room ideally should be at the back, so that parents with small children can leave early. Be sure that baby-sitters arrive early and have all the supplies they need.

Refreshments (two people) — Coffee, tea, punch, cookies, etc., should be next to the kitchen. Greeters should make sure that new people get refreshments and meet veterans who show them the . . .

Display of clippings, photos, and interesting facts about the organization and the issue — This area needs no volunteer. Shy people will huddle here, so keep an eye out for them. Because they obviously would enjoy being a part of an exciting organization, show them the . . .

Membership table (two people) — Have membership applications, current newsletters and brochures, blank receipt forms, and a cashbox with cash in it for making change. When people are new members, show them the . . .

Sales table (two people) — Where people buy membership supplies such as buttons, bumper stickers, T-shirts, cookbooks, and tickets for the spaghetti supper. Have a cashbox with cash in it and blank receipt forms. Now show them to the . . .

Chairs — Get people seated and reading the agenda so that the meeting can start on time.

The exception is if someone who comes in is a member of the press. Send the press immediately to the . . .

Press table (two people) — Give press releases, current newsletters, and brochures to the press. One person should watch the table while the other person introduces press people to the president and chairs for the meeting. Be sure television people have enough space for their equipment.

You also will need a *table and chair for the secretary.* This is because the secretary will take much better minutes if any person who wants the group to vote on something gives the text of this motion to the secretary in writing. The secretary should be seated away from the head table so that people can go over to him or her during the meeting with their motions without interrupting the meeting.

If someone — for example, the fire commissioner — is going to be "on the spot" at this meeting, put a *chair for the guest* at the front of the room but away from the head table. He or she probably will bring several people for moral support. Let these extra people take chairs in the audience. You want to focus on the one person who has power, not on subordinates. If this person is an adversary, you want to isolate him or her as much as possible. On the other hand, if you have invited an honored guest, put him or her at the head table with your leaders.

Be sure your *organization's name* is visible at the front and sides of the room. If you can, frame your leaders between the American

flag and your own banner. If there is a podium, cover the front with
the name of the organization. Find photos of big meetings in the
newspaper, and study them to see how the groups decorated the
rooms so that their names and slogans would appear in any photo of
a speaker or the crowd.

Set Up Early

Everything should be set up at least one-half hour before the time
to start, and even earlier for an especially big crowd or a meeting at
which there will be many senior citizens. If any worker does not
show up, the chair of the meeting should find a substitute. Once
everything is set up, walk through the room once as though you
were a newcomer, check the washrooms, and then get ready to meet
your public.

Crises

Murphy's Law states: "Anything that can go wrong, will."
Flanagan's Corollary states: "Things that can't go wrong, will."
This is always true of big meetings. No matter how carefully
planned a meeting is, something unexpected will happen. I have
had the first car stall in the entrance of the only parking lot so that
no one else could park. I have had three people show up with six
keys to the meeting room, only to discover that none of the keys
worked. I have had the speaker get lost and miss the meeting; and
once — honestly — lightning even struck the building. That is why
you have to get there early, keep your sense of humor, and use your
imagination. Whatever happens, you will have to think on your feet
and quickly create an alternative to keep people there and stay on
your timetable. Involve other local leaders early in your planning,
so that you have many resources available to help in a crisis.

HOW TO CHAIR A LARGE MEETING

If you are the chair, ask four people to be your helpers. The day
of the meeting, review what you want them to do. The chair's
helpers are people in the audience whose job, like the chair's, is to
watch the movement of the meeting rather than the content of the

FIGURE 14–1
Sample Floor Plan for Large Community Meeting

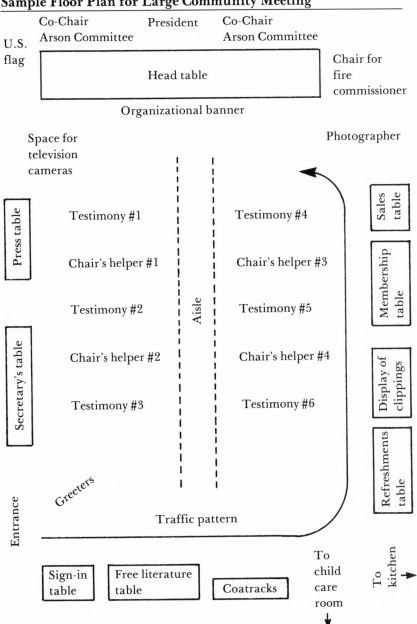

discussion. They help to answer questions from people around them, help to keep people following the agenda, and do whatever they can to make the chair's job easier. Being a chair's helper is an excellent way to learn to be a chair, because you have to think, "What does the chair want to do next? What does he or she need to make that work?"

The chair's helpers are not the floor team. The floor team is the group of people who give testimony, make motions, or give reports. For example, six people know they will testify on a particular subject. They are the floor team. They practice ahead of time so that their remarks will be short and dramatic and will cover all the points they want to make. When they are not testifying they concentrate on what is said, while the four chair's helpers concentrate on how it is said and how it is heard. Together these two groups are at all times alert to the needs of the chair and the audience.

STARTING THE MEETING

The chair must be ready at least fifteen minutes before the meeting. When other people arrive, they will look to the chair to see if they should get to work. If you are the chair for the meeting, five minutes before starting time, say, "We will start in five minutes. Please take your seats." This gives people time to get their coffee and wrap up their conversations.

Start on time! Starting on time helps this meeting a little and helps every future meeting a lot. If you start late, the people who are on time will resent it, and the people who are late will be even later next time. If you want people to believe that you are an effective organization, act like an effective organization—start on time.

Welcome everyone to the meeting. Introduce yourself if you are the top officer; then introduce the other officers. If you are not the top officer, have that person introduce you to the audience, nominate you as chair for the meeting, and give you the gavel.

Call the meeting to order. This is the official beginning of the meeting. Pound your gavel two times, and say, "The meeting will come to order." This tells people that you know what to do and that the meeting has begun. It also adds a little excitement to the start, the "curtain going up" on your meeting.

Announce the quorum. The quorum is the number of people

who must attend before the group can do business. This number is written into your bylaws. Tell the group, "Our quorum is one-tenth of the voting members, or forty people. Will the voting members please stand and be counted?" (You already will have counted to confirm the number.) This gives the members a chance to act as a group right at the beginning and gives them a feeling of unity. It also shows the members that their presence is important and recognized as necessary to do business, and it shows the nonmembers that members are important. Now say, "A quorum is present. We may proceed."

Next, you may ask for a roll call, during which the leader of each group will announce the name of the group and the number of people it represents. This makes a nice show of strength at a large meeting and gives many people a chance to speak. As an alternative, the chair can recognize the leaders at the meeting, thank anyone who worked, and introduce any visiting dignitaries.

The chair sets the tone for the meeting. First, tell people the purpose of the meeting; for example, "We are here tonight to find out what Commissioner Burns will do about arson in Akron." Handle all "housekeeping" matters early and quickly. Tell people the location of the washrooms, telephones, lost and found, child care, and refreshments. This will prevent interruptions later. Point out the membership table, and urge people to become members or volunteer for committees. If the meeting is very large, point out your helpers, and ask people to ask the helpers if they have questions about how the meeting is run.

At a large meeting, you want the group to focus on the goal of the meeting—not on the process of meeting itself. Planning must be done in advance by a small committee, so that later your goals can be accomplished by a large group in a small amount of time.

At the meeting, ask the group to look at the agenda. Explain that the agenda was planned by the ten people at the planning meeting. Have two people from the planning committee ready to move and second that the agenda be adopted as written. Vote to approve the agenda. If anyone protests that he or she wants to add something, say that the last section is "open discussion," and new business will be discussed then if there is enough time.

Now tell the group the rules of the meeting. Have printed copies available. This is your opportunity to tell people how you see your role as chair. Tell them that your job is to help them conduct business fairly and productively. The reason for the agenda, the chair, and the rules is the same: to do first things first, handle one thing at a time, and be sure that something gets done on each issue. Point out the helpers again.

Several times during the meeting, refer to the agenda, the rules, and your role. Keep telling the group how well they are doing and how well the meeting is going. Then it will.

If you like, you can now call on a minister or rabbi to give a prayer, lead the Pledge of Allegiance, or begin a song. For some meetings, these activities even may be expanded. This will set the tone of the meeting, give people something to do as a group, and provide a way to involve clergy or other community leaders.

DURING THE MEETING

When you start the business part of the meeting, review the rules as briefly as possible. It is a good idea to have some guidelines for discussion, especially during a heated debate. For example, many groups alternate the pros and cons. A person who is in favor of the motion speaks, followed by a person who is against the motion. No person may speak twice until everyone who wants to speak has been heard once. If one side runs out of speakers, the other side may continue to have speakers recognized only if the speakers are offering *new* arguments.

Sometimes the chair will assign numbers to the hands raised— "One, two, three, four, five"—make a list, and then call on people in order. Say, "Tony, you were one. Sally, you will be next." Then say, "Sally, you were two, Juan, you will be next." This way everyone knows when they are to speak.

The chair also may announce a time limit, such as ten minutes on discussion. Then, after ten minutes of discussion, take a "sense vote." For example, say, "Our time for discussion is up. How many would like to extend the time to allow Senator Smith to finish her remarks?" If the majority wants to continue discussion, allow five more minutes. If the majority wants to vote, move to the vote. This way everyone at the meeting understands what is happening and how long everything will take. This procedure also reminds them that the purpose of the rules is to accomplish business and at the same time to do the will of the people at the meeting. Like a good judge, a good chair will protect the rights of all sides so that they get equal chances to present their points of view.

The chair can insure a good discussion by watching and listening.

Watch for people who look as though they want to speak. They may be shaking their heads in disagreement or nodding in agreement. They may be smiling or frowning. Others in the group may look to one person, expecting him or her to speak. Especially when you know most of the people at the meeting, you know whose opinions are respected. If one of these people does not volunteer, call on him or her. Say, "You look as though you want to say something . . ." or "Didn't you study this problem last year? What do you think?" At a large meeting, the helpers should encourage people to speak. The helpers also watch for distractions — people talking to each other, not following the agenda, getting fidgety. They tell people why this part of the agenda is important to them.

Listen to the speakers. Everyone has something to say and a reason for saying it. Remember that not everyone comes to your meeting just because he or she cares about the agenda. Some people come because they are looking for status, affection, importance, an outlet for their anger, or a chance to show off. Whenever someone is speaking, ask yourself: What is he or she saying? Why? Why now? What does he or she want? How can he or she get that from this meeting? Who is listening to this speaker? Why? During the discussion, make a list of the people who speak and are listened to. A total stranger may get up, say two sentences, and get the biggest applause of the evening. It is the job of the helpers to be sure than an officer introduces himself or herself to that person, gets his or her name, and invites him or her to the next meeting.

AT THE END OF THE MEETING

At the end of the meeting, make sense of what has happened. The chair frames the meeting by reminding people of the purpose of the meeting, recapping what went on, praising the group for the work done, and pointing out the accomplishments of the evening. If specific people have taken assignments, review the people, tasks, and deadlines. Point out the date, time, and place of the next meeting. Use a very upbeat and positive closing. Tell people why the meeting was important and effective. Plant a thought in their minds so that they will answer enthusiastically when their neighbors or co-workers ask, "What happened at the meeting?" You want them to say, "It was exciting! This was the first time the fire commissioner has ever come to a meeting in our neighborhood. We got everything we wanted. He will be back to report on the twelfth, and you ought to be there." Or "We saw an unbelievable slide show! This is going to be the most important exhibit in the history of Cincinnati. The next meeting is Tuesday. You should come, too."

Try to have each person leave the meeting with something to do. A person can simply take a leaflet, put a poster in a window, or wear a button. Anyone can collect signatures on a petition or sell raffle tickets. You can ask each person to call one neighbor to report on the meeting, or ask people to call an appropriate politician. The last step before adjourning is to ask each person at the meeting to take one specific action for the organization the following day.

End on time! Like starting on time, ending on time will pay off because it shows people that you respect their time. If they have to arrange rides, hire baby-sitters, or get to work, they will be counting on you to end on time. If necessary, defer business to another meeting. Send it to a committee, or postpone it. Ending on time is more important.

If you reach the time for adjournment, the chair can simply adjourn. If you finish the business early, one of the floor team can move to adjourn. This will mark the end of business, and relaxed conversation can begin again.

AFTER A LARGE MEETING

The board's work is not over when the meeting adjourns. This is when the audience can leave, but there is still plenty for the leaders to do. The officers should talk to anyone new who made a good comment or brought other new people. Personally thank the people who worked, and pitch in with the cleanup. Be available to members who want to give you suggestions.

Anyone who made a motion that passed must give a copy of the final motion to the secretary, with the correct spelling of the name of the person who made the motion and of the person who seconded the motion. The chair's helpers can help to find the people who made motions and help them do this. The secretary and the publicity committee should make sure they know the correct spellings of names that will go in the minutes or in the newsletter.

The publicity committee and photographer should set a time to choose photos and write the story and photo captions for the newsletter. They can watch any television coverage, then clip, date, and save all the newspaper and magazine articles about the meeting.

The treasurer should record and deposit all cash and checks from new memberships, sales, and donations.

Ask volunteers to call active members who were absent to tell them about the meeting. (Urge enthusiastic members to call or write the speakers the next day to congratulate them on a job well done.)

Divide assignments for sending thank-you notes. The president can thank the host organization, any guest speakers, and any big donors. The chair can thank all the people who worked. The two people who worked at the membership table should write to welcome new members and thank them for joining. The two people who worked at the sales table should thank everyone who made a purchase. The names and addresses will be on the receipts. All of these thank-you notes should be in the mail the day after the meeting. If you know you will have a long list of notes to write, you can write the envelopes or even the notes in advance. Then add a "PS" about anything special that happened at the meeting.

After the meeting, the leaders of the meeting also should get together to discuss what worked and what did not work. Who produced people? Who got a big hand for a comment? Who said something good? Who was listened to? Then discuss what to do next. Review assignments and deadlines. Right after the meeting is the best time to hold the evaluation. However, if the meeting ends too late, schedule an evaluation session for the following day.

STEPS TO CHAIRING
A LARGE COMMUNITY MEETING

THE CHAIR OF THE MEETING WILL:

1. Start on time!
2. Welcome everyone to the meeting.

3. Introduce the officers of the organization and the chair of the meeting.
4. Announce the quorum.
5. Ask for a roll call or make introductions.
6. Explain the purpose of the meeting.
7. Explain the agenda.
8. Explain the role of the chair.
9. Explain the rules.
10. Ask for the Pledge of Allegiance, benediction, or other unifying ceremony.
11. Chair while motions are made, seconded, discussed, and voted on.
12. Frame the meeting at the end. Tell people what happened and why their attendance was important.
13. Recognize and praise the workers.
14. Recap all assignments and deadlines.
15. Ask each person in the audience to do one task tomorrow.
16. Announce the next meeting or action.
17. End on time!

15

The Publicity Committee

"The world speaks back to you in the tone of your own voice."

— Lupe Guajardo
Oregon Fair Share

When you start your organization, eight people may meet each week, make the plans, and do the work. Everyone knows everything about the organization. As the organization grows, there is more to do and more people to do it, so naturally you divide the work force into committees. As the committees meet regularly, they know what their own committees are doing but not all of the work of the other committees. This is the time to start a publicity committee. It may also be called the communications committee, information committee, or outreach committee.

Whatever you call it, the publicity committee helps all of the active members become as well informed about all the activities of the organization now as the founding members were at the beginning. Many people like starting new organizations because they like the close fellowship, and they like seeing results quickly. As the organization grows, the publicity committee will maintain this feeling of solidarity and accomplishment. Well-planned publicity makes all members feel as much a "part of the family" as the founders did.

The publicity committee also is the press agent for all of the other committees. This committee persuades a reporter to write a feature story on the president, promotes the fish fry, helps prepare the membership brochure, and publishes the newsletter. It makes the members and leaders feel good about themselves and look good to the public.

The publicity committee has five major jobs. These may be scheduled at different times of the year so that you can vary your work, or you may choose to create a special subcommittee to handle each task. The jobs are:

1. Internal communications — especially the volunteers' telephone network and internal publications.

2. External communications — especially the newsletter, annual report, and speakers' bureau.

3. Public relations — making it pleasant and productive for the public to work with your organization.

4. Promotion — making your organization the one people want to join and your events the places to be.

5. Press and publicity — telling your story to the news media.

These jobs combine to create a strong campaign to inform the public and your members about who you are, what you do, and how you do it.

The publicity committee may be relatively small, perhaps from two to four people to do the year-round work with another twenty people "on call" to handle bigger jobs like newsletter mailings and promotion of special events. It is easier for the news people if working reporters and editors know one person as the contact person for your organizations. So the publicity committee chairs often serve longer terms than other committee chairs. You could have publicity chairs who serve as long as five years, even if the other officers change every year.

INTERNAL COMMUNICATIONS

Every group needs good internal communications among its members, committees, and board members. You have several tools to keep everyone informed. The cheapest, quickest, and most popular is word of mouth. This is the grapevine that is always at work in any organization. It moves news, facts, and gossip. Because people already know how to use it and want to use it, the publicity committee can make sure that the information *you* want is moving on the grapevine.

Make the Grapevine a Telephone Network

Take what you already have, an informal grapevine, and make it a telephone network — a well-organized grapevine. Choose two dependable people, and ask them to coordinate the network. They can divide the work however they like. Some coordinators divide the names; others alternate months on duty. Through trial and error you will learn how many people one member can call in a day or evening. Usually the number is around four or five. Once you learn who is dependable, put the best people at the top. These coordinators each call four people; each of these people calls four people; they each call four people; and so on. So one calls four people who can call 16 who can call 64. Just four levels of calls will get your message to 256 people!

You can use the telephone network to inform people about big meetings or actions, encourage them to call or write their legislators, tell members about last-minute meeting changes, or ask for emergency funds. The strength of the system is that it is fast and free. The weakness is that it will work well only to convey short, simple, urgent messages. If the message is long, complicated, or dull, the telephone chain will not work.

During the blizzards of 1979, some groups that had to cancel meetings used their telephone chains for two-way communications. They could warn members to stay home and, at the same time, take a sense vote on urgent matters to guide the leaders between meetings. This is much more difficult, because it requires working the chain all the way down, then all the way back up again; however, it will work in a crisis.

Internal Publications

Once the telephone network is in place, the publicity committee works with the board and other committees to prepare publications for use inside the organization. Each committee can prepare information, then get help from the publicity committee in writing, designing, printing, and publication. For example, the membership committee can prepare a "Welcome to the Organization" brochure, the nominating committee can prepare a "Should I be a Candidate for the Board?" pamphlet, the personnel committee can prepare a personnel manual, the active program committees can produce testimony and research reports, and the fund-raising committee can make up foundation and corporation proposals. The job of each committee is to choose the content. The job of the publicity committee is to make sure that the publications are clear, attractive, easy-to-read, and fair presentations of the organization.

EXTERNAL COMMUNICATIONS

Newsletter

Your newsletter is your organization's newspaper. Every member gets a copy. The newsletter is one way you keep the active members well informed so that they stay involved. Most groups also send their newsletter to people who give money but are not active in the organization. These people are actually subscribers, although you may choose to call them members to make them feel a part of the organization. The newsletter permits large numbers of people — the subscribers — to share the excitement of your organization.

Whereas the membership committee asks individuals to become active members in the organization, the publicity committee asks large numbers of people to buy subscriptions to the newsletter. The members are your retail business; the subscribers are your wholesale business. Although there are limits on how many people can participate in your organization in a meaningful way, there are no limits to how many people can read your newsletter and share your work that way. It is much easier to get subscribers than members because you are asking them to do so little. You may call them members to make them happy, but for your own planning you have to separate the people who *read* from the people who *do*. Keep them separated as "active members" and "subscribers."

WHO CAN SUBSCRIBE?

Potential subscribers are all the people who like the idea of what you are doing, want to read about your work, and are willing to give you a small amount of money but little or no time. Virtually anyone can be a subscriber. As a rule of thumb, you could expect to have at least ten times as many subscribers as members. So, if ten people are active, you can have one hundred subscribers. When one hundred people are active, you can have one thousand subscribers. When you have six hundred active members, you can have six thousand readers.

WHY SELL SUBSCRIPTIONS?

Say that your organization chooses to give each member a newsletter four times a year, and this will cost you $1,200. If you now have six hundred members, the cost per member is $2 per year. If each member pays $10 in dues, the organization nets $8 per year per member. This $8 must cover the costs of running the organization. However, for every subscriber, you net the same $8 with no additional costs, since they do not come to meetings or use any services. So the more subscribers you can sign up, the more money you will make. Newsletter subscriptions are a dependable source of income. Just remember that you get what you ask for. These people are *readers*. If you want active members, the membership committee has to *ask* for active members.

HOW TO GET SUBSCRIBERS

How can you sell many subscriptions to your newsletter? According to sales whiz Richard Steckel, the first rule of marketing is "Never retail when you can wholesale." Think of ways to sell one hundred or one thousand subscriptions at a time. For example, a local church could buy one hundred subscriptions, and a local corporation could buy even more to give to employees. You can offer half-price subscriptions to big subscribers.

The second Steckel rule of marketing is "Never set up your own network when somebody else's is already in place, and it's free." In other words, do not buy mailing lists or advertising space unless you are a well-endowed charity. Ask other organizations to give you space. Ask other groups to include your flier in their regular mailings or to run your advertisement in their newsletters for free if you do the same for them. Make an attractive "Half-price Subscription Offer" flier to be sent out by other organizations or passed out at their meetings. Ask an advertising agency to design an advertisement to get subscribers. Put a code letter on each subscription coupon so that you will know how the subscriber got your ad or flier.

You can put your subscription blanks on anything that is printed. The Children's Museum of Denver persuaded a grocery store to print their membership blanks on one million shopping bags, a hot dog company to put the blank on the carton around the hot dogs, and a fast-food place to print the blank on the place mats. In this way, the museum has asked millions of people to join at almost no expense to itself. Most of the people who fill in the blanks become subscribers. A handful also will become active volunteers at the museum. Most, however, are interested only in supporting the museum and getting the publications.

HANDLING RENEWALS

The secret to a successful newsletter is renewals. Once you have subscribers, organize a system so that you know which subscriptions expire each month. Two months in advance of expiration, send each subscriber a "time to renew" notice. One month in advance, send another notice. Then send a "last chance to get this terrific newsletter, renew today!" notice. Three notices seem to make about the best balance between economy and effectiveness. If you have a very large list of subscribers, you may find that it pays to send more notices. Some local public television stations will send you nine renewal notices; some political campaigns will send even more. Ask the members of the publicity committee to let all their own subscriptions and memberships run out this year. Do not renew, then collect the renewal notices to see how other charities and publishers ask you to renew and how many times they write. After three to six months, the big ones will offer a premium to get you to join again, so you will get not only a free lesson in selling through the mail, but also a free promotional gimmick when you rejoin!

You need a very dependable group of people to handle renewals each month. If volunteers want to help the organization but shy away from a public leadership role, this is a perfect task for them.

Find all the people who are conscientious, dependable, thorough, patient, and good with details. Make this an important committee. Be sure the renewal committee's picture is in the newsletter at least once a year and that the top officers help the committee at least once a year. Once you have more than three thousand names on your list, you may want to hire a professional service to handle your mailing list and renewals. However, you will lose the advantage of using local people who know the people in the organization who died, moved, married, divorced, or changed names. A small, local organization particularly should avoid using a mailing service. But if your list gets so large that you have to hire an outside firm, the publicity committee chairs should review your list at least quarterly.

THE MAILING LISTS

The list of the names and addresses of subscribers and members can be maintained by the secretary, the membership committee, or the publicity committee. If you do not have paid staff, an easy way to divide the work is for the secretary to handle smaller, specialized mailing lists such as the lists of members of the board, advisory board, major donors, politicians and other influential neighbors, local clergy, and other organizations in the state or national network. The membership committee can keep track of active members, including committee assignments. The publicity committee can maintain a list of local and national press people as well as the list of subscribers. Ask an experienced office manager or secretary how to keep names, make labels, and bill renewals.

Your board will have to set a policy about whether to trade or sell your list. Most organizations trade their lists with other, similar organizations, and they all benefit. Sometimes groups fear that if they give out their lists, they will lose subscribers. Actually, the opposite is true. Every time nonprofit groups trade or combine their lists, they all make more money. If you share your list with other groups or trade fliers or ads to include in your newsletters, you will all get more subscribers. So you have nothing to fear from an economic or business standpoint. However, for other reasons your own members may say that they do not want you to give out the mailing list. In this case, you must honor the request.

Many groups include the cost of a subscription to the newsletter in the membership dues. Most subscriptions will be sold to people who have not paid dues. In addition, the board may decide to give some copies away free. These free subscriptions are a promotional expense and must be included in the budget each year.

You can send a newsletter to your large donors as a repeated thank-you with news about what they are getting for their donations. Send it to people you plan to ask for money or services, to prepare them to say yes to your request. You can exchange copies of the newsletter with local organizations and groups doing the same kind of work. Many publicity committees send free newsletters to local clergy; local, state, and federal politicians; and local libraries. Most send free newsletters to the editors of local newspapers and magazines, to the assignment editors of local radio and television stations, and to reporters or freelance journalists who cover your type of organization. Otherwise, never give the newsletter away except as a promotional tool to get paid subscribers. For example, you may give newsletters away at a state or national conference, but keep track of how many paid subscribers you get as a result. If the new subscribers do not pay for the copies you gave away, do not give them away next year.

CONTENT OF A NEWSLETTER

Ask everyone on the publicity committee to collect one copy of each newsletter they get for three months. Ask your friends and family to save samples, too. Gather all your samples at one meeting and talk about what you like and what you want to copy. Some features shared by most good newsletters are:

1. Many clear, action photos. Recruit good photographers right away.

2. Names. Names are news. Put in as many names of your own people as you can.

3. Information on how to join the organization. Include a choice of committees, and ask for a donation to support the work.

4. A brief description of how the organization was started and what it does now.

5. The names of the people who write, edit, and mail the newsletter. Names of the people who took photos or created artwork go next to the photo or art.

6. Many quotes from your leaders and other celebrities.

7. A column from the president. This explains the spirit and philosophy behind the news of the organization.

The rest of the content will be decided by the audience and the purpose of the newsletter. If the audience will be people who are active members of the organization, you can include news that would be of interest only to your own membership—such as news of committee elections, social notes, names of new members, interesting anecdotes, and news of social events. On the other hand, if the audience of the newsletter includes people who are not active members as well as donors, the working press, members of similar organizations, or area politicians, then you can include news stories of interest to the public at large. Many organizations consider their newsletters news sources that will print the news that the commercial news media will not print. They use their newsletters to cover their issues in depth. Especially if you do original research, the print media often will not, and radio and television cannot, cover it in detail. Your newsletter will tell the complete and correct story.

Some organizations publish two kinds of newsletters. The internal newsletter goes out from four to twelve times a year, is produced inexpensively, and goes only to the active members. The external newsletter goes to the larger audience from two to six times a year.

DIVIDING THE WORK

The newsletter needs two subcommittees: (1) an editorial committee to write, edit, design, and produce the newsletter and (2) a business committee to sell subscriptions and bill renewals. The newsletter offers a perfect job for every volunteer! The creative people who like to draw, photograph, write, and edit put out the newsletter. The confident salespeople can sell subscriptions. The well-organized office workers can record and renew subscriptions.

Annual Report

After the newsletter committees are running well, the publicity committee can consider what else you want to publish for the organization. Many groups publish annual reports in which they record their histories and recognize their supporters. For both members and donors, the annual report answers the question "What have you done for me recently?" You can describe your accomplishments, add many action photos, list everyone who gave you money or supplies, and announce your goals for next year. The publicity committee can put it out when you hold your annual meeting or at the beginning of the calendar year. (See Chapter 21 for more advice on annual reports required by the state and federal governments.)

A good-looking annual report is especially effective for raising money from corporations, because many for-profit corporations publish annual reports. To get samples, you can call ten of the largest corporations with headquarters in your town and ask for copies of their annual reports. Tell them you are an investor. If some of your committee members own stock in a company, they will get its annual report automatically. A friendly broker or the business columnist for your newspaper may also be able to give you examples of corporate annual reports. Look at the styles of these reports. Pick one you like, and then call the company's director of public relations and tell him or her how much you admire the last annual report. Ask if you can borrow the person responsible to help you design your own report. Get the artist excited about your project, then ask the corporation to produce your annual report or underwrite the expense of production.

Quarterly Reports

Quarterly reports are another type of publication copied from for-profit corporations. Many groups that receive large grants from foundations or government agencies prepare quarterly reports for the staff people who handle their accounts. Especially if you are in Wyoming and your checks come from New York, you should make contact with your funding sources at least every three months. Send a package of your best reports, clippings, thank-you letters, and photos along with a personal letter from the president to keep your group in the minds of the funders.

The Speakers' Bureau

In the organization's first year, the publicity committee can handle requests for speakers from other organizations. As you become well known and your issues become *the* exciting issues in your town, you will get more requests for speakers. If you get a lot of invitations or if you want to make money from your speakers, set up a committee called the speakers' bureau to handle speaking engagements.

It is often difficult for a leader to ask for money for his or her own speech. So the speakers' bureau serves as your leaders' agent, asking for money and weeding out undesirable invitations. The committee books the speeches, prepares materials for the audiences, sets and collects the fees, trains speakers, matches speakers to audiences, and handles any follow-up.

If you have a story that is easy to photograph, such as a program about sports, pollution, children, or art, the speakers' bureau can prepare a slide show. This will help new speakers by serving as an outline for remarks. As long as the speakers follow the slides, they cannot leave anything out. But each speaker can make the talk personal by telling a story about how he or she got involved in the organization and what the group means to him or her today. Slide shows are especially good for showing contrasts. For example, one senior citizens' group prepared slides of their small city bungalows on which they paid high property taxes, then contrasted them with large suburban homes of the county commissioners, who paid low taxes.

In the first year, you may take all speaking engagements for free so that your leaders can get experience. Ask for contributions at the end of each speech, and be sure each person in the audience gets the current newsletter and a membership blank.

After the first year, set a policy about speeches. If you can fill all the requests and you are getting new members, you can continue the "free for all" policy. On the other hand, you may find that you want to make fewer demands on your leaders. In that case, list the groups you want to reach, and rank them A, B, or C. The A's are the people you want to reach this year. Plan to call them and ask to speak at their biggest meetings. B's are groups whose invitations you will accept but not pursue. C's are groups that will not be worth your time. For example, a new health clinic may actively pursue chances to talk to doctors, nurses, social workers, police, and clergy (A's), all of whom may refer people to the clinic and support the clinic in other ways. The clinic will accept speaking engagements from any group of adults within its designated boundaries (B's). But it will not accept engagements from school groups or groups outside the clinic boundaries (C's).

The easiest way to limit your speaking engagements is to charge money for your speakers. If your speaker is new, you can charge $1 per person in the audience. Then you will get about $35 if you talk to a college class, perhaps $50 to talk to a neighborhood organization, and $150 to talk to a citywide group. If your officers have established reputations as experts, ask a minimum of $100 for them, and more if the group can pay more. The beauty of this system is that your leaders will speak only to people who want to hear them. You may choose to waive your speaker's fee if you will get an organizational benefit from talking to the group, such as a group you want to join a new coalition. Otherwise, you have nothing to lose and much to gain by limiting your speeches to groups that want you enough to pay. They pay to hear sports stars, politicians, newscasters, and authors. They can pay for your stars, too.

PUBLIC RELATIONS

Public relations includes all "the activities undertaken by an organization to promote a favorable relationship with the public."[1] Your newsletter and annual reports tell the public about the work of your organization. Now consider other ways the public meets your organization each week. What can you do to assure that the public likes the experience and wants to meet your organization again?

Current members come in contact with potential future members whenever they answer the phone at the office, collect signatures on petitions, or speak at public hearings. The publicity committee can help everyone make the organization sound good and look good to potential members. This does not mean that you should put on a false front or do anything phony. It does mean that you exert yourself to make sure that strangers get a good first impression of your organization. For example, the publicity committee can ask the telephone company to send one of their free teachers to show everyone the most effective way to answer the phone and take clear messages. Remember, you never get a second chance to make a first impression!

Recruit a Professional Artist

If none of your members is a trained artist, search until you find one to volunteer. Professional design will improve everything from your stationery to the sign on your office door. These details introduce you to the public and create a good first impression.

Ask the artist to design a logo, which is a visual symbol for your organization. This logo can go on everything that you print. Then ask the artist to design your stationery, envelopes, membership brochures, and any other paper products.

If you do not know any artists, look in your daily newspaper and list the businesses that run the largest advertisements each week. Start with the biggest advertiser and work your way down. Call the company's advertising director, and ask him or her to donate one artist's time to your organization. Or ask a local art school or the art department of a high school or college for a teacher or talented student.

If you live in a small, rural community, you may have to make a trip to the nearest city to find an artist to help you with your most important jobs, such as your stationery or your brochures. Ask him or her to teach the publicity committee some tricks of the trade so you can do your own fliers and bulletins in emergencies.

Besides a good graphic artist, you also will want to recruit at least one good volunteer photographer. If your organization is very active, you may have to find more than one. You should pay all the expenses and costs for supplies of your artist or photographer, but try to get the time donated.

Complaints

As part of its public relations, the publicity committee also can handle suggestions and complaints. Of course, a major problem or complaint from a major supporter should be handled by the president or another officer. But day-to-day matters can be part of the job of the publicity committee.

Especially if you get coverage in the local papers, radio, and television, local people will call and write to your headquarters with advice, suggestions, and criticism. Consider this to be an excellent, free, ongoing evaluation of your work.

One or two people should take the task of answering all letters and calls. Complaints should receive the "two-for-one treatment." If you get a one-page complaint write a two-page answer; a two-page complaint gets a four-page answer, and so forth. Even a popular organization will get a few hate letters and a few crazy letters that can be filed under "Correspondence — Not Answered." But the serious people who have taken the time to call or write with well-thought-out criticism should be answered seriously and courteously. Do not argue. Simply explain what the group is, how you make decisions, and why you think the decision is best for this purpose at this time. Thank the writer for his or her suggestions, and say that, as an open democratic organization, you want and need honest expression of differing viewpoints. Enclose a membership blank and a donation envelope. Even if you do not convert the person who wrote the complaint, you at least will have shown that you are a reasonable organization that can accept criticism and welcomes suggestions from the community. After you answer a suggestion or complaint, forward the letter and a copy of your response to the appropriate committee or officer.

Fortunately, the same people get to handle thank-you letters and fan mail. Anyone who writes in commending the leaders, congratulating you on a victory, or praising your work should get an answer right away from the publicity committee. Send a personal letter and a membership blank. Forward the letter and a copy of your answer to the appropriate person.

PROMOTION

Be creative about getting your name out to the public. For example, the Seattle Opera persuaded the local cement company to promote the opera on the big cement trucks that drive around town.

The back part of these trucks rotates as the truck drives, keeping the cement mixed up. The trucks all were painted pale blue with black lettering that said: "Get mixed up in the Seattle Opera." The Friends of the Parks (FOP) group got a call on the Friday of one Memorial Day weekend from an alarmed animal lover. He was concerned because little boys were throwing stones at the baby ducks in the park. FOP persuaded the park rowboat concession to give the organization rowboats for the weekend. They decked out the animal lover and other members in green Friends of the Parks T-shirts and had them row around all weekend, protecting the baby ducks. Meanwhile, other volunteers on the shore told people about the organization and sold T-shirts and memberships. The 9-to-5 organization of women office workers in Boston was founded with the slogan "Raises, not roses." The organization collects money on the streets of downtown Boston each April during Secretaries' Week. Each donor gets a red button with a white rose, but no words, on it. Women can join without fear of antagonizing a conservative boss, but all members recognize each other. The Ravinia music festival persuaded local department stores to decorate their windows with fashion mannequins portraying people picnicking at the Ravinia concerts. Notice how other groups in your own town get attention, and dream up new ways to promote your own group.

THE PRESS AND PUBLICITY

Working with the press is one of the best jobs of the publicity committee. This work introduces you to the celebrities, workers, and workings of local newspapers, magazines, radio and television stations, and wire services. If your organization is the first or best of its kind, and you are bold and lucky, you also will get to meet national press people.

As in fund raising, in publicity you get what you ask for. You will get your story on "60 Minutes" or in *Newsweek* if you sell the producer or editor on the national significance of your story.

You should aim high and be bold! As an amateur publicist working for your favorite organization, you have two advantages over the professional publicist who works for several paying clients. Most of all, you have the conviction and enthusiasm of a volunteer who

240   The Successful Volunteer Organization

wants to tell the story of your group. Second, you have only one organization to publicize, so you can focus all your efforts on getting the best possible coverage for your group. You do not need any special skills to promote your organization. As long as you believe that this is the most worthwhile organization in town with the most inspiring leaders, you can tell your story to the press.

There are several excellent booklets written about publicity and the press. See Chapter 24 for recommended publications to help the publicity committee do this work. If you follow the advice in these books, you soon will be able to tell your story in a form that is easy for the newspapers, radio, and television to use. As in any other work with professionals, your job is to make their job easy. If you prepare all your materials the way the press wants them prepared and meet their deadlines, you will find that it is a pleasure working with them. If you need more help with your writing, recruit an editor or an English teacher to give you advice. Many high schools and community colleges offer reading and writing classes for adults. Some also offer special classes in public relations for community groups. Best of all, recruit an experienced public relations professional to review your work and give you a personal introduction to the working press. If you work hard and remember that honesty is *always* the best policy, you soon will have a good working relationship with the news people.

PUBLICITY IS FREEDOM

A hardworking publicity committee is essential to an effective, open, and democratic organization. A democratic organization is built on the idea that most people will make the right decisions most of the time. The publicity committee helps get people to the meetings, educates them so they will have the knowledge to make the best decisions, and then publicizes those decisions so that the entire membership shares the knowledge. The more public you are, the stronger you are. *Especially* if your organization has a bold, controversial program or if you have powerful enemies, you must promote your organization as publicly and aggressively as possible.

Some organizations fear negative publicity or fear that if they open their meetings to the public, they will be spied on. Honest communications and open meetings will neutralize both threats. Journalist Vernon Jarrett interviewed "the forgotten heroes of the Montgomery Bus Boycott" and tells this story:

> Robert Nesbitt was the chair of the pulpit committee of the Dexter Avenue Baptist Church in Montgomery, Alabama, in 1955. When he was on a business trip to Atlanta, a co-worker suggested he hire "Mike King" as their minister. Mike King would become known to the world as Dr. Martin Luther King, Jr., leader of the Montgomery Improvement Association (MIA), which organized the successful boycott that forced desegregation of city buses. Nesbitt says, "The movement (bus boycott) had few secrets, if any. In fact, we never had a public meeting that the governor did not have his white police representatives there in the front seats taking notes of everything we did. They became so familiar to us that we knew them by name and frequently called upon them to make a contribution since they were taking up space. At every meeting, mind you, they were there reporting everything we said and did.
>
> "Yet they couldn't stop our movement because everything we did was open. We met every Monday night at a publicly announced church. (Later the meetings were extended to twice a week.) They spied on us, spit on us, pushed us around physically, but they couldn't defeat us."[2]

Coaches say that the best defense is a good offense, and the best offense against negative publicity is to tell your own story to the public. Proud publicity will tell your story the way *you* want it told. Let your members, friends, neighbors, donors, supporters, and your enemies know what you are doing. A democratic organization with open meetings, elected officers, open membership, and clear communications never can be seriously harmed by criticism or by spying from the outside.

TEAMWORK

Publicity is "information that attracts public notice."[3] Good publicity will make the public notice you, which is the first step to building your group. Then the other committees get them to join and enjoy the organization. A good publicity committee makes it easier for the other committees to do their jobs. But it needs the membership committee to sell memberships, the fund-raising committee to ask for money, and other committees to organize. Publicity will not sell memberships, raise money, or activate citizens by itself. As publicity expert Don Rose says, "A good story about you in the newspaper is no substitute for the basic job of organizing the community."[4]

The publicity committee will only introduce your organization to the community. The value of the organization itself "sells" it to your neighbors. Regardless of what the publicity committee does, your organization will be judged on its intelligence, energy, determination, integrity, and sincerity. As Ralph Waldo Emerson said, "Use what language you will, you can never say anything but what you are."

16

How to Hire and Supervise Paid Staff

"First-rate people hire first-rate people;
second-rate people hire third-rate people.
Hire the best you can."
— Robert Townsend
Up the Organization

Once your organization has been around for a year or two, you will be well on your way to creating a strong board of community leaders, a dependable funding system, and popular programs. You may find that the organization and the work it does have grown so much that you want to hire paid staff. Then the board can hire skilled professionals to do specific jobs or to provide full-time attention to the entire organization.

Good employees are always available to work for a good organization. The people who choose to work for nonprofit groups are often the most idealistic, energetic, and creative workers around. Because they are committed to doing this kind of work, they can improve the program and challenge the best leaders. Paid staff can complete your team to help make your goals reality.

However, when the board believes that it is ready to hire staff, it should have one meeting to discuss whether the organization really needs paid staff now. Is this the right step? This exercise is also valuable if the organization has paid staff members who were hired before anyone on the present board joined the board.

DO YOU WANT TO HIRE PAID STAFF?

First, review your mission. What does the organization do for the community, and how do you do it? What can you do here that no one else can do? Second, discuss your goals. How can you reach them better? More work is not necessarily better work.

Alternatives to Staff

If you have more work to do than the current board and committees can do, you can:

Do less work. Give away or stop some of your programs.

Work more efficiently. Reorganize or simplify the work so that you can do more with the same people. For example, can you buy training for your people so that you will get more out of them than you now do? Perhaps instead of buying staff, you ought to buy training.

Recruit more volunteers. If you were to recruit more members, expand your current committees, or start other committees, could the work be done? Members are always less expensive and more plentiful than professionals.

Share the work. Perhaps you are trying to do more than one organization can do. Would the work be done better if you did it as part of a coalition of organizations?

WHAT DO YOU WANT STAFF TO DO?

If the board decides that hiring paid staff *is* the best way to do the work and achieve your goals, then it should consider exactly what it wants the future staff to do. At the same time, discuss what the board, committees, and members will continue to do for themselves. Even if you hire paid staff, the board still will have to develop new leaders and recruit new members. Hiring paid staff should not reduce importance of the elected leaders or the enthusiasm of the membership committee. Begin by discussing what the board does now, what you want to continue to do, and then what you want the staff to do.

Decide what kind of staff you want based on the strengths of the board. If you can hire only one person, consider the strengths of the board, especially the president, and then decide to hire a person to complement those strengths. If your board has been working efficiently for some time, you may want to hire a staff person who will serve as an organizer to motivate the board and members to take new risks and try new ideas. If the board is newer, it may be enthusiastic about the program and purpose of the organization but uncertain about record keeping and tax paying. In that case, hire a person who is a strong administrator to organize the finances and record keeping and meet deadlines.

At first, you may want to hire staff who will enable the board and members to do more of what they do best. Later, you may want to hire people with more specific skills to do certain jobs for the organization. Depending on the goals of the group, you may need to hire a nurse, doctor, counselor, teacher, bookkeeper, secretary, scientist, researcher, lawyer, economist, accountant, publicist, organizer, lobbyist, editor, or fund raiser. In any case, the board has to decide exactly what it wants the staff to do and what it will continue to do for itself. Ask other grass roots organizations for advice on the kind of staff to hire first and how the board and staff can work together best.

CAN YOU AFFORD STAFF?

First, interview other organizations to find out their *total cost* of hiring staff. This includes salaries, federal and state taxes, health insurance, disability insurance, pension plan, paid vacations, training, and expenses such as travel and meals. Find out what they paid for staff in the most recent year. An experienced bookkeeper can help you figure out a staff budget for your own organization.

Once you hire staff, your budget will double, triple, or go up even more. At most organizations with paid staff, salaries, taxes, insurance, and other staff costs make up from 60 to 90 percent of the budget. Be sure that you can raise the money you need each year from renewable sources so that you can get and keep the best staff.

As you prepare the budget, you will be making choices that will become part of your personnel policy. These include what you will offer in addition to salary. The bookkeeper can tell you which state and federal taxes you legally must pay, as well as your local tax obligations, if any, and insurance such as unemployment insurance and workers' compensation. Each state has different requirements based on the number of employees you hire. Ask what else the best employees will get besides money. You want to be able to hire the best possible employees, so you want to be able to offer a package to compete with the best nonprofit and for-profit organizations. This could include a health plan, disability insurance, life insurance, and a pension plan or annuity. If the staff gets a paid vacation, will you have to budget for a temporary replacement, or can the board fill in?

Table 16-1 is a sample of what it could cost you to hire an employee at fifteen thousand dollars, with the minimum package of benefits. This does not include other costs such as a desk, a chair, a telephone, the desk supplies this person will need, or the monthly expense account. This is just the cost of staff in 1980 in Illinois, determined by Gloria Varona, consultant on financial management for the W. Clement & Jessie V. Stone Foundation.

You see that a $15,000 employee is not really a $15,000 employee. Someone who is married with two dependents can cost $17,694. But that person can take home only $11,719. A single employee with no dependents can cost you $16,746. That person can take home $10,737. So you must budget more than just salary and buy someone who is able to live on the *net* after taxes.

A 501(c)(3) organization legally is exempt from paying Social Security taxes. In the example above, the group has chosen to pay Social Security. If it had kept the exemption and chosen *not* to pay into Social Security, the cost to the organization would have gone down by $919, and the employee's take-home pay would have gone up by $919. Ask your insurance agent and your banker about alternatives to Social Security. You may find that you can invest the same amount of money in a pension plan, annuity, or life insurance plan, which you control and which will give you a better return for your investment.

TABLE 16-1   Sample Budget For Paid Staff (1980)

Employee	Cost to the Organization	Employee's Take-home Pay
Married — two dependents		
Gross salary	$15,000	$15,000
Federal income tax	--	(1,794)
Illinois state income tax	--	(388)
Insurance — health	1,560	(180)
Pension	optional	
*Social Security (FICA)	919	(919)
†State unemployment compensation (Ill.)	195	--
Federal unemployment compensation	Exempt-------------------------------	
‡Workers' Compensation	20	--
	$17,694	$11,719
Single — No dependents		
Gross salary	$15,000	$15,000
Federal income tax	--	(2,860)
Illinois state income tax	--	(364)
Insurance — health	612	(120)
Pension	optional	
*Social Security (FICA)	919	(919)
†State unemployment compensation (Ill.)	195	--
Federal unemployment compensation	Exempt-------------------------------	
‡Workers' Compensation	20	--
	$16,746	$10,737

* The Federal Insurance Contributions Act (FICA), or Social Security Act, was enacted to insure an income for retired persons who work for a certain period of time before their retirement. FICA taxes are paid by both the employer and the employee. These payments are optional for 501(c)(3) organizations. In this example, the organization has chosen to pay FICA taxes rather than have a pension plan. Thus the organization will have to deduct 6.13 percent from each employee's gross pay, so the staff person will take home $919 less. Then the organization must match that amount, so it must pay out $919 over the salary it pays the employee. This example is based on the FICA rate of 6.13 percent of the first $25,900, which was current in 1980. The amount due for FICA taxes will increase every year.

† This example is based on the first $6,500 at the Illinois rate for 1980. The rate is based on how many of your organization's former employees collect unemployment.

‡ Workers' compensation can be purchased through your insurance agent.

If you decide that you *do* want to pay into Social Security, you must waive the exemption given to 501(c)(3) organizations. File Forms SS-15 and SS-15A with the IRS, telling it that you are waiving the exemption.

Once you know the total cost of staff, look at your fund-raising strategy. Can you raise this much money from dependable, renewable sources? If you receive a grant for the first year, can you add that much money from your renewable sources for the second and subsequent years? The board and the staff member will probably want to have at least a two-year contract. If you cannot guarantee that you can pay a full-time employee for two years, do not hire the person until you can. Once you know how much you need, begin raising the money. You should have at least six months' salary in the bank before you advertise your job.

WHOM DO YOU WANT TO HIRE?

If you decide that your organization needs and wants paid staff now, discuss what staff you want. Talk to older organizations and get their evaluations of the advantages and disadvantages of their staffing arrangements. If you are still small, you may want to start by hiring services from outside your organization, such as a telephone answering service, then hire part-time staff, and then hire full-time staff. Each step will be determined by your needs and income.

Decide what staff you want to do your work right now. Your options include:

People to provide *special services,* such as to answer telephones, audit your books, or prepare bulk mailings. You can get these services from people outside your organization, contracted for a certain amount of time or by the job.

Part-time staff. This is staff that you hire to work less than forty hours a week or fifty-two weeks a year. When you are starting, you may find that part-time staff can handle your office work or seasonal work. For example, an emergency hunger project knows its work will skyrocket around Christmas, at the very time it is most difficult to get volunteers. You can plan ahead to hire staff for December and January.

Full-time staff. These are employees who work forty hours a week all year. They receive full pay and benefits.

You also may want to decide whom you do *not* want to hire. For example, many organizations will not hire friends or relatives of board members. Of course, in a small town it may be impossible to find people who are *not* friends or relatives, so you may not be able to have such a policy. You also may want to decide that you *do* want to hire the kind of people you are trying to reach. For example, you would hire disabled veterans to work with disabled veterans.

It is important to create an equal opportunity employment policy. As an organization working for positive goals, your hiring should reflect your commitment to social progress. Any organization that hires more than fifteen people is legally required to meet the federal laws against discrimination in hiring. To get the current regulations governing your responsibilities as an employer, contact the Equal Employment Opportunities Commission (EEOC) and ask for the pamphlet on record-keeping and reporting requirements. In large cities, the EEOC is listed in the telephone book under "United States Government," or you can write to the Associate General Counsel, Legal Counsel Division, Equal Employment Opportunities Commission, 2401 E St., NW, Washington, DC 20506. Some states have equal opportunity laws that are stronger than the federal law, so contact your state Fair Employment Practices Commission or Human Relations Commission and ask for current regulations. Remember that *all* labor laws apply to all employers, whether they are for-profit or nonprofit. When you hire staff, you must know and obey the laws.

PAPERWORK TO DO BEFORE YOU INTERVIEW

Once you know the real cost of hiring the staff you want, get the rest of your ideas down on paper. The board should collect samples of the documents you will want when you hire staff. These are the budget, a personnel policy, a job description, a contract, and job application forms. Check the organization's bylaws to see if they specify what paid staff may or may not do. If the bylaws do not mention staff, or if the current provisions are not what you want, revise the bylaws when you prepare the other documents.

The first time you hire staff, all of these documents should be prepared by the board of directors, because these decisions will affect how much money the board has to raise and may change the basic structure of the organization. Once you have established the organization's employment policies, the board can create a personnel committee to review the personnel policies and salaries once a year. The personnel committee will need to do this each year before the board prepares the budget.

The Personnel Policy

Most big companies have written personnel policies, which tell employees all the rules governing pay, work, and time. Ask your members to bring in samples from their employers, or order the materials listed in the Bibliography. Use them as guidelines in making your policy. Most groups put this in a loose-leaf notebook so that it can easily be updated. You may believe that your small group does not need a policy in writing, but it is much better to decide these questions in advance and put the decisions in writing than to wait for a crisis and force the president to make a difficult decision. Two members can make a draft; the entire board can read, revise, and adopt it. Then print enough copies for all employees, the board, and future job applicants. Review the policy once a year, and make any changes you like. Ask the staff to recommend improvements, too.

The Job Description

A job description outlines the job's responsibilities and the kind of employee you want to hire. This is one page that you can send to encourage people to apply for the job. A job description includes:

1. The purpose and goals of the organization.
2. The duties and responsibilities of this job.
3. Where and when the staff member is needed.
4. To whom he or she is accountable.
5. The experience and skills you want for the job.
6. The salary range.
7. How to apply for the job. The deadline, if any.

8. The name, address, and phone number of the person to contact for more information.

A Contract

You may want to spell out in a written contract what you want an employee to do and what the organization, as the employer, will do in return. This would include how long the staff member will work for you, what he or she must do, and what he or she may not do. The organization would be responsible for paying a certain salary, reviewing the salary after a set period, and providing other benefits. A written contract gives both the staff and the organization precise protections and guarantees. Ask your lawyer and other nonprofit and for-profit groups for samples of contracts. Some groups hire their first staff for a three-month trial period, then decide if they want to make them permanent employees. At that time the board can give them two- or three-year contracts. If you are hiring someone for more than two years, such as a lawyer or scientist, you should set up a system to review and revise the contract every two years. If you are hiring someone for a job that will last less than one year, you may not want or need a written contract. In that case, prepare a "pay authorization" letter to instruct the treasurer when and how much to pay the employee.

Job Application Forms

You can write your own job application forms, or you can buy a standard one-page form at an office supply store. These ask questions about the applicant's history, schooling, and job experience. Always ask for and *always check references* of everyone you want to hire. Discuss the applicant's work with former employers and co-workers. If you have to make some long-distance phone calls, do so, because this is the best way to find out what the applicant does best.

Revising the Bylaws

Finally, the board and your lawyer must review the bylaws before you hire staff. Put in writing what the staff may and may not do. See Chapter 3 for information on how to amend your bylaws.

HOW DO YOU HIRE?

Very often a small group hiring its first staff will simply put a member of the board on the payroll. The board knows that he or she already knows the people in the organization, he or she can start immediately, and he or she wants the job. Former board members can be the best staff if you keep the jobs of leader and staff separate.

A community-controlled volunteer group must distinguish between leaders, who have a following in the community, and employees hired to do the work. A board member who joins the staff should resign from the board. Elect a new board member to complete his or her term of office.

If you hire a board member, remember that you still will need the written personnel policy and contract. You also owe it to the organization to interview at least two or three other candidates to make *sure* the board member is the best person for the job.

Finding Applicants

There are two ways to find applicants. Either go out and find them, or publicize the job so that they find you. Do both. First, the board goes looking for the person it wants. Ask everyone to suggest names of potential staff members. Word of mouth usually produces the best candidates. Follow up every lead. There may be someone who already has a job—with either a nonprofit or for-profit organization—who would rather work for you. As in fund raising, you get what you ask for, so aim high and keep trying until you get the person you want.

Also publicize your job so that good workers can find you. Send a job description to community leaders, such as clergy, foundation staff, and directors of the large agencies such as the YMCA or YWCA, who know both your organization and the labor market. List your job with city and state job services, high school and college job counselors, and private job services. In large cities, the mayor's office may be able to direct you to special job programs for people who are disabled, veterans, ex-offenders, or senior citizens. Advertise in local newspapers and magazines, as well as the trade papers for your sort of organization. Ask other groups where they advertise. Do not forget other publicity opportunities in your own community, such as church bulletins and local organizations' news-letters. If you want to hire someone from your own community, these will be your best bet.

If your organization is in a remote area, you may have to use national networks to find the staff you want. Try your own national organization first, as well as the staff of national foundations. Some large national organizations have hired professional search firms to find employees for them. They can reach more people than you can. Of course, you must pay for this service, so use your own re-sources first.

Interviews

Before people apply for your job, decide who will do interviews. Form a subcommittee of the board with the president, another of-ficer, and at least one member of the board who has had experience interviewing job applicants. If no one on the board has any ex-perience doing interviews, ask a local businessperson who hires staff to teach you how. Show the business adviser your application forms and the questions you intend to ask. The businessperson can suggest other questions for the form and the interview. Practice a few times in front of the businessperson; then, use his or her suggestions.

Ask each applicant to fill out your application form. Then, ask him or her questions, and give him or her a chance to ask you about the organizaton and the job.

You will want to find out:

Will this person be able to accomplish what you want?

Does this person understand the mission of the organization?

Will he or she respect your members?

Will he or she stay in this job for two years or the length of the contract?

Do you want this person to work for you?

Does this person *want* this job?

In *The Effective Executive,* Peter Drucker suggests these ques-tions: "What has he or she done well? What, therefore, is he or she likely to be able to do well? What does he or she have to learn? If I had a son or daughter, would I be willing to have him or her work under this person?"[1]

All job interviews should be conducted in private. If you do not have an office, meet at a church or another group's office. Do not interview people in your home. At the end of the interview, thank the person for applying for the job, and say when you will tell him or her your decision.

When you choose the person you want, submit the person's application form and the interviewing committee's recommendation to the board of directors. The board as a whole must approve the choice, because it is responsible for raising the salary. Once the board approves the decision, the president should call the person who was chosen for the job. The president should call the other candidates to say that they were not chosen and send each one a personal letter thanking him or her for applying for your job. You may want to hire these people in the future, so give them every courtesy, even if you hire someone else.

ORIENT YOUR NEW STAFF

The president should meet the new staff person to officially welcome him or her to the organization. Explain your goals and your plans for the next year, and say how you want the staff member to fit in. Give the staff member the same background materials you give new board members: your budget, financial reports, fundraising strategy, bylaws, newsletters and annual reports, and any current newspaper clippings or foundation proposals. The treasurer will have collected the tax forms necessary for employers in your state. Ask the employee to sign Form W-4 for the IRS and your state W-4, if there is one. The W-4 is the form you use to collect information necessary to calculate the amount of money for taxes you must deduct from the staff member's salary. Also ask the employee to sign any necessary insurance forms at this time.

Give the staff person a copy of your personnel policies. Ask him or her to read all of the materials and make sure that this system will be all right for both of you. Explain that he or she will work for a three-month trial period and that, after three months, if you both think this arrangement is working well, you will give the staff person a contract for the agreed-upon length of service.

Then give the staff person the names, addresses, and phone numbers of the members of the board of directors. If possible, it is nice to have a reception to welcome the staff person and introduce him or her to the members of the board. Explain that the board is legally and morally responsible for the organization. So the first job you should ask the new staff person to do is to interview each member of the board in person.

Interview the Board

The interview with the new staff person will give each member of the board an opportunity to discuss at length the problems of and possibilities for the organization. This procedure is recommended when you hire your first staff person, a staff director, or executive director. If you hire additional staff—such as a fund-raising assistant or public relations specialist—who are expected to work with all of the board, these people also should meet the board members to be sure you all know who does what. See the sample interview form in Figure 16-1.

Personal interviews will help you to avoid the most common problem facing boards that hire staff for the first time—a sharp decline in volunteer work. Each board member thinks, "Well, now we have staff. He or she can do this job." All twelve of them give the new staff person part of their work loads and start to coast. The new staff person cannot possibly do *all* of this work as well as the board can! The president must set an example by doing *more* work once the staff person is hired and working more efficiently, too. Check with the other officers at least weekly to be sure they continue to do the jobs they do best.

The board interviews give each person on the board a chance to tell the new staff member exactly what they think the strengths and weaknesses of the organization are right now. Once you all get a say, the staff person and president can create a realistic work plan so that the staff person can do first things first. The staff person will report directly to the president, but the work plan is based on the ideas of all the board. This helps you avoid two common problems—either the staff reports to the president and the rest of the board feels ignored, or else the staff tries to do something for everyone and ends up without direction. Your staff person cannot serve twelve masters. Let the president and the staff member work out a monthly work plan based on the board's opinions. Then let the staff person do his or her job.

FIGURE 16-1   Sample of Board of Directors' Interview Sheet
for Use by new Staff Director*

1. How long have you been on the board?
2. How did you come to be a board member?
3. What is the *most* satisfying part of your participation in the organization?
4. What is the *least* satisfying part of your participation in the organization?
5. What specific day-to-day tasks have you been doing to date?
6. Which of your present tasks do you wish to continue?
7. What do you want the office staff to undertake?
8. What do you think is the most important thing for this organization to be doing now? In six months? In one year? In three years? In five years?
9. When the staff director was hired, what did you expect his/her job to be?
10. How does the board's job differ from the staff's job?
11. Have you done fund raising in the past? What kind?
12. Can you open doors for the organization? Where?
13. Whom do you know through business or friendships who has talents or resources we can use?
14. Please prepare a list of fund-raising prospects.

Sent one week before interview to board member with confirmation of date, time, and place of meeting. Allow at least two hours for in-person interview.

* Adapted from interview sheet written by Sally Owen-Still for Horizon Hospice. Reprinted with permission.

SUPERVISING YOUR STAFF

Decide how your staff person will fit into the current structure of the organization. Groups with one staff member usually make that person accountable directly to the president. Groups with more than one staff member usually make all staff accountable to one person, who is called the staff director or executive director, and that person is accountable to the president. Sometimes you may prefer to make specific staff members accountable to specific officers. For example, a bookkeeper would be accountable to the treasurer, and a researcher would be accountable to the head of a specific task force. In any case, the staff needs monthly supervision so that it will be accountable to the board, happy and effective in its work, and productive.

Supervision is a three-step process. First, you set goals and prepare a written work plan. Second, the staff does the work on the plan. Third, you evaluate the work done. Did it accomplish its goals? What worked well, and what did not work well? What needs to be changed? How does this piece of work fit into the overall goals of the organization? As with your program plan, effective work plans require clear goals.

The Importance of Goals

One challenge facing a volunteer organization is that the board is the "boss," but often some of the people on the board never have supervised anyone else. If this is the first time you are responsible for supervising staff, you may be too timid and polite to tell the staff exactly what it is to do.

You may think that, because the staff members are "professionals" or "college people," they will know what to do. On the other hand, a staff member may think, "The board did not tell me what to do, so I guess I can do whatever seems most urgent. It is up to me to plan my work." The staff people cannot read your mind. If the board does not say what it wants, it will not get what it wants.

Without clear goals, the staff ends up *reacting* to requests from many people and being very busy, but it may not move you and your organization toward your goals. With clear goals and a written plan, the staff people know what they are supposed to do and when. Clear goals mean:

You are advancing the goals and purpose of the organization. The work done will accomplish your mission.

You get your money's worth out of your employees. They are doing the work you want done.

The staff has the satisfaction of knowing what they are supposed to do. They can do first things first.

Staff members can decide what they should *not* do. It is easier for them to say no to requests that do not fit into their work plans.

It is easier to evaluate employees. Especially in a small organization, leaders and staff can become close friends, and it can become very difficult to evaluate staff work objectively. If you have clear, written goals and frequent evaluations, this is easier and fairer for both of you.

Making the Written Work Plan

A written work plan is a plan for what work will be done in a certain time period. It is agreed upon by the staff director and the president. When you start, you may want to make monthly work plans. During especially hectic times, such as before your convention or toward the end of the legislative session, you may need weekly work plans.

The work plan says what the goals of the staff will be for a time period. Like your program goals, they must be described with a *number* and ranked in order of importance.

Let us say that your board wants to expand the Akron Arson Committee into the Forty-third Ward. You have hired an organizer to find interested citizens and create a committee to work on the arson issue in the Forty-third Ward. The president and the organizer make a work plan for June. The organizer will plan to do the following:

Set up one house meeting per week, for a total of four house meetings.

Recruit at least twelve people to come to each house meeting. The arson committee co-chairs will speak at each meeting.

By the end of the month, prepare a report on the number of people who came to house meetings, possibilities for future meetings, the cost of starting a new committee in the Forty-third Ward, suggestions for temporary co-chairs for the Forty-third Ward committee, and recommended next steps.

The Evaluation

At the end of the month, it will be easy to see if the staff person lived up to his or her plan:

Plan
1. Four house meetings.
2. Twelve people per meeting for a total of forty-eight people.
3. Report prepared.

Results
1. Five house meetings.
2. Ten people per meeting for a total of fifty people.
3. Report prepared.

This system of written work plans is especially valuable during the three-month trial period for new staff. It gives you an objective and accurate way to measure the work of the staff. Based on the work plans and results, after the first three months the board can decide if it wants to make the staff person a permanent employee and decide if a contract for a specific length of time would be appropriate.

WHAT TO DO ABOUT SUCCESS

If the staff has succeeded, give lots of praise. Say you like the monthly report, out loud, at the first paragraph. Never think it is obvious that a staff member is doing a good job. *Say so.* Say that others think he or she is doing a good job. Pass along a compliment. Build on strengths and accomplishments.

WITH MIXED REVIEWS

If the staff succeeded at part of the job but not all, focus on the successes. As Peter Drucker says, the job of the president is "to feed opportunities and to starve problems." So expand the successes. Give the staff member more of the work he or she is good at and lots of praise for it. Then consider the problems. How can they be solved? Does this staff person need and want more training? Was the goal unclear? Did he or she understand why the work is important and how it fits into the mission of the organization? On the other hand, is it really important? Perhaps you, as the president, need to reevaluate this goal. Maybe it does not matter now and can be postponed until another time. If you decide that the goal is important but that this staff person has other talents, then reassign the job. Give the job to a dependable volunteer, or assign a different staff person. Do *not* do it yourself. If you do every job the staff fumbles, you will not have time to do your job as president.

Sometimes it will take persistence for the staff to succeed. Give the staff your wholehearted support so they keep trying. If a staff person is afraid of one job or unsure of his or her abilities, give him or her encouragement, break the job into smaller pieces, build on smaller successes, and keep sending him or her out.

End the evaluation with praise. As expert Karen Thomas says, "Make a 'praise sandwich' when you do an evaluation of a work plan. Begin and end by talking about what went *right*. Then the staff members will have more confidence to tackle the work they need to improve."

WITH FAILURE

After two months, it will be obvious if you made a mistake hiring a particular person. You will know this is the wrong job for this person if he or she is not meeting goals, is making excuses without trying harder, or is not trying to improve skills. If a staff member fails to achieve the written goals two months in a row, meet with him or her and talk about your disappointment. Explain that the mission of the organization is dependent on having staff work. So far, you are not getting results for your money, and the staff member obviously cannot be happy in a job in which he or she is not working well. Ask the staff member if he or she wants to resign now or try one more month with the understanding that, if he or she cannot meet goals, this will be the last month. Together, set clear goals and double-check that these are fair. Then reevaluate at the end of the month.

Sometimes even well-meaning, intelligent people go to work for a volunteer organization and act as though they were in summer camp. They think they do not need to produce because "this is a nonprofit group." This can usually be solved by a heart-to-heart talk and clear, written goals. Most of all, they must know that the staff works for you and for the organization, salary is paid in exchange for specific labor, and this job is not a scholarship. Once the staff member is serious and on track, he or she will be much happier, because he or she will be getting results. You can spend the organization's money in good faith.

On the other hand, sometimes a job is wrong for a person, or an employee is wrong for your organization. You will have to fire the staff person. At your third meeting, say you regret this, but you have to fire the person and look for a replacement. Discuss any work that was done well. Discuss other work for which you think the person would be better suited, and say that you will be glad to recommend him or her to a more suitable employer.

FIRING VETERAN STAFF

Written work plans, careful hiring, and caring supervison will help the board and the staff form an effective team to reach the goals of the organization. As the board gets more experience working with staff, it will find that all of this gets easier and easier. However, the one part that will become *more* difficult after a few years is firing your staff. If you fire someone who has only worked for the organization two months, it will be obvious to both of you that the firing is the right thing to do. On the other hand, when you have to fire someone who has worked for the organization for two *years,* it becomes much more difficult. The staff member who has invested time and emotions in this group may want to stay. You may have become friends, too. However, it is still the responsibility of the president to fire any staff member who is not necessary for next year's program or who is not meeting your goals right now.

Honesty is the best policy when you have to fire veteran staff. If the board has evaluated the work for the previous year and has decided to stop a program, it either can transfer the staff members to other programs or fire them. If you follow the planning system model in this book, you can plan your programs in September for the calendar year starting in January. If you decide to stop a program at the end of the year and have to fire staff, tell the staff members immediately so they will have three months to look for other jobs. Long-range planning gives the staff members you have to fire a chance to find another job while they still have jobs. Do everything you can to help them look for jobs.

How to Be a Great Supervisor

Once you know you have the right employee, you want to continue your supervision so that you, the staff, and the organization all keep getting better and better. This is an ongoing effort. Most leaders of volunteer organizations have little experience supervising staff, so you will learn and grow together. The best source of advice is any executive who manages a small business in your neighborhood. He or she already has learned many of the skills you need to know, such as how to interview, how to train on the job, how to balance being both the boss and a friend, and how to handle specific problems, such as a request for a loan. Do not expect to know the answers if you have never supervised people before. Ask for help, and be honest with your staff. Explain that you want to work with each staff person to be sure that you both will enjoy this experience and do the most for the good of the organization.

As the president, your responsibility is to the organization and its goals. It is up to you to set a high standard for current and future officers. Treat everyone fairly. Never play favorites, and never get intimately involved with your staff. If you think you are getting too involved with a member of your staff, ask yourself which is more important to you right now—your responsibility as president of the organization or the relationship with the individual. Then give up one or the other.

Most of all, realize that the board's responsibility for raising money must go on. It is tempting to think, "Well, the money goes for *their* salaries. Let *them* raise it!" This is not fair to you, to the staff, or to the organization. If you want to get the best possible staff members, you must offer them dependable income for the length of their contracts. If the board does not do this, the staff can and should work somewhere else. If you let the staff members raise their own salaries, they act as though they are self-employed. They do not work for you, your members, your organization, or your community. They work for themselves, and they can do whatever they want. Power in any organization goes to the people who raise the money. The board must keep raising the money if it wants to keep control over the decisions of the organization and the work of the staff.

RESPONSIBILITIES OF THE BOARD
WHEN YOU HIRE STAFF

Legally, the board is responsible for making sure that all the taxes due to the state and the IRS are paid on time. If you choose to give your employees Social Security coverage or a pension plan, you are legally responsible for making sure that it is paid in full, on time. If the money is not paid, you personally will have to pay the amount due to the government, plus penalties. The IRS says, "A 5 percent penalty is charged when taxes aren't deposited when due, . . . fines and other criminal penalties may be charged."[2] In legal terms, the board of directors is the employer responsible for paying taxes. The fines and penalties apply to *you*—not the staff. Pay on time.

Your treasurer can learn to do the payroll if you have fewer than five staff members. He or she can calculate the salary and deductions, pay the staff, and deposit the taxes due in the bank each time they are due. If you have more than five staff members, you may want to hire a bookkeeper to handle the payroll and write checks. In that case, be sure that two officers sign the checks. Do not let members of the staff sign checks. Ask the bookkeeper, read the IRS booklets, and check with your volunteer accountant to be sure that you always pay the full amount of taxes due on time.

If you ever have cash flow problems, which is a fancy way of saying that you are spending money faster than you are making money, the staff may suggest you postpone paying federal income taxes. Say no. If you cannot afford the taxes, you cannot afford the staff. Either put aside your other work and focus on fund raising for a month, or reevaluate the need for staff. If the board does not think that the staff's work is worth raising money for, then it is time to fire the staff. Cut back until you can be confident you can pay all of your bills, salaries, and taxes on time. If this means firing all the staff and becoming an all-volunteer organization again, do it. You will learn either that paid staff are a luxury you can do without or that they are vital—in which case you will raise the money to pay for them. In that case, reorganize your fund-raising strategy to create a dependable cash flow. Once money comes in faster than it goes out, rehire your old staff or hire new people.

The board is also responsible for the growth of your staff members. Encourage them to shop around for the best possible training to improve their skills. In many communities, the United Way, foundations, colleges, and professional associations offer workshops for staff members. Your state or national network may offer training through its own staff or at annual conventions. Your job as the board is to give the staff the time and money to take advantage of the training. Put training money in the budget, and plan the annual calendar so that the staff can attend workshops or conferences. You will reap the advantages of their increased knowledge and confidence, so this is a good investment for you.

If your budget is too small to buy training for your staff members, you can still help them to improve their skills in two very inexpensive but effective ways. First, encourage them to find or set up support groups of other people doing the same kind of work. The organizer can meet other organizers and the teacher can meet other teachers at a regularly scheduled meeting. Your staff members need to share their ideas, anxieties, hopes, and dreams with other people who do the same kind of work. They will learn more by helping others and being helped. You can help by encouraging the staff and giving them the time to participate.

Second, you can help your staff by giving them good books to read. This is so simple and obvious that it is easily overlooked. Because it is easy for staff members to get bogged down in day-to-day work and swamped by technical reading, they need inspirational books that will suggest new methods and nourish their spirits. Even if you cannot afford to train your staff members, you can give them the best ideas in book form. Virtually all of the most effective self-help books are in paperback, and many are available at the public library for free. Share the books that have made a difference in your own life, or start with some of the books recommended in the Bibliography. Each person will adapt the advice to suit his or her own goals and style, and they all will be happier and more successful workers.

HOW TO PREVENT "BURNOUT"

"There is no doubt that residents [the staff] in a Settlement too often move towards their ends 'with hurried and ignoble gait,' putting forth thorns in their eagerness to bear grapes. It is always easy for those in pursuit of ends which they consider of overwhelming importance to become themselves thin and impoverished in spirit and temper, to gradually develop a dark mistaken eagerness alternating with fatigue, which supersedes the 'great and gracious ways' so much more congruous with worthy aims."

—Jane Addams
Twenty Years at Hull-House

Jane Addams wrote that in 1910, but she would find the same problem today. The single most common problem with staff in a volunteer organization is what the staff calls *burnout*. This can range from discouragement because they thought the work would be easier, go faster, or be more fun, to complete exhaustion resulting from nonstop work.

It is never too early to consider that your staff members could experience burnout, because "an ounce of prevention is worth a pound of cure." Remember that the board is responsible for the growth, integrity, and health of yourselves, your organization, and your staff. Decide that you want to protect the staff members; then make a plan to keep them healthy, happy, and eager to work for your group. The experts recommend that the board of directors:

Pay enough money. It will not help you to over-economize. Pay a fair living wage.

Give staff a comprehensive health plan. Include all dental and other preventive care. It is a good investment for you.

Require paid vacations at least two weeks a year. It is a good idea for you to plan ahead, and then force the staff to go. It is *always* a "bad time" to take a vacation, there is *always* an important meeting to go to, and there is *always* a crisis going on. Budget money to hire vacation substitutes, divide the work among board members, or close the office.

Give staff members jobs worth doing. Write monthly work plans, share goal setting, and give supervision based on results. If the staff members understand the goals, they are less likely to waste their time and energy on "busyness" that may wear them out but that will not get done what needs doing.

Be available. Return phone calls promptly. Answer mail. If you do not know, cannot do it, or will not do it, say so immediately; then get a substitute. There is nothing worse for a staff person than to be left dangling without response or guidance.

Be lavish with praise. Give lots of compliments and recognition. Do so early and often. Tell each staff person each month that you are proud of his or her work. Show how it has helped the mission of the organization. Send thank-you notes for special efforts.

Provide a chance for employees to get away from the day-to-day grind and talk about larger issues. If you run a crisis nursery, you could take a day or two for a retreat to discuss the future of the family. For that matter, what *is* the family? Getting away for retreats enables people to talk about what they are doing, what it means to them, why they see it as important, what makes them discouraged, why they are optimistic, and what they hope to do next. You also could devote one session to long-range planning, or discuss your group's role in the national or international movement.

Plan the fun. Once a year the board can have a party for the staff members and their families. Have a potluck dinner, picnic, or celebration so that you can share good times together without having "to get through the agenda."

Provide support from other professionals as necessary. This could be in the form of a weekly meeting with a mental health professional or a monthly meeting with an organizing consultant. The board's job is to raise money to buy the best support personnel.

Listen. Listen. Listen.

Best of all, as an exciting grass roots organization, you can give your staff the opportunity to work with an organization that does worthwhile work. Give staff members a chance to do their jobs, encourage them to take risks, listen and act when they encourage you to take risks, and give them your complete support. The ideal relationship between the board and the staff is for the board to set high standards for work, raise enough money to hire and keep the best possible staff, and then have enough confidence to let staff members do their jobs. Bill Draves's praise of Free Universities holds for all healthy community groups: "The free u. offers the kind of atmosphere which encourages individual development and growth, and in return gets creative ideas, dedication and commitment, and a lively and exciting organization."[3]

STEPS TO HIRING AND SUPERVISING STAFF

THE BOARD OF DIRECTORS WILL:

1. Consider alternatives to hiring paid staff.
2. Decide what they want the staff to do.
3. Calculate the total cost of hiring staff.
4. Decide whom they want to hire.
5. Prepare a budget, personnel policy, job description, contract, and job applications. Revise the bylaws if necessary.
6. Advertise for staff. Interview and hire staff.
7. Orient the new staff.
8. Prepare monthly work plans and give supervision.

THE NEW STAFF WILL:

1. Interview every member of the board of directors.
2. Work with the president to prepare a work plan based on the information collected from the interviews of the members of the board of directors, the mission and the current goals of the organization, and the talents of the staff.

17

Change—The Only Constant

"There are three kinds of people;
Those who make things happen!
Those who let things happen.
and
Those who say, 'What happened?' "
— Richard Chavez, Founder,
Chavez & Associates

The only thing you will be sure to face as the years pass is change. The members of your board, the committees, the issues, the resources, the competition, and the community you serve are all changing constantly. What works today may be obsolete tomorrow; the person who is a major leader in your group today may drop out to run for mayor tomorrow; your best source of funds may move out of town tomorrow. Only the people you serve and the problems you want to solve will remain.

How can you provide leadership to keep the organization going? What can you do today to make sure that your group can do its job in five years or ten years? How can you plan to keep the organization fresh, vital, and important to the community?

If you could gaze into a crystal ball to see the future of your organization, you would see one of three fates for your group. It can stay the same in its purpose and structure, but the people involved may keep changing. It can go through a period of decline, losing

268

money and members and limiting its programs. Or it can grow. Most organizations go through cycles of rapid growth followed by a plateau, followed by more growth. But even the best organization will sometimes suffer brief periods of decline. As a leader, your job is to keep the organization fresh during periods of stability, keep control of the organization during periods of rapid growth, and keep your confidence and convictions during periods of decline. Let us look at each one of these periods to see what you can do.

ENOUGH IS ENOUGH

Let us say the organization has grown to a size that is just right for your board and members. You know what you want to do and how you want to do it. You know that there are people in your community who want what you do and will support you with their time, money, and ideas. How do you keep the enthusiasm and vitality?

Even if everything is working well, you still must stop from time to time to evaluate your work seriously. Every five or ten years—for example, when you update the history for the anniversary celebration—think about your mission and your future. Ask yourself, "*Why* are we doing this? Why are we *not* doing something else?" This will give the board a chance to end any programs that are no longer of interest to the members and give you a way to test your current ideas. Try to budget money so that you can bring in an outside consultant to give you a fresh look at your work. It is easy to miss the obvious when you are deeply involved with the program and have done the same work for years. If you have not hired outside help to evaluate your goals in the last ten years, put it in your budget and your calendar for next year.

An organization that has reached a stable size and style can remain an important influence in the community and an invaluable training ground for new leaders. It is possible to keep your organization as it is now and keep your vision intact over the long run. A good example is the thousands of nonprofit amateur theaters in the United States. They choose to stay the same size and do the same sort of work every year. But because of their enthusiasm and dedication, amateur theaters can continue to attract enough money, talent, and commitment to produce top quality theater year after year, decade after decade. One example is the Thalian Association in Wilmington, North Carolina, the oldest nonprofit theater in the United States. It was founded as an amateur theatrical society in 1788, opened its own theater in a building shared with the city hall in 1858, and still produces live theater each year!

A stable, self-sufficient organization can work effectively with other organizations in a statewide or national network. You can help newer organizations get started and become stronger, too. For example, the Thalian Association renovated its theater building in the thirties and had it beautifully restored in the seventies. Today it shares its stage with two children's theaters, a Black theater, the civic ballet, a summer stock theater, two concert series, a film series, and the historic building tour. In a coalition, each organization benefits from sharing the work with others.

Be who you are, and celebrate your stability! As you master the skills to do your program, raise increasing amounts of money, and plan smooth transitions, your organization will get better and better every year. As coach George Halas once said, "In any game, you do the things you do best, and you do them over and over and over."

LESS IS MORE

What do you do if your organization suddenly shrinks in size? Perhaps you neglected your fund raising because of a big grant. It ran out, and you had to cut your program back. Or perhaps you were undone by success. You won a big victory or solved the problem, only to discover that most of your members then were ready to go back to their everyday lives rather than continue coming to your meetings. Sometimes the change is communitywide. If most people are employed, they may see recreation as an important community goal. But if the major employer in town shuts down, people will be interested in finding new jobs rather than filling their leisure time.

How do you avoid discouragement when your group faces a slow or sudden decline in membership, income, or program interest? How can you make a negative a positive? How can you regain your confidence and momentum?

First, realize that at any time, your organization is just what *you* choose to make it. Wonderful organizations have been begun or re-vitalized in times of depression, recession, war, or unrest. If you want this organization to succeed, you can find a way for it to suc-ceed. Make up your mind to make the group as it is now into what you want it to be.

Take inventory of what you have now. Who is involved, and why? What do they get out of belonging to this group? How could other people get the same satisfaction out of belonging to this group?

Next, take stock of the reasons for the decline. Where did your planning go wrong? Were you too dependent on just one source of money? Was your program limited to just one campaign or just one issue? Were your members joining to solve the problem rather than to build the organization?

To regain your morale and momentum, you have to pinpoint the problems and then find the solutions. Nonprofit organizations tend to attract people who are very idealistic. If they believe that every-thing is going to work well because they are "good" or "right," they will be crushed down when they discover that people who are good and right can make mistakes just as often as the people who are bad and wrong. What matters is how you use the knowledge you gain from this. The most important quality for anyone on your board is curiosity. Even when you make mistakes, you want to say, "What went wrong? How can we do it differently next time? What did we skip in our planning? Who else can help us?"

One of the best lessons in W. Clement Stone's books is that any adversity holds the seed of equal or greater opportunity. When something goes wrong, follow Mr. Stone's example. Say, "We have a problem? That's great!!!! Let's find out why and let's find out how we can use this information to get better!"

If the board has a problem, talk about it. Discuss it with your key professional advisers or other community leaders. *Never* just sit and stew. You are never alone. Pick up the phone and call *someone* to get advice. Listen, talk it over at board meetings, plan the next step, and then get going.

Emphasize that the purpose of looking at problems is to find ways to make the organization *better*. It is not to cast blame or wallow in guilt. The Greek philosopher Heraclitus said, "You can't step in the same stream twice." My friend Beryl McCleary says, "Don't recycle your old decisions." Do not keep saying, "If only we had . . ." or "Why didn't we . . ." Learn from your mistakes, but do not dwell on them. Learn when you can, and then go on to the job of building for tomorrow.

Once you know the problems, the board can plan to solve them. Go back through this book, and review the areas in which you need to strengthen the organization to work better. Do you need more members? Activate the membership committee, and focus on a full-time membership drive for the next two months. Do you need more dependable funds? Expand your fund-raising strategy to get more money from dependable, renewable sources. Did your program suffer because you put all your resources into one idea and then, win or lose, left yourself with nothing to do? Redo your program plans. Test two or three activities to reach your goals. This time, map out a five-year plan so you have other plans going if you win or lose on one issue.

Above all, have the courage of your convictions. Be consistent. Review your mission statement before you do any plans. Revise it if you truly believe that your organization should change its purpose. If you still believe in your original mission, keep your belief in your ability to achieve it. Do not give in to the temptation to do something else in the short run in order to get money. Trust yourself, and trust your fellow board members to make the right decisions. It will be hard work, but if you believe your goals are worth it, you will be able to achieve them. You need the courage to say no to the easy solutions and yes to the hard work that will make your organization succeed at the job that *it* wants to do. The secret is to keep trying. Never give up, and never sell out.

Keep your sense of humor and your perspective. Every mature organization, like every mature person, will have some setbacks and disappointments. If you want to achieve great goals, you will have to take big risks. As Henry David Thoreau said, "Don't worry when you stumble. Remember a worm is the only thing that can't fall down." Seize this opportunity to reevaluate, reorganize, and rejuvenate the organization. Keep your vision, stop the unsuccessful work, and revitalize the effective parts of your organization. Personally set an example of courage and conviction. The rest of the organization will rise to the challenge and emerge from the problem period stronger and more confident than ever before.

MORE IS NOT ENOUGH

Architect Mies van der Rohe said "Less is more," but hundreds of Victorian architects would have said "More is not enough!" Like the Victorian homes that are so covered with gingerbread trim that you can barely make out the house, some organizations grow so fast in so many ways that after several years it is difficult to discern the idea behind it all. Today's organization may be much larger than and very different from the one planned by the founders.

Especially if you have done your work so well that the group is growing fast, the board needs to stop from time to time to get control of the process. A strong and active organization especially may grow so fast that the members no longer can see the big picture behind the many committees and activities. Your job as the leader is to make the work and the organization make sense. Remind everyone of the original design and the ultimate goals of the group. Emphasize the philosophy of the group. Keep your mission in sight.

Growth is good only as long as it is growth you can choose, control, and understand. You *can* run this organization. Do not let the organization run *you!* The board needs clear thinking and careful planning to be sure the organization remains true to its mission, controlled by the elected leaders, and accountable to its own community. Put in the time to do the planning you need. Do not just react to other people's plans, offers, or ideas.

The leaders also need to make time for yourselves, to make sense out of all the activities going on. Get control of your own schedule. Time management experts suggest that you make a "to do" list each day. Put on it only those activities that will move you toward your most important goals. Taking time to plan each day will help you do first things first and make your work more effective. Sometimes a leader will keep a journal to help review his or her work, growth, and development. Making time for yourself also could include taking a day or two each month to write a column for your newsletter. This is your chance to integrate the spirit and philosophy of the organization into the day-to-day activities. The philosophy will have to make sense to you before you will be able to explain it to your readers. If you are having trouble explaining how last month's work fits into the organization's philosophy, perhaps you need to schedule a meeting to review the program plan.

Teaching others is an excellent way to clarify your own thinking about what you do, how you do it, why you do it, and what it means to you personally. Be an active part of the speakers' bureau, and offer workshops to newer organizations on how you work. If possible, accept invitations from similar organizations in other locations, so that you can compare your ideas and your results with theirs. Taking turns doing evaluations for other organizations will help all of you clarify what you want to do, what works, what does not work, and how to get things done.

At least once a year, plan a retreat or brainstorming session for the top leadership. Before meeting, clarify your own thinking on your plans and goals for the next year. You may need to go into hiding for a day or two, but it is worth it. You cannot lead anyone else if you do not know where you are going.

Continue your own education and study. If you can get the time and money, go to the best classes available. If you have a more limited calendar and budget, at least share advice with others in your field, and read the best self-help books you can find. Set aside time to think, study, and plan your work. Saul Alinsky said, "Organizing is action and reflection, action and reflection. You can't have one without the other." Especially if your work is in an emotionally charged field, it is even more important for the effectiveness of your work and your own self-confidence that you get and continue to get the best possible training. As Dr. Thomas West, deputy medical director of St. Christopher's Hospice, says, "Competence is very comforting. There is no place for tender loving care without a background of sheer hard knowledge."

Do your homework, and then use your new knowledge to improve the organization. Keep finding new ways to clarify the work of the organization as it grows. Your job is to draw the connections between the different parts of the organization so that everyone will know where you are going. This is a continuous process. The growth is not going to stop so that you can study it. You have chosen to be a leader in your community, a job that requires you to analyze and explain your organization today at the same time you are inventing something better for tomorrow.

Have the courage to be you. Think your own thoughts, and make your own plans. Even rapid growth can be controlled and understood if you know who you are and what you want to do. *Make* it happen! Choose to control your own group; then teach your skills to the next generation of leaders. You will know that the group is getting bigger *and* better every year!

Part III
Getting Organized

18

The Job of the Secretary

"We make a living by what we get, but we make a life by what we give."
—Winston Churchill

It is the job of the secretary to create a system to collect, store, and retrieve all nonfinancial information important to the organization. The secretary must set up files for all legal papers, such as signed copies of the minutes of board meetings; business documents, such as contracts and leases; correspondence; and any other information that current or future officers may want. The secretary serves as the recorder and preserver of organizational history, as well as the hub of all communication among board members.

The state laws for nonprofit corporations specify what records the organization must keep. In most states, the secretary must take minutes at board meetings, send them to all board members, and preserve a copy for the audit and history. See "Minutes" in Chapter 14 for advice on taking minutes. Besides the minutes, the secretary can handle most of the internal communication. The secretary can make telephone calls before meetings, follow up deadlines, and send out copies of newspaper clippings, research papers, and meeting notices. In addition, the secretary can help produce the internal publications of the organization, such as a newsletter for and about the active members, a ten-year history, or a membership brochure.

The secretary can serve as the organization's liaison with other organizations — trading newsletters, special event fliers, and meeting
notices with local groups and similar organizations in the state and
the rest of the country.

Many secretaries collect and organize background information
for the group. They recruit housebound parents to read and clip
newspapers and magazines and recruit a librarian to organize your
research materials. The secretary can ask members with video recorders or tape recorders to tape your meetings and television and
radio coverage.

HISTORIAN

The secretary can serve as historian for the organization. In addition to the minutes of the board meetings, he or she can keep two
copies of every piece of paper with the group's name on it; all clippings about the group, labeled and dated; photographs; promotional materials such as buttons and bumber stickers, dated and
labeled with the name and address of the slogan creator and the artist; copies of letters to and from the group; copies of all public
testimony and original research; newsletters; and annual reports.
Find the person who writes the annual report for a well-established
organization that has just celebrated their fiftieth or one hundredth
anniversary. Ask him or her what earlier members *should* have
kept.

After a few years, the secretary may end up with more boxes of
files than you can fit in your home or office. Keep all legal and
business files in the office, as well as current files and lists. Sort out-
of-date material into two categories: sentimental and historical. Use
the sentimental material for a "Memorabilia Auction" at your fifth
anniversary party or when you need an emergency fund raiser.
Make arrangements with the local historical society, museum, or
college history department to take historical materials. You can
watch the librarian or archivist to learn how to organize historical
materials and control their use. The advantage of leaving your
documents at a central, staffed location is that they are safe and ac-
cessible to all students.

FILES

While the treasurer maintains financial records, the secretary must set up files for the organization's nonfinancial records. At the beginning, the secretary would file:

1. Copies of written notices of board meetings and signed copies of the minutes of board meetings. Legally, these must be kept by nonprofit corporations in Illinois. Check your state laws for similar provisions.

2. Permanent legal papers, including the originals of the organization's bylaws, the state certificate of nonprofit incorporation, the federal employer identification number letter, the federal tax exemption ruling letter, a copy of the application to make expenditures to lobby, leases, contracts, copyrights, and other legal papers. Mark the file "Do not take," or frame the originals for the office walls.

3. Photocopies of legal papers for volunteers' use. This would include copies of the federal employer identification number to use when shopping and copies of the federal tax ruling letter to send with foundation proposals.

4. Correspondence. File letters alphabetically by the name of the person or the group.

5. Original research and testimony.

6. Samples of all materials from similar organizations filed by the name of the group.

7. Samples the board may want to copy now or later. File these by the name of the item, such as "annual report," "thank-you letters," or "personnel policy."

8. All publications, permits, and records from the post office.

9. Annual reports and other material from the annual meetings.

10. Newsletters, brochures, and fact sheets.

11. Clippings of news stories about the group and recordings of television and radio reports.

MAILING LISTS

The secretary can coordinate all large mailings. The work will go much more smoothly if one person keeps track of all the permits, supplies, and accounting for the post office. The first secretary can collect all the information from the mailing permits department of the main post office, apply for bulk mail and business reply permits when necessary, and learn how to prepare bulk mailings. Then he or she can help the committees put out major mailings, such as the newsletter, annual report, convention or retreat invitations, or membership drive. As part of this job, the secretary can maintain the mailing lists of the organization.

In addition to the files, the secretary will want to create a system to store and retrieve the names and addresses of people. Ask the secretaries of other local organizations for advice on the most versatile and least expensive system for you. Depending on which system you use and how much you mail, you can set up the following lists:

1. Board of directors.
2. Advisory board.
3. Honorary board.
4. Committees.
5. Donors of money, talent, or things.
6. Similar groups in your town, state, and the rest of the country.
7. Politicians representing your city, county, state, and congressional district(s).
8. Press and publicity outlets.
9. Prospects—people you want to keep informed because you want to ask them for their money or talent in the future.
10. People to whom the newsletter must be mailed. This can include all of the people above, plus the dues-paying members and subscribers. You may choose to give free subscriptions to local clergy, press, or donors and exchange newsletters with other organizations.

19

The Job of the Treasurer

*"Give cheerfully with one hand, and you
will gather well with two."*

—*Irish proverb*

It is the job of the treasurer to create a system to collect, store,
and retrive all financial information important for the organization. The treasurer will set up the books and records for the organization, open and maintain bank accounts, supervise investments,
help prepare the budget, and handle the payroll for staff, if any. If
the organization hires a bookkeeper to handle the money and
books, it is still the responsibility of the treasurer to make sure that
all records and reports are accurate and up-to-date.

The treasurer works as a partner to the board of directors as a
whole. He or she will record all money raised and spent by the
organization and prepare reports each month, quarter, and year to
enable the board to make and review its plans. These reports are explained in Chapter 20. The treasurer also will prepare annual
reports for the IRS and most states. The government annual reports
and annual audits are explained in Chapter 21.

SETTING UP BOOKS

Several very good books on bookkeeping and accounting for nonprofit organizations are listed in Chapter 24. These will tell you how to set up books. Each group will need different books, depending on where its money comes from. As long as you are raising your own money, you can choose your own style of bookkeeping. But if you raise money outside the organization, the funding source may require certain books or records. Some United Ways demand a bookkeeping system in detail that extends down to seventeen-digit account codes. Other funders may require only evidence of sensible internal controls, such as asking for receipts for expenditures.

The state laws on nonprofit corporations will require certain records. For example, Illinois law requires a nonprofit corporation to keep "correct and complete books and records of account, minutes of meetings, and the names and addresses of its members entitled to vote. All books and records of a corporation may be inspected by any member . . . for any proper purpose at any reasonable time."[1]

If you are the new treasurer of your group, meet with the president, the volunteer CPA, and the bookkeeper for a similar nonprofit group. They may recommend certain kinds of books available at a local office supply store, or they may have developed a system that will be easy for you to copy. Or ask your church how it handles its money. The church has a system for collecting, counting, recording, and depositing money every week. It is probably handled by volunteers and can be copied.

Why Keep Books?

As a successful organization asking the people in your community to give you money, you have a responsibility to take good care of the organization's money. This is the job of the treasurer, who must keep clear, written financial records. Your organization wants a complete accounting system because:

1. You know where your money is now.

2. You know where your money went. You can tell the value of the things you own and the cost for things you buy.

3. You know the sources of your money, so you may be able to go back for more.

4. You can tell the people who gave last year exactly what you did with their money. Because the best people to ask for money are the people who have already given you money, clear records make it easier to ask.

5. You can tell members how much it costs to run your program, what they get for their dues, and why they should pay.

6. You make it easier to do fund-raising benefits, because you will have seed money to support your plans.

7. You can be a better shopper, because you can buy in bulk for the entire year's needs.

8. You can accurately estimate how much money you will need next month or next year.

9. You will be confident that all of the money is going where it is supposed to go. Sensible systems for handling the money help reduce the temptation to anyone to use any of the organization's money improperly.

10. You will have clear, accurate information when you have to fill out the annual reports required by the state or federal governments.

11. You will make it easier, quicker, and less expensive to get an audit.

12. The biggest advantage of written books and records is that they make it possible for a large group of people to share the ownership of the group. In some for-profit companies, many people buy shares of stock in the company and then are paid a percentage of the profits. In a nonprofit corporation, you also want a large number of people to buy in to the group. This is the most dependable way to raise renewable money, it is the most accurate proof that your group is needed, and it is the best way to show the members that you want their participation.

A successful organization will require the treasurer to use great care in managing its money. A strong organization requires many members, a bold program, and a dependable income. These, in turn, create the need for good books.

What Do We Need?

Set up your books so that you can easily and quickly retrieve the information you will need for the monthly, quarterly, and yearly reports. As a minimum you will need:

1. A checking account.
2. A savings account.
3. A petty cash system.
4. Receipts for every donation.
5. An income journal to record all income and its source.
6. An expense journal to record all payments and where they go.
7. Files for bills paid; bills due; tax reports; monthly, quarterly, and annual reports; and letters.
8. A record of donors. This can consist of cards on which you write the name of each donor and how much he or she gave. If you have the information, also include the home and work address and phone number, volunteer commitments, when the donor joined, and who recruited him or her. Each time you receive a donation of money or anything else from this person, write it on the card. This will help you next year when it is time to ask for new donations.

When your organization is bigger, or if you take foundation grants or government contracts, you may have to expand your system. If you hire staff, you have to add bookkeeping for payroll, benefits, and taxes. If you want an audit, you will need the advice of a CPA to set up your books so they are easy to audit. Be sure to get advice from a CPA and other treasurers to keep your system up-to-date.

HOW TO HANDLE THE MONEY

Because everyone on the board will be selling memberships, asking for donations, and helping with fund-raising events, they all have to know what to do with the money they will be receiving. It will make their job easier if the board agrees to turn money and checks over to the treasurer at their regular meeting. The treasurer will record the source and amount of each donation, make out a receipt, and deposit the money in the bank.

The board should set a policy on what is and is not a reimbursable expense. For example, the organization may choose to reimburse leaders for postage because they can get a receipt from the post office, but not for local phone bills because there is no way to know how much of a bill is for calls for the organization. The board's decision should be put in writing and passed out at the next meeting so everyone knows what the policy is. It is not fair to leave this decision up to the treasurer.

OPENING BANK ACCOUNTS

The board will choose a bank or savings and loan association for its checking and savings accounts according to the questions suggested in Chapter 8. Once the organization has decided to become a nonprofit corporation and applied for its federal employer identification number, it can apply for a corporate checking account. Ask the officer at the bank to waive the charges for this account because you are a nonprofit organization doing good work for the benefit of the community.

Most groups recommend having two officers sign the checks. This way more than one person sees each check. You may decide to make the president, vice-president, treasurer, and secretary your "approved signatures" and rule that any two of them may sign the checks. If the treasurer actually writes the checks and pays the bills, it is wise to have another officer reconcile the bank statement. This means he or she will compare the bank's record of your checks and deposits against your record, then make sure that your record is up-to-date and accurate. Whenever you elect new officers, you will have to get and fill out new "signature cards" from the bank so that the new officers can sign checks.

You also can open a savings account so you can deposit any funds you do not need to meet current expenses. Then you can begin to save toward a long-term goal, such as opening an office or hiring staff. Ask your banker for advice on the best way to save or invest your funds.

BONDING THE TREASURER

Regardless of who is elected the first treasurer, it is in the best interest of the organization to buy a bond to cover the person for his or her term of office. A bond can be purchased through your insurance agent. Unlike insurance, which is a two-way agreement between the insurance company and the organization, a bond is a three-way agreement. The bonding company agrees to pay for any loss to the organization because of dishonesty or default of the treasurer.

Buy a bond right after electing the first treasurer in order to avoid any hurt feelings or financial losses later on. If you have more than one treasurer or more than one officer who handles money or other valuables, they all should be covered by a surety bond. If you also hire paid staff to handle your money and valuables, they should be covered by a fidelity bond. Ask your insurance agent to explain surety bonds, fidelity bonds, and insurance coverage. A good agent will design the best package to meet your needs based on who the people are and how much money they handle.

Buy a bond for the first treasurer for the following reasons.

Your treasurer is trusted with both the funds and the good will of everyone who gives money to the organization. Like getting an annual audit, buying a bond for the treasurer is a way to show your supporters that you are a responsible organization that is serious about the stewardship of their money.

The bond is based on the job rather than the person doing the job. Some groups are reluctant to bond their treasurer because they fear it will look as though they do not trust the individual. Fortunately, you can say that buying a bond is actually a compliment to the treasurer, because bonding is granted only after the person fills out a questionnaire on himself or herself. The bonding company grants the bond only if the company assumes that, if the application is correct, the company never will have to pay on the bond. So a bond for the treasurer is an endorsement from the bonding company that he or she is above suspicion and therefore bondable. If you bond the first treasurer and every treasurer, no one will have to feel insulted.

The cost is based on the risk. As long as your budget is small, you will qualify for the minimum premium. As your budget grows, so will your coverage and your cost. Because your budget can grow quickly during the first few years, the board will be saved from any unpleasant arguments over "how much is too much" to trust to the treasurer. You will have established a tradition that will protect the organization, whether the budget is $500 or $500,000.

In the unlikely event that you and the bonding company misjudge a treasurer who turns out to be dishonest, if you prove that the person took your money or valuables, the bonding company will pay you and then try to get the money back from the thief.

20

Budgets and Financial Reports for the Board

" 'I can' is the greatest cage-breaker of them all. Tattoo it on your soul."
—Tish Sommers
The Not-So-Helpless Female

A budget is the board's estimate of how much money the organization will spend in the coming year. It is the basis for the board's fund-raising strategy—the plan of who will raise the money and how and when they will raise it. The budget and fund-raising strategy are prepared by the board with help from the treasurer. The board uses these tools to make sure that it will have all the money it needs for the coming year.

Throughout the year, the treasurer will prepare financial reports to show the board how much money is being raised and spent. Every month, quarter, and year, the board will compare actual income and expenses to the budget, so the board is sure that enough money is coming in to meet projected expenses *before* they arise. Although budgets and financial reports may be new to the board, it is easy to learn how to use them.

Set aside one board meeting to work on next year's budget. Many groups plan in the fall of one year for the work of the next year.

Under this system, the board would begin in September by considering exactly what it wants to do in the next calendar year. Review Chapter 13 for information on how to evaluate this year's and plan next year's program.

In October, once you know what you want to do, make a budget — a list of what you will need to buy and how much you expect it to cost. In November, the board will design a strategy to raise the money needed to meet the budget. In December, the program plan, the budget, and the fund-raising strategy will be adopted by the board. Each board member will make a personal commitment to raise his or her fair share of the budget.

Here is a sample budget. To design it, the board looked at how much it spent this year, then estimated its expenses for the next year. After you add up all the expenses you can predict, add 10 percent for items you cannot anticipate. Then add at least 10 percent to allow for inflation. This gives you the total amount the board will have to raise next year. Table 20-1 is a sample for a small organization with no paid staff. For advice on preparing a budget for an organization with paid staff, see Chapter 16.

TABLE 20-1   Sample Budget

Purpose	Expenses
Program meetings (10)	$ 500
Board meetings (11)	110
Newsletters (4)	1,200
Supplies	300
Printing	300
Phone and Postage	200
	$2,610
Unanticipated + 10 percent	260
	$2,870
Inflation + 10 percent	290
	$3,160

This organization decided to raise all of its budget from dues from the members. This is the easiest, quickest, and most democratic way to raise money. Since they will not do any special fund-raising events, the officers and members of the organization can devote all of their time to achieving the goals of the group.

Here are two sample time lines for this budget and fund-raising strategy. Table 20-2 shows projected expenses. The most money will go out in March, because the group will have to pay for printing and buy supplies for the April annual meeting as well as publish the quarterly newsletter. Table 20-3 compares expenses to income from dues. The group will sell memberships every month except July and August. To meet its goals, the members will have to sell forty memberships each month. Because the group gets $8 per membership, it will earn $320 per month for ten months. The time line shows that this will cover expenses every month. But it also shows the importance of starting to raise money right away—in January— and of making the quota each month. The difference between the income and expenses at the end of the year will be used up by unanticipated expenses and inflation.

TABLE 20–2   Sample Time Line for Expenses

Month	Program meeting	Board meeting	News-letter	Supplies	Print-ing	Phone and Postage	Total
January	$ 50	$ 10		$ 20	$ 10	$ 10	$ 100
February	50	10		20	10	10	100
March	50	10	$ 300	80	190	30	660
April Annual meeting	50	10		20	10	10	100
May	50	10		20	10	10	100
June	50	10	300	20	10	30	420
July	50	10		20	10	10	100
August	—	—		20	10	10	40
September	50	10	300	20	10	30	420
October	50	10		20	10	10	100
November	50	10		20	10	10	100
December	—	10	300	20	10	30	370
TOTAL	$500	$110	$1,200	$300	$300	$200	$2,610

TABLE 20-3   Sample Time Line for Income and Expenses—Operating Budget

Month	Expenses	Income from dues	Balance
January	$ 100	$ 320	$220
February	100	320	440
March	660	320	100
April	100	320	320
May	100	320	540
June	420	320	440
July	100	—	340
August	40	—	300
September	420	320	200
October	100	320	420
November	100	320	640
December	370	320	590
TOTAL	$2,610	$3,200	$590*

* Balance gives you a cushion against unforeseen expenses and price increases.

Plan your fund-raising strategy so money comes in throughout the year. It will help to make a chart showing when you will have to pay out money and when you expect money to come in. This will show you if you will need more money than usual during one part of the year, such as around the annual meeting or at the end of the legislative session. Then you can plan ahead to raise money *before* it is needed.

YOU ONLY GET THE NET!

Remember that you only get to spend the *net,* which is the amount you raised minus what it cost to get the money. The net will vary, depending on how you raise money. From individual donations, the net is 100 percent, because it does not cost you anything to get them. The president and other officers can ask individuals, in person, to make generous donations. This is all profit.

In this example, each member pays $8 dues per year. The organization chooses to send members a quarterly newsletter. Divide the cost of the newsletter ($1,200) by the number of members (400); it costs the group $3 per member. They will net $5 per member to do the work of the group. If you want to operate on the income from dues, be sure to find the exact amount you will net per member after subtracting the cost of everything you give to members.

If you raise money at special events, such as a dance, you may only net 50 percent. You may raise $1,000 but spend $500 on the band, hall, decorations, and refreshments—net, $500. From an ad book, you may have to spend $400 from the gross $2,400 in order to net $2,000. In planning, be sure that you use only the net figures.

FINANCIAL REPORTS

To do its job well, the board needs three kinds of reports from the treasurer. First is the monthly report, which shows how much the board raised and spent in the previous month. This is your "early warning system" to tell you whether you are raising enough money or need to step up your fund raising.

The board also needs quarterly reports comparing actual income and expenses to the income and expenses projected in the budget. Because the organization always is changing, the economy in which it operates always is changing, and the people involved always are changing, the quarterly reviews of the income and expenses enable the board to keep its plans up-to-date. Especially in the first year, you very possibly may raise less money or spend more money than you anticipated. Quarterly reviews will help you revise your plans based on current, accurate data so that you can catch up and be solvent at the end of the year.

Finally, annual reports serve as the basis for the next year's plans. These are the yearly financial reports you use for your own evaluation and planning. The annual reports due to the IRS and the state are explained in Chapter 21.

Cash Basis Versus Accrual Basis Reports

Most experienced treasurers and boards recommend that you ask the treasurer to prepare the reports for the board on what is called an *accrual basis,* even though he or she may keep the books on what is called a *cash basis.* At the very least, the annual report should be done on an accrual basis.

WHAT IS THE DIFFERENCE?

Most people run their personal accounts on a cash basis. Most new organizations also start their books this way. A cash basis accounting system shows all of the transactions as if they were conducted in cash, recording money when you receive it and when you pay it out. This gives you an accurate record of where your money comes from and where it goes. But it does not record outstanding obligations, such as taxes due but not paid, and other debts that you have not paid. It also does not show money owed to the organization, such as a payment due for sales or services.

Most for-profit companies run their accounts on an accrual basis, and most successful nonprofit organizations recommend accrual basis accounting. This means that you run the books based on the agreements you make when you make them, whether or not money actually changes hands. So you record income when you earn it, and you record expenses when you incur the expenses. This kind of a report will tell the board not only what it raised and what it spent, but also how much money others owe you and how much money you owe others. Especially if you hire staff, receive large grants, or handle a lot of money, an accrual style of reports will give the board a much more accurate picture of the financial status of the organization. Ask a veteran bookkeeper or your CPA to show you how to produce reports on an accrual basis from your books and records. See Chapter 24 for recommended reading to help the treasurer set up the books and prepare the reports.

21

Annual Reports and Audits

.

*"The years teach us much which
the days never know."*
— Ralph Waldo Emerson

Do not be confused by the words *tax-exempt*. A tax-exempt nonprofit corporation is exempt from *paying* corporate income taxes, but it is not exempt from *reporting* every year to the IRS. Most states also require annual reports from nonprofit corporations. The annual reports are supposed to help protect citizens from fraudulent charities. The benefit to the board is that they force you to keep your records up-to-date and to create one concise financial report every year. They give you a short, accurate record to compare year-to-year finances.

The IRS requires that tax-exempt nonprofit corporations file a written report each year. The report states the source and amount of the money the corporation raises and spends. The IRS will automatically send the correct forms to your organization's registered address near the end of your fiscal year. But do not wait until you receive the forms to start keeping the records you will need in order to fill them out. Ask for samples of the forms and instructions for filling out the forms as soon as you incorporate; these will tell the officers what records to keep. The forms and instructions are free. Ask other nonprofit corporations, your lawyer, or your accountant which reports are required in your state. See Chapter 23 for information on how to order the federal forms and instructions.

Once you have the forms, read them all the way through. Pay attention to the following:

1. Who has to sign them? This usually is the president and the treasurer or secretary. If you hold one of these offices, protect yourself by being sure you know what the forms say and require you to do.

2. When are they due? This usually is a date after the end of your fiscal year or before the anniversary of your incorporation. It is your responsibility to meet these deadlines. The state agencies may not remind you. Write the deadline on next year's calendar, and plan to start work on the reports at least two months ahead of the deadline.

3. What information will you have to have next year in order to fill this out? Set your books and files up right the first time. Make sure you have a system established to record all the data that will be needed for the form. This will include both financial and historical data, such as minutes of your board meetings.

4. Do you need any special help? Under some state laws, you will need a CPA to prepare an audit for you. If this is the case, plan to recruit a CPA immediately to show you how to set up your records so the audit will be easy, quick, and inexpensive.

ADVICE TO THE TREASURER

If you have to prepare the annual tax reports for your group, you will save yourself a lot of frustration if you start early and get advice from someone who has prepared these reports in the past, your lawyer, or your accountant. Give yourself enough time to read all the forms and instructions. Then meet with the IRS to clear up any questions. If you need more help with the IRS, ask the staff of your U.S. senator or member of Congress to intervene on your behalf. This service is free to taxpayers and usually gets results.

INTERNAL REVENUE SERVICE ANNUAL REPORTS

IRS Form 990 and Schedule A

The following refers to the 1980 IRS reports. Be sure to check the current year's forms and instructions for changes.

Form 990 is a four-page report that the IRS requires of all tax-exempt organizations. It asks where you get your money, where you spend it, what you have, and what you owe. *Every* tax-exempt non-profit corporation must file a Form 990 with the IRS every year. Smaller groups can fill in only the top part, as instructed. If you raised less than ten thousand dollars, you only have to give your address, identification number, and IRS code number. See the sample below.

Form **990** Department of the Treasury Internal Revenue Service	**Return of Organization Exempt from Income Tax** Under section 501(c) (except black lung benefit trust or private foundation), 501(e) or (f) of the Internal Revenue Code	**1980**

For the calendar year 1980, or fiscal year beginning	, 1980, and ending	, 19

Use IRS label. Other-wise, please print or type.	Name of organization	A Employer identification number (see instructions)
	Address (number and street)	B If exemption application is pending, check here . . . . ▶
	City or town, State, and ZIP code	C If address changed check here . . . ▶

D Check applicable box—Exempt under section ▶ ☐ 501(c) ( ) (insert number), ☐ 501(e) OR ☐ 501(f).

E Is this a group return (see instruction I) filed for affiliates? . . ☐ Yes ☐ No   If "Yes" to either, give four-digit group exemption
    Is this a separate return filed by a group affiliate? . . . . . ☐ Yes ☐ No   number (GEN) ▶

☐ Check here if gross receipts are normally not more than $10,000 and do not complete the rest of this return (see instruction B(1)).
☐ Check here if gross receipts are normally more than $10,000 and line 12 is $25,000 or less. Complete Parts I, II, IV, and VI and only the indicated items in Parts III and V (see instruction H). If line 12 is more than $25,000, complete the entire return.

Schedule A of Form 990 is another four-page report that is required of 501(c)(3) tax-exempt organizations. It asks the names of the members of your board, names of staff paid more than thirty thousand dollars, and arithmetic to show that you are a public charity rather than a private foundation. In part 4 of Schedule A you report the amount of money you spend on lobbying, if you filed Form 5768 as discussed in Chapter 9.

Form 990 and Schedule A are due to the IRS 5½ months after the end of your fiscal year.

Unrelated Business Income and IRS Form 990T

If you sell anything to the public, be sure to protect yourself by finding out if the IRS is going to consider these sales "unrelated business" income." When you apply for a 501(c)(3) ruling, you are asking the federal government to exempt your nonprofit corporation from corporate income taxes. The government says yes to this request because it wants to encourage certain charitable, educational, or scientific work. The government calls this work your *exempt function*. As long as the money you raise goes toward accomplishing this exempt function, it will be exempt from corporate income taxes.

However, the IRS will *not* consider some sources of money as "substantially related to" your exempt function. This money is called *unrelated business income.* It can include sales, advertising, and rent. If the IRS rules that this money is taxable income, then you must pay taxes on it. Unfortunately, the law is vague and confusing, so protect yourself by getting advice from an experienced CPA and also asking someone at the IRS office.

It is important that you find out as soon as possible whether your source of income will be considered unrelated business income by the IRS. Even if you are a tax-exempt nonprofit corporation, you will have to pay corporate income taxes on that income, at the same rate as a for-profit corporation does. In 1980, this ranged from 17 percent of the first $25,000 of net income to 46 percent of net income more than $100,000. Obviously, this can add up if you are successful. If your CPA and the IRS say the income from your sales will be taxed as unrelated business income, you have to plan ahead to pay the taxes as a cost of doing business. It is in your interest to learn about these taxes as soon as possible so that you do not overestimate your profits or underestimate your taxes.

You are required to file a Form 990T with the IRS if you raise more than one thousand dollars in money considered unrelated business income. This is a very complicated, four-page form, so you will have to recruit help early to be sure that you keep the information needed to fill out the form.

This Form 990T is due to the IRS 5½ months after the close of the fiscal year, at the same time as Form 990 and Schedule A. Plan ahead; you want everything done in time so that the officers can review and sign the forms.

REPORTS TO THE STATE

As of 1981, thirty-eight states and the District of Columbia required nonprofit corporations to register when they begin and to report every year after that if they solicit funds, do business, or own property in the state. You will have to register with the secretary of state (sixteen states), and/or the attorney general (eight states), or another department.

To find out what you have to do, write or call the secretary of state's corporate division and the attorney general's charities division to ask how to report. Ask to be referred to the correct department if the office you call does not regulate nonprofit corporations. In some states, one department may regulate the organization because it is a corporation doing business and another because it is a charity soliciting funds from the citizens. It is your responsibility to find both forms and meet both deadlines. The best place to get help is from a treasurer or bookkeeper of an organization similar to yours who has made out annual reports for your state.

Most states do not require very small organizations to report. If you raise less than a set dollar amount, you will not have to report to the state or get an audit. For example, in Maine, if you raise less than two thousand dollars, you do not have to report; and if you raise less than ten thousand dollars, you do not have to have an audit. Check with your state for the current regulations.

STARTING IN THE MIDDLE — ANNUAL REPORTS

If you are the newly elected president or treasurer of an established organization, ask last year's officer if he or she remembers filling out these forms and sending them in. If previous officers did not do it, get the forms immediately and send them in at the right time. Even if the officers did send in the forms, the forms change very often. Compare this year's forms to last year's forms to see if anything has changed. Be sure to use the current instructions as a reference rather than a general accounting reference book, which will probably be out-of-date.

AUDIT

In addition to the state and federal annual tax reports, you may need or want an audit of your books each year. An audit is an inspection of your books and records by an independent CPA. The auditor will look at your bookkeeping and accounting systems, test the accuracy of the records, and give you a written opinion of your system. This opinion is written in special words that have a specific meaning to auditors and people who read financial reports. Your officers and board can learn the language, too.

The advantage of an annual audit is that you will have an independent outside opinion of your system. This can tell you better ways of doing your work and provide an incentive to keep your system efficient. An audit gives you a check on paid staff and volunteers who handle money. It gives an independent opinion of your fiscal integrity that you can show to people you want to ask for money. Getting an audit once a year helps you revise the bookkeeping system as the group grows and changes. Then you know your books or records can give the board the data it needs to plan for the organization.

The disadvantage of an audit is that it is expensive and time-consuming. Because it is written in a very special language, the board may not understand what it says or why it is beneficial. So you must hire an auditor who has experience with nonprofit organizations, and ask your volunteer CPA to help translate and mediate as the work goes on. (See Chapter 4 for advice on recruiting a volunteer CPA.)

An audit is well worth the trouble even when you are small, because it will produce the best accounting system for the group each year. If the board is unconvinced, ask your volunteer CPA to tell a few stories about groups that were "penny wise and pound foolish" and decided to do without an audit. Here are some examples.

A dance company needs an audit in order to apply for a federal grant. The group has not had an audit in six years, its records are a shambles, and it has a deadline. The auditors have the group over a barrel. It will cost more than fifteen thousand dollars to make up for lost time. This is a lot of money to gamble on one grant; if the group is turned down, it will go out of business.

A church did not want to get an audit because the members were afraid "It will hurt the treasurer's feelings. He will think we do not trust him." That was before the church found out that the treasurer, seemingly honest and a former mayor of the town, had embezzled forty thousand dollars from the church over several years.

A social service agency was audited by twenty-seven state and federal agencies in one year because its books were such a mess that the government assumed it was hiding something. Although the group had nothing to hide, without a current audit it had nothing to show. It wasted most of its office staff's time for a year catering to government auditors.

Do We Need an Audit?

You need an audit if:

1. State law requires one because of the amount and method of your fund raising.
2. Your funding source requires one.
3. Your national organization or network requires one.
4. You want to get a mortgage or a loan.
5. Your board wants one.

It would be very, very smart to get an audit if:

1. Your budget grew by more than 50 percent last year.
2. You take money from outside your membership.

3. You plan to ask for money from foundations, corporations, or government agencies.
4. You hire paid staff to handle your money.
5. You have had the same bookkeeper or treasurer for more than five years.
6. You handle a lot of cash from a lot of people.
7. You run a business.
8. Your board wants one.

In fact, you may *not* want to get an audit every year *only* if you have established a dependable funding base that produces the same amount of money every year from the same sources, and if this amount is less than the minimum that would cause the state to require an audit. For example, say you are a block club and raise two thousand dollars every year from dues, the summer block party, and the Christmas tree sale. In that case, the board may vote to have an audit every ten years just to update the system and get fresh advice on how to use the money.

How to Choose an Auditor

If the board wants an audit, the president, the treasurer, and your volunteer CPA can ask other local nonprofit groups that have operations the same size as yours for recommendations. Ask three firms to come in, look at your system, and give you an estimate of how much it will cost to do an audit. The board can review the bids and choose a firm at least three months before the close of your fiscal year. Then the treasurer and the auditor can plan the audit work over the next six months. Some work may be done even before you close the books, such as sending out letters to verify the sources of your income. After the treasurer closes the books, he or she will have to work closely with the auditor to be sure everything is done the way you want it done. Ask the auditor to attend a board meeting to explain the audit and his or her opinion. If the auditor has any suggestions for ways to improve the financial system, the board members should hear those suggestions at the same time.

Because the board needs accurate, useful data in order to make workable plans and budgets, any improvements suggested by the auditor should be welcome. It will be easier to improve your accounting system if you review and revise the system every year with independent professional advice. This will help you avoid one common problem of groups that choose someone to be treasurer because the group knows that he or she is conservative and will keep tight control of the money. The group often discovers that the negative side of this conservatism is that the treasurer may be reluctant to change the accounting system, even if the change obviously seems to be an improvement. Asking for, listening to, and applying the advice of your auditor will help you avoid hurt feelings or the inadequate bookkeeping that can come from the conservative treasurer's seven last words: "We never did it that way before."

How to Pay for It

The best way to "pay" for an audit is to get an accounting firm to donate the audit to your organization. If someone on your board has influence in the business community, he or she may be able to request a free audit for you, at least if you are small and the books are done well. But the firm may not want to do the audit for free every year. A free audit may not seem as "independent" as it should, and you may have trouble getting it done on time.

Another way to pay for an audit is to hire an auditor who will let you pay one-twelfth of the expense every month, all year. Although you only get an audit once a year, you pay a little each month. This gives the group a monthly reminder of the importance of keeping the system up-to-date, and the group is not faced with having to pay a huge sum once a year—which might tempt you to postpone the audit. Ask the CPAs if they will let you pay on a year-round basis. If a CPA knows that he or she can count on the income, he or she may be willing to discount the price.

Always ask if there is any way to make the audit less expensive. The auditor may recommend a different fiscal year or a different bookkeeping system. Although it may cost you some money to set up the recommended books, the expense probably will pay off in the long run.

The last resort is simply to buy the best possible audit once a year.

Consider it a cost of doing business. Because you want to get bigger and better every year, the audit is a tool you use to guarantee control. It is money well spent.

The advantage of paying the CPA is that you have an incentive to be ready for the work and to cooperate with the audit. When you pay, it is easier to make sure the audit will meet your standards and your deadlines. In the interest of getting your money's worth, you are likely to ask more questions, learn more, and put your findings to use right away to improve your system. Especially if the officers and the board are not accustomed to handling large amounts of money, it is in your interest to buy the best advice you can get, listen to it, and use it each year.

STEPS TO COMPLETING ANNUAL REPORTS

THE TREASURER WILL:

1. Ask the bookkeeper of a nonprofit organization of your type in your state to give you advice. Also ask your lawyer and accountant.
2. Collect all necessary government forms and instructions.
3. Set up books and records to collect necessary information.
4. Set a date on next year's calendar so that you will begin to prepare forms at least two months in advance.
5. Fill in the forms.
6. Have officers sign the forms.
7. Copy and file a copy of the completed form for next year's officers.
8. If you also need or want an audit, ask three CPAs to bid on your job.
9. Choose a CPA, and begin work early.
10. Ask the auditor to explain the audit to the board.
11. Implement suggested improvements in your accounting system.

22

Calendars: How to Get Control of Your Time

*"Better now than tomorrow,
better tomorrow than the day after."*
—Joan of Arc

As leaders of a community organization, you will meet many exciting challenges during your term of office. Obviously, the first thing you will want to do is to attract members and hold meetings to create a strong organization. But before you plunge into the excitement of meetings and members, plan your calendar to get the most from your time, money, and energy.

After each election, the new officers and board members can schedule one meeting just to make up a calendar for the next year. The calendar will help to make sure that everything is done, that nothing is left out, and that everyone knows what everyone else is doing. It distributes the work so that you do not end up with more work than you can do in April and nothing to do in August. It also divides the work so that everyone does his or her fair share.

PLANNING YOUR TIME

Before the calendar planning meeting, the president, treasurer, and secretary can meet with the organization's volunteer lawyer and

306

accountant to create a work plan to accomplish the year's legal and accounting tasks. They will plan when to find a CPA, do the audit, and prepare annual tax reports. Any other legal or accounting work can be scheduled according to the advice of officers of similar organizations.

Then the officers can research other important dates that the group will want to include in its calendar. These could include legal holidays; religious holidays; family days; or dates of important local, state, or national meetings of groups with the same purpose. Ask a friendly lobbyist or legislator if any relevant bills will be coming up during the year's state legislative session. If the officers want to testify in hearings on the legislation, they can plan to send a delegation at the right time.

Depending on your goals and your resources, you may even need to plan for longer than one year. For example, a madrigal singing group could believe that it is good enough to compete in the international choral group contest in Llangollen, Wales. But the members of the group cannot afford to pay their own way. So they decide to have a special fund-raising concert each summer at the same time as the Welsh festival, featuring the songs they will perform in competition. After the concert, they will host an international food feast to represent the chance to compete and share with the groups from other countries. On the advice of their travel agent, they decide to raffle off a trip to Wales. Each year the concert, the dinner, and the raffle will make a little more than one-third of the amount needed. So the group plans special concerts for three summers and plans to go to Wales to compete during the fourth summer.

Once the officers have learned all of the religious and secular holidays, politically important dates, convention and training dates, and long-range opportunities that must be considered, it is time to plan the calendar. Get twenty calendars with boxes you can write in. Give one to each officer, board member, and committee chair. Use the calendars to write the work plan for the board, the officers, and the committees.

MAKING THE CALENDARS

First schedule regular monthly meetings. For example, this could include a regular board meeting the second Thursday of every month and a regular program meeting the fourth Thursday of every month. When you put these dates on the calendar, you see that the fourth Thursday in November is Thanksgiving, and the fourth Thursday in December is Christmas. So you move the November program meeting to the third Thursday and decide to cancel the December program meeting. Instead, you will hold a party on the second Thursday. If you combine the regular board meeting and Christmas party, there will be one less meeting when people are most busy. You may decide to skip meetings in August, also, because you know that attendance is usually so low in August that all the business is put off to September anyway.

After you have planned the monthly meetings for the year, schedule four quarterly meetings to review the budget. It is especially easy for a new group to outgrow its budget. In order to control your fund raising and spending, plan one meeting every three months so that officers and top fund raisers can, if necessary, revise the budget and the fund-raising plan.

Then plan once-a-year events, such as your official annual meeting at which you will elect officers for the next year. If you know that you want to elect officers in April, you will have to create a nominating committee and review the bylaws in December, revise the bylaws in January if necessary, and choose a slate of candidates in February and March. The advantage to writing all this out in advance is that the work will begin in December. Otherwise, it is easy to think, "Gee, the annual meeting isn't until April; we have plenty of time." But soon it is March, and you have to change the bylaws and find good people to run for office. The work may be done too fast, so that some people are dissatisfied, or it may not be done at all. Planning a year ahead will seem to "make more time," so that everything will be done in an orderly way, with plenty of opportunity for everyone involved to express opinions in enough time to act on them.

Other once-a-year activities to plan are your regular fund-raising events and "fun" membership activities. You could plan on an ad book that you will sell in the summer and give out at a Halloween party. Then plan a summer picnic and a Christmas party for the members.

Don't forget to schedule your planning meetings for the year. Evaluation and planning are so important to the health of the organization that these meetings should be put on the calendar first and other work planned around them. Many groups plan in the fall for the next calendar year. In this system, you would do program planning in September, budget planning in October, fundraising strategy planning in November, then combine the plans for the board to adopt in December.

After you have planned the monthly, quarterly, and yearly meetings and parties for the organization, go through the calendar again and plan the regular committee activities. This will let all the committees work best. For example, the publicity committee may say it will put out the newsletter every three months—in March, June, September, and December. Then the president must write a column two months before each of these dates, the treasurer must have checks ready to pay the post office and the printer, the secretary must have the post office permits and all the mailing paraphernalia ready, and the membership committee must have a current list of mailing labels. Planning the year's work in advance will make the work easier for everyone.

The biggest advantage to planning the administrative work a year in advance is that the work needed for the organization itself will not be neglected, even if your program activities multiply. Advocacy groups, lobbying groups, and direct-action groups especially must be able to react to city hall, the state legislature, or Congress. You cannot control these powers, so you should have the rest of your work under control.

Part IV
Getting Advice

23

Free Government
Publications and Services

Your federal, state, and local governments can give you and your volunteer organization many free publications and services. Ask other organizations like your own to recommend the best people in government agencies and the most useful publications. Get to know the elected officials from your district and their staff. Helping good volunteer organizations get started and get results is good for all the voters in their district, so they should be eager to help you. Here are some suggestions of the most useful publications and services available for free in 1981. Also ask each agency for their current list of publications to order newer titles.

UNITED STATES GOVERNMENT

Internal Revenue Service (IRS)

The IRS is listed in most telephone books under "Internal Revenue Service" and "United States Government." In large telephone directories, the government offices are all listed in the blue pages in the front. If the IRS is not listed in your telephone book, call the toll-free number for your state from the list below. Contact the office of your U.S. senator or member of Congress if you need more help.

ALABAMA

Birmingham, 252-1155
Huntsville, 539-2751
Mobile, 433-5532
Montgomery, 264-8441

Elsewhere in Alabama,
  1-800-292-6300

ALASKA

Anchorage, 276-1040

Elsewhere in Alaska, call operator
  and ask for Zenith 3700

ARIZONA

Phoenix, 257-1233
Tucson, 882-4181

Elsewhere in Arizona,
  1-800-352-6911

ARKANSAS

Little Rock, 376-4401

Elsewhere in Arkansas,
  1-800-482-9350

CALIFORNIA

Please call the telephone number shown in the white pages of your local telephone directory under U.S. Government, Internal Revenue Service, Federal Tax Assistance.

COLORADO

Denver, 825-7041

Elsewhere in Colorado,
  1-800-332-2060

CONNECTICUT

Hartford, 249-8251

Elsewhere in Connecticut,
  1-800-343-9000

DELAWARE

Wilmington, 573-6400

Elsewhere in Delaware,
  1-800-292-9575

DISTRICT OF COLUMBIA

Call 488-3100

FLORIDA

Fort Lauderdale, 522-0704
Jacksonville, 354-1760
Miami, 358-5072
Orlando, 422-2550
St. Petersburg, 823-7459
Sarasota, 371-4526
Tampa, 223-9741
West Palm Beach,
  655-7250

Elsewhere in Florida,
  1-800-342-8300

GEORGIA

Atlanta, 522-0050
Augusta, 724-9946
Columbus, 327-7491
Macon, 746-4993
Savannah, 355-1045

Elsewhere in Georgia,
  1-800-222-1040

HAWAII

Hawaii, 935-4895
Oahu, 546-8660
Kauai, 245-2731
Lanai, call operator and ask
  for Enterprise 8036
Maui, 244-7654
Molokai, call operator and ask
  for Enterprise 8034

IDAHO

Boise, 336-1040
Elsewhere in Idaho,
  1-800-632-5990

ILLINOIS

Chicago, 435-1040
Elsewhere in area code
  312 (except city of
  Chicago) and residents in
  Joliet Region Telephone
  Directory, 800-972-5400
Springfield, 789-4220
Elsewhere in all other locations
  in Illinois,
  1-800-252-2921

INDIANA

Evansville, 424-6481
Fort Wayne, 426-8300
Gary, 938-0560
Hammond, 938-0560
Indianapolis, 269-5477
South Bend, 232-3981
Elsewhere in Indiana,
  1-800-382-9740

IOWA

Des Moines, 284-4850
Elsewhere in Iowa,
  1-800-362-2600

KANSAS

Wichita, 263-2161
Elsewhere in Kansas,
  1-800-362-2190

KENTUCKY

Lexington, 255-2333
Louisville, 584-1361
Northern Kentucky
  (Covington dialing area),
  628-0055
Elsewhere in Kentucky,
  1-800-428-9100

LOUISIANA

New Orleans, 531-2440
Elsewhere in Louisiana,
  1-800-362-6900

MAINE

Augusta, 622-7101
Elsewhere in Maine,
  1-800-452-8750

MARYLAND

Baltimore, 962-2590
Prince Georges County,
  488-3100
Montgomery County,
  488-3100
Elsewhere in Maryland,
  1-800-492-0460

MASSACHUSETTS

Boston, 523-1040
Elsewhere in Massachusetts,
  1-800-392-6288

MICHIGAN

Ann Arbor, 769-9850
Detroit, 237-0800
Flint, 767-8830
Grand Rapids, 774-8300
Mount Clemens, 469-4200
Pontiac, 858-2530

Elsewhere in area code 313,
    call 1-800-462-0830

Elsewhere in area codes
    517, 616, and 906, call
    1-800-482-0670

MINNESOTA

Minneapolis, 291-1422
St. Paul, 291-1422

Elsewhere in Minnesota,
    1-800-652-9062

MISSISSIPPI

Biloxi, 868-2122
Gulfport, 868-2122
Jackson, 948-4500

Elsewhere in Mississippi,
    1-800-241-3868

MISSOURI

Columbia, 874-4040
Jefferson City, 635-9141
Joplin, 781-8500
Kansas City, 474-0350
St. Joseph, 364-3111
St. Louis, 342-1040
Springfield, 887-5000

Elsewhere in Missouri,
    1-800-392-4200

MONTANA

Helena, 443-2320

Elsewhere in Montana,
    1-800-332-2275

NEBRASKA

Lincoln, 477-6081
Omaha, 422-1500

Elsewhere in Nebraska,
    1-800-642-9960

NEVADA

Las Vegas, 385-6291
Reno, 784-5521

Elsewhere in Nevada,
    1-800-492-6552

NEW HAMPSHIRE

Portsmouth, 436-8810

Elsewhere in New Hampshire,
    1-800-582-7200

NEW JERSEY

Camden, 966-7333
Hackensack, 646-1919
Jersey City, 622-0600
Newark, 622-0600
Paterson, 279-9400
Trenton, 394-7113

Elsewhere in New Jersey,
    1-800-242-6750

NEW MEXICO

Albuquerque, 243-8641

Elsewhere in New Mexico,
    1-800-242-5750

NEW YORK

Albany District (Eastern
    Upstate New York)
Albany, 449-3120

Elsewhere in Eastern Upstate
    New York
    1-800-342-3700

Brooklyn District
Brooklyn, 596-3770
Nassau, 294-3600
Queens, 596-3770
Suffolk, 724-5000

Buffalo District (Central
and Western New York)
Buffalo, 855-3955
Rochester, 263-6770
Syracuse, 425-8111

Elsewhere in Central and
Western New York,
1-800-462-1560

Manhattan District
Bronx, 732-0100
Manhattan, 732-0100
Rockland County, 352-8900
Staten Island, 732-0100
Westchester County,
997-1510

NORTH CAROLINA

Charlotte, 372-7750
Greensboro, 274-3711
Raleigh, 828-6278

Elsewhere in North Carolina,
1-800-822-8800

NORTH DAKOTA

Fargo, 293-0650

Elsewhere in North Dakota,
1-800-342-4710

OHIO

Cleveland District
Akron, 253-1141
Canton, 455-6781
Cleveland, 522-3000
Toledo, 255-3730
Youngstown, 746-1811

Elsewhere in Northern Ohio,
1-800-362-9050

Cincinnati District
Cincinnati, 621-6281
Columbus, 228-0520
Dayton, 228-0557

Elsewhere in Southern Ohio,
1-800-582-1700

OKLAHOMA

Oklahoma City, 272-9531
Tulsa, 583-5121

Elsewhere in Oklahoma,
1-800-962-3456

OREGON

Eugene, 485-8285
Medford, 779-3375
Portland, 221-3960
Salem, 581-8720

Elsewhere in Oregon,
1-800-452-1980

PENNSYLVANIA

Allentown, 437-6966
Bethlehem, 437-6966
Erie, 453-5671
Harrisburg, 783-8700
Philadelphia, 574-9900
Pittsburgh, 281-0112

Elsewhere in area codes
215 and 717, call
1-800-462-4000

Elsewhere in area codes
412 and 814, call
1-800-242-0250

RHODE ISLAND

Providence, 274-1040

Elsewhere in Rhode Island,
1-800-662-5055

SOUTH CAROLINA

Charleston, 722-1601
Columbia, 799-1040
Greenville, 242-5434

Elsewhere in South Carolina,
  1-800-241-3868

SOUTH DAKOTA

Aberdeen, 225-9112

Elsewhere in South Dakota,
  1-800-592-1870

TENNESSEE

Chattanooga, 892-3010
Knoxville, 637-0190
Memphis, 522-1250
Nashville, 259-4601

Elsewhere in Tennessee,
  1-800-342-8420

TEXAS

Austin, 472-1974
Corpus Christi, 888-9431
Dallas, 742-2440
El Paso, 532-6116
Ft. Worth, 335-1370
Houston, 965-0440
San Antonio, 229-1700

Elsewhere in Texas,
  1-800-492-4830

UTAH

Salt Lake City, 524-4060

Elsewhere in Utah,
  1-800-662-5370

VERMONT

Burlington, 658-1870

Elsewhere in Vermont,
  1-800-642-3110

VIRGINIA

Baileys Crossroads (North-
  ern Virginia), 557-9230
Chesapeake, 461-3770
Norfolk, 461-3770
Portsmouth, 461-3770
Richmond, 649-2361
Virginia Beach, 461-3770

Elsewhere in Virginia,
  1-800-552-9500

WASHINGTON

Everett, 259-0861
Seattle, 442-1040
Spokane, 456-8350
Tacoma, 383-2021

Elsewhere in Washington,
  1-800-732-1040

WEST VIRGINIA

Charleston, 345-2210
Huntington, 523-0213
Parkersburg, 485-1601
Wheeling, 233-4210

Elsewhere in West Virginia,
  1-800-642-1931

WISCONSIN

Milwaukee, 271-3780

Elsewhere in Wisconsin,
  1-800-452-9100

WYOMING

Call 1-800-525-6060

Telephone Assistance
Services for Deaf/Hearing
Impaired Taxpayers Who
Have Access to TV/
Telephone—TTY Equipment

Hours of Operation
8:30 A.M. to 6:45 P.M. EST

Indiana residents,
  1-800-382-4059

Elsewhere in U.S., including
  Alaska, Hawaii, Virgin
  Islands, and Puerto Rico,
  1-800-428-4732

GETTING STARTED:

Publication 557 — *How to Apply for and Retain Exempt Status for Your Organization.* (82 pp.)

Form 1023 — "Application for Recognition of Exemption Under Section 501(c)(3) of the Internal Revenue Code." (22 pp.)

Form SS-4 — "Application for Employer Identification Number." (4 pp.)

Form 5768 — "Election/Revocation of Election by an Eligible Section 501(c)(3) Organization to Make Expenditures to Influence Legislation." (1 p.)

ANNUAL REPORTS:

Form 990 — "Return of Organization Exempt from Income Tax." (4 pp.)

Instructions for Form 990. (8 pp.)

Schedule A (Form 990) — "Organization Exempt Under 501(c)(3) Supplementary Information." (4 pp.)

Instructions for Schedule A (Form 990). (8 pp.)

Form 990T — "Exempt Organization Business Tax Return." (4 pp.)

Instructions for Form 990T. (10 pp.)

Publication 598 — *Tax on Unrelated Business Income of Exempt Organizations.* (32 pp.)

TO ANSWER QUESTIONS ABOUT DONATIONS:

Publication 526 — *Income Tax Deduction for Contributions.* (8 pp.)
Publication 561 — *Valuation of Donated Property.* (12 pp.)

STARTING IN THE MIDDLE:

If you are a new officer of a tax-exempt nonprofit corporation and cannot find copies of the organization's IRS form or reports, call the IRS immediately to get copies so you can plan your work for your own term of office. Call the IRS, ask for "Exempt Organizations," and tell them the group's federal employer identification number if you can. Explain you are the new officer of a tax-exempt nonprofit corporation and ask for copies of the forms filed by the organization in the past. The IRS will refer you to the correct office. If you need a copy of the group's Form 1023 or Form 990 and Schedule A, they will send you to your Key District Office. If you need a copy of the group's Form SS-4 or Form 5768, they will send you to your Internal Revenue Service Center.

If you want to change your fiscal year and reporting dates, ask for:
Form 1128 — "Application for Change in Accounting Period." (4 pp.)

Post Office

Call the main post office and ask for mailing requirements.
Publication 13 — *Mailing Permits.* (40 pp.)
Form 3624 — "Application to Mail at Special Bulk Third-Class Rates for Qualified Nonprofit Organizations or Associations." (2 pp.)
Form 3614 — "Application to Distribute Business Reply Cards, Envelopes and Labels." (1 p.)

Small Business Administration (SBA)

Write the SBA at the Small Business Administration, P.O. Box 15434, Fort Worth, TX 76119, or call the SBA office in large cities.
SBA 115A — *Free Management Assistance Publications.* (4 pp.)
SBA 115B — *For-Sale Management Assistance Booklets.* (4 pp.)

STATE GOVERNMENT

Look in the telephone directory under the name of the state, write to the state capital, or contact your state senator or representative.

Secretary of State, Corporate Division

Ask for the law governing nonprofit corporations, an application to become a nonprofit corporation, and all instructions for the application. The law and instructions will tell you the legal requirements for creating and operating a nonprofit corporation in your state.

Ask if there is an annual report form due to the secretary of state. If there is, ask for the form and instructions.

The State Department that Regulates Charities

This could be the secretary of state (sixteen states), the attorney general (eight states), or another state department. Ask for information and forms to register as a charity. Also ask for the annual report form.

Department of Revenue—Sales Tax Division

Ask for information and forms to apply for an exemption from your state sales tax. Also ask the Department of Revenue to send you information on any forms on fund raising that they regulate. For example, in Illinois they could send you the regulations for Bingo and the lottery.

COUNTY GOVERNMENT

Look in the telephone directory under the name of your county, or contact your county commissioner.

Recorder of Deeds

If the organization becomes a nonprofit corporation, you will have to file a copy of your certificate of incorporation with the county recorder of deeds.

County Clerk

If the organization does not want to incorporate, but does want to be a legal entity with a protected name, ask the county clerk to send you an application to become an unincorporated association.

If none of your members is a notary public, you may want the secretary to become one. Ask the county clerk for an application to become a notary public.

The Election Department, which may be under the county clerk or may be a separate department, is an excellent place to get up-to-date lists of registered voters and detailed maps. Ask for the precincts or townships where you will be working. They are usually free.

Some counties exempt nonprofit groups from paying either real estate property taxes or personal property taxes. This may also fall under the jurisdiction of the city. Ask for information on your responsibilities and possibilities of exemption.

CITY, TOWN, OR VILLAGE GOVERNMENT

Look in the telephone directory under the name of your city, town, or village, or contact your mayor, city manager, or member of the town council.

Department of Revenue

If you have a city sales tax or income tax, ask if it is possible for a nonprofit group to apply for an exemption. If so, ask for the rules and forms.

If you want to solicit money either door-to-door or on street corners, you may have to apply for permission from the city. Ask for the forms.

Police

Ask for regulations for crowds, meetings, and traffic control.

Member of the City Council

This person can give you the information on signs, traffic, parking, curfews, garbage pickup, litter control, and other local service problems that may affect your office or meeting place.

Other

Ask similar organizations for advice on other government agencies that regulate your enterprise. For example, a food co-op must work with the City Department of Health, the City Department of Weights and Measures, and the local United States Department of Agriculture Food Stamp Office.

Politicians

In some areas, the smaller the government unit, the more possible it is that the real work of government will be done by the political party in power. Thus you may have to request services from ward or township committee persons of the dominant political party. Ask experienced officers from older organizations for advice on working with the local politicians.

24

Bibliography and Resources

*"The first time I read an excellent book, it is
to me just as if I had gained a new friend.
When I read over a book I have perused before, it resembles meeting with an old one."*
— Oliver Goldsmith

Here are more books to help you start and strengthen an effective
volunteer organization. These are all good values, easy to read,
and easy to use. For each topic, I recommend the books that give
you the most information for the least money. These are how-to
books, with information you can use immediately.

Most of them also include bibliographies recommending further
reading in the same field. For example, *The Food Co-op
Handbook*'s chapter on federations and warehouses refers the
reader to publications on credit unions, yogurt making, herb and
sprout growing, "cooperating with bees," and starting community
canneries. The publications can also refer you to sources of more
advice.

All addresses are U.S. unless indicated, and all prices are as of
1980. For any publication from a nonprofit organization, payment
must be sent with your order. Make your check or money order pay-
able to the name of the organization or publisher. If the price has
gone up, they will notify you. If the publication is out of print, they
should send your check back to you.

Publications and resources are listed under the following head-
lines:

THE BASICS
Part I: Getting Started
How to Start a Volunteer Organization
Adult Education
Arts
Business
Children/Families
Community Organization
Cooperatives
Foundations
Historic Preservation
Housing
Mediation
Politics
Professionals
Rural Organizing
Self-Help
Women
Inspiration/Motivation
Chapter 9: Choosing a Method to Report Lobbying Expenses
Part II: Getting Results
Chapter 10: Members, Committees, and the Board of
                 Directors
Chapter 11: Program Planning and Evaluation
Chapter 13: Fund Raising — How to Ask for Money
Chapter 14: Making Meetings Fair and Effective
Chapter 15: The Publicity Committee
Chapter 16: How to Hire and Supervise Paid Staff
Insurance
Research
Training
Part III: Getting Organized
Chapter 19: The Job of the Treasurer
Chapter 20: Budgets and Financial Reports for the Board

Chapter 22: Calendars: How to Get Control of Your Time

THE BASICS

You must have these and know how to use them. If you cannot buy your own books, the public library will have copies of all of these that you can use.

1. Dictionary. Any current and complete paperback.

2. Thesaurus. Any current and complete paperback.

3. Etiquette. Any paperback such as *Amy Vanderbilt's Everyday Etiquette.* Especially useful for letters and invitations.

4. Media directory. A list of the working press in your community, including the names of current staff, with addresses and telephone numbers of newspapers, wire services, radio, and television. This may be published by the local public relations professionals' association, the telephone company, the Newspaper Guild, or a clipping service. Ask a local public relations professional where to get one.

5. Telephone directories for your town and any suburbs or towns that affect your group. If you lobby, you should also get the telephone directories (both white and Yellow Pages) for your state capital and Washington, D.C. All are free from your local telephone company office. In large cities, the Yellow Pages often include a street guide, a directory of federal, state, and local government offices, professional sports schedules, and other helpful information.

6. Current postal regulations. Free from your local post office. These will tell you how to prepare bulk mailings (second or third class) and first-class mailings.

7. Subscriptions to the daily newspapers, local weeklies, and anything else your membership reads.

8. A current library card. Read magazines and books there. Get to know the reference room librarian. Ask him or her to teach you how to find and use current reference books such as almanacs, atlases, dictionaries, directories, and encyclopedias.

9. Calendars. A twelve-month calendar posted in the office or meeting place with important organizational dates marked on it tells all members that the organization has ambitious goals for the year and that newcomers are welcome. Each member of the board

and any staff should also have calendars they can carry at all times.

10. Address book or card file to store and retrieve names, addresses, and phone numbers.

11. Police and fire regulations for crowds. Emergency numbers for local police, fire departments, hospital, paramedics, and ambulance.

PART I—GETTING STARTED

How to Start a Volunteer Organization

ADULT EDUCATION

How to Start a Free University. Greg Marsello. 1976. 24 pp. $2.50. Lifelong Learning Resources, 1221 Thurston, Manhattan, KS 66502. How to create new Free Universities, defined as "organizations offering ungraded, unaccredited classes, activities, and programs to the general public." Recommended to any group that offers classes or workshops for free or for sale, for adults.

The Learning Exchange. G. Robert Lewis and Diane R. Kinishi. 1977. 151 pp. $6.50. The Learning Exchange, P.O. Box 920, Evanston, IL 60204. How to set up and operate a phone referral service to connect teachers and learners. Based on the highly successful program that has 3,000 teachers on file, from "accordion" and "animals—chimp trainer" to "yoga" and "zoology." Features how to set up and use a voluntary membership program. Includes 78 pages of samples including a corporate support brochure, public service announcements, and thank-you letters.

See also publications listed later under "Training."

ARTS

Arts Administration: How to Set Up and Run a Successful Non-Profit Arts Organization. Tem Horwitz. 1978. 256 pp. $7.95. Chicago Review Press, 215 W. Ohio St., Chicago, IL 60610. Overview of setting up an arts organization, from the board of directors to the building. Excellent chapters on financial management, budgeting and bookkeeping, and law and the arts.

Beginning a Community Museum. Howard Levy and Lynn Ross-Molloy. 1975. 84 pp. $3. The Publishing Center for Cultural Resources, 152 W. Forty-second St., New York, NY 10036. Excellent book on getting money, especially government and foundation money, and involving community people in planning and running a community museum. Features information on finding, evaluating, and remodeling a building.

See also *Subscribe Now! Building Arts Audiences Through Dynamic Subscription Promotion* later in this chapter under "Chapter 13. Fund Raising — How to Ask for Money."

BUSINESS

Checklist for Going into Business: Small Business Administration. Small Marketers Aid No. 71. 1970. 12 pp. Free. Small Business Administration (SBA) P.O. Box 15434, Fort Worth, TX 76119, or your local SBA field office. Good checklists and work sheets to use to find out if you have the right personality and enough money to go into business for yourself.

Starting and Managing a Small Business of Your Own. Wendell O. Melcalf. 1973. 96 pp. $2.40. Small Business Administration Publications, U.S. Superintendent of Documents, Washington, DC 20402. Excellent introduction to starting a business, including many work sheets and questions. Best buy.

CHILDREN/FAMILIES

"I Love My Child But I Need Help . . .": How to Develop a Crisis Nursery. Joan C. Curtis. 1977. 24 pp. Free. National Center on Child Abuse and Neglect, Children's Bureau, P.O. Box 1182, Washington, DC 20013. Introduction to starting a crisis nursery, with discussion of types of nurseries, especially the emergency shel-

ter and the residential treatment center, funding, staff, policies, and procedures.

If We Think We Can . . . Organizing Community-Based Family Services. Leslie Lilly, Ruth Mather, and Jim Clark. 1979. 16 pp. $1. Southern Appalachian Ministry, 1931 Laurel Ave., Knoxville, TN 37916. Excellent description of a day-care center and parent education center in two small Southern communities. Outlines the evolution of an organization from an idea, finding resources, hiring staff, and growing pains. Recommended to any rural group.

Creating Drop-In Centers: The Family Focus Model. Lorraine B. Wallach and Bernice Weissbourd. 1980. 48 pp. $5. Family Focus, Inc., 2300 Green Bay Rd., Evanston, IL 60201. Excellent introduction to creating a community-based drop-in center for families of young children based on the Family Focus model. Each chapter has sections on "things to think about" and "things to do." Especially good on relationships with staff, people under stress, and planning your program. Recommended to any community-based, family-oriented, high-use center.

How to Grow a Parents' Group. Diane Mason, Gayle Jensen, and Carolyn Ryzewocz. 1979. 211 pp. $5.95. CDG Enterprises, P.O. Box 97, Western Springs, IL 60558. Excellent, very readable account of how three women began a Mothers' Hot Line that grew into a comprehensive countywide program for new parents. Excellent chapters on planning, budgets, setting goals and objectives, preparing newsletters, and avoiding burnout and attrition. Recommended to volunteer groups with no staff.

COMMUNITY ORGANIZATION

Rules for Radicals. Saul D. Alinsky. 1971. 196 pp. $2.45. Vintage Paperbacks, 201 E. Fiftieth St., New York, NY 10022. Do not be put off by the title; if you liked Thomas Paine, you will love Saul Alinsky. An inspiring and patriotic book that emphasizes values, communication, realism, and humor. Especially good on choosing tactics. Based on forty years of experience from the man who taught the men and women who are teaching today's organizers. Recommended to any group that wants to build a powerful organization. Especially recommended to any leader who hires someone who calls himself or herself an "organizer." He or she has read this book; you should, too.

COOPERATIVES

The Food Co-op Handbook: How to Bypass Supermarkets to Control the Quality and Price of the Food You Eat. The Co-op Handbook Collective. 1975. 382 pp. $4.95. Houghton Mifflin Co., 2 Park St., Boston, MA 02107. Excellent book on organizing food co-ops, from the first meeting to expanding into federations. Take advantage of the firsthand experience of the dozens of people who helped with the book. Recommended to any group that wants to initiate, organize, or expand a cooperative.

Management Manual For Co-operative Houses. Max Kummerow and NASCO. 1972. 18 pp. 75¢. North America Students of Co-operation (NASCO), Box 7293, Ann Arbor, MI 48107. Written for people who want to start or manage a student housing co-op. Recommended to anyone trying to do the long-range fiscal planning if you own (or want to own) real estate that is owned and operated by a group.

FOUNDATIONS

The Handbook for Community Foundations: Their Formation, Development and Operation. Eugene C. Struckhoff. 1977. Vol. I, 303 pp. Vol. 2, 757 pp. in two loose-leaf binders. $40. Council on Foundations, Inc., 1828 L St., NW, Washington, DC 20036. Complete manual for setting up and running a community foundation.

Robin Hood Was Right: A Guide for Giving Your Money for Social Change. 1977. 148 pp. $5. Vanguard Public Foundation, 4111 Twenty-fourth St., San Francisco, CA 94114. Written for and by young people who have inherited wealth and want to fund social change projects instead of more traditional philanthropy. How to set up or join an "alternative foundation."

Why Establish a Private Foundation? Patricia Thomas. 1980. 26 pp. $3. Southeastern Council of Foundations, 134 Peachtree St., NE, Atlanta, GA 30303. Why and how to organize and operate a private foundation.

HISTORIC PRESERVATION

Information: A Preservation Sourcebook. National Trust for Historic Preservation. 1979. 437 pp. in a loose-leaf binder. $16.50. Preservation Shops, 1600 H Street, NW, Washington, DC 20006. A collection of twenty-three articles on preservation techniques, funding programs, economics, legalities, and building types. Includes sections on neighborhood conservation, rural conservation, and education projects. Very thorough, with excellent bibliography.

HOUSING

The People Fight Back: Building a Tenant Union. Mike Miller et al. 1979. 68 pp. $4.50. Organize Training Center, 1208 Market St., San Francisco, CA 94110. The tale of organizing the Geneva Towers Tenant Association in San Francisco. Clear analysis of what worked and what did not, and why.

MEDIATION

Organizing for Neighborhood Justice. James H. Klein and John W. Payton. 1980. 70 pp. $5. The Center for Urban Policy, Loyola University of Chicago, 820 N. Michigan Ave., Chicago, IL 60611. Study of several models of neighborhood justice centers, which provide arbitration, mediation, and referrals. Description of the creation and first-year operation of the Uptown-Edgewater Neighborhood Justice Center. A neighborhood justice center provides an effective alternative to the civil courts, which often cost too much and take too much time to fulfill the community's desire for justice.

POLITICS

Campaign Workbook. Betsy Wright. 1978. 202 pp. in a loose-leaf binder. $15. National Women's Education Fund, 1410 Q

Street, NW, Washington, DC 20009. How to put together a winning political campaign. Covers planning, targeting public opinion
surveys, support operation, individual voter contact, political
media, candidate activity, fund raising, and windup.

See also the section on "Chapter 9: Choose Method to Report
Lobbying Expenses" later in this chapter.

PROFESSIONALS

*Anatomy of a Counter-Bar Association: The Chicago Council of
Lawyers.* Michael Powell. 1979. 42 pp. $3. *ABA Foundation Jour-
nal* reprint. Vol. 1979, Summer, No. 3. The American Bar Foundation, 1155 E. 60th St., Chicago, IL 60637. Study of the start and
early years of an alternative bar association. Recommended to anyone trying to start a new group of professionals.

See also *To Light One Candle* in the section on "Chapter 13:
Fund Raising—How to Ask for Money" later in this chapter.

RURAL ORGANIZING

*How People Get Power: Organizing Oppressed Communities for
Action.* Si Kahn. 1970. 128 pp. $2.95. McGraw-Hill Paperbacks,
1221 Avenue of the Americas, New York, NY 10020. Excellent
book on community organizations, building political power, and
leading the community. Recommended to any rural organization.

See also *If We Think We Can* in the section "How to Start a
Volunteer Organization: Children/Families" earlier in this chapter
and *Training Guide* listed later under "Training."

SELF-HELP

The Family Circle Guide to Self-Help. Glen Evans. 1979. 240 pp.
$2.25. Ballantine Books, 201 E. 50th St., New York, NY 10022.
The theory of self-help, case histories, and "The ABC's of Beginning Your Own Self-Help Group." Sixty-five pages listing self-help

groups in the United States and thirty-five pages on self-help groups in Canada. May tell you about the group you need so that you will not have to start your own.

How to Organize a Self-Help Group. Andy Humm. 1979. 50 pp. $3. National Self-Help Clearinghouse, Graduate School and University Center of the City University of New York, Room 1227, 33 W. Forty-second St., New York, NY 10036. Good introduction to starting a self-help group like Alcoholics Anonymous, including group discussions, people chains, and use or nonuse of professionals.

WOMEN

How to Set Up a Community Based Program for Battered Women and Their Families: Project Manual. 1980. 154 pp. $5. Park Slope Homes Project, P.O. Box 429, Van Brunt Station, Brooklyn, NY 11215. How this Brooklyn community set up a network of homes to provide shelter for battered women and their children for three-day periods.

How to Start a Rape Crisis Center. 1977. 54 pp. $4. Rape Crisis Center, P.O. Box 21005, Washington, DC 20009. Excellent information on starting and running a crisis center, including counseling, community education, the criminal justice system, self-defense, fund raising, media, and resources, Appendixes include office procedures, bylaws, meeting procedures, policy statements, a volunteer report form, becoming a member, and "What to do if you can't start a rape crisis center." Recommended to any group starting a community-controlled crisis center.

How to Start a Women Office Workers Group in Your City. 1980. 4 pp. $1. Working Women, 1224 Huron Rd., Cleveland, OH 44115. How to organize a new group to win rights and respect for women office workers. Tested advice on running meetings, filing charges, local resources, legal rights, and more from the groups that inspired the movie *Nine to Five.*

Wife Beating: How to Develop a Wife Assault Task Force and Project. Kathleen M. Fojtik. 1976. 42 pp. $3. Domestic Violence Project, Inc., 202 E. Huron, Suite 101, Ann Arbor, MI 48104. A step-by-step approach to setting up a task force and project to help wives who have been assaulted by their husbands. Includes excellent bibliography and appendix.

Women's Networks: The Complete Guide to Getting a Better Job, Advancing Your Career and Feeling Great as a Woman Through Networking. Carol Kleiman. 1980. 210 pp. $5.95. Lippincott & Crowell, 521 Fifth Ave., New York, NY 10017. What Kleiman calls *networks* others call *self-help groups.* Excellent section on "how to set up your own network" and listings of national, state, and local networks.

See also *The Bucks Start Here: How to Fund Social Service Projects* under "Chapter 13: Fund Raising: How to Ask for Money" later in this chapter.

Inspiration/Motivation

Alcoholics Anonymous: The Story of How Many Thousands of Men and Women Have Recovered from Alcoholism. Third Edition. 1976. 575 pp. $9. Alcoholics Anonymous World Services, Box 459, Grand Central Station, New York, NY 10017. Forty-four personal stories of members of Alcoholics Anonymous, including the founders, plus the Twelve Traditions, which are basis of A.A.'s success.

American Dreams: Lost and Found. Studs Terkel. 1980. 470 pp. $14.95. Pantheon Books, 201 E. 50th St., New York, NY 10022. Also available in paperback. Hear Americans talking about their hopes and dreams for themselves and their country. See especially "Stirrings in the Neighborhood," featuring the growth of Mary Lou Wolff from housebound mother of nine to leader of the most successful community organization in Chicago.

Benjamin Franklin: The Autobiography (and Other Writings).

Benjamin Franklin. Signet Classics, 1301 Avenue of the Americas, New York, NY 10019. 1961 (written in 1771). 350 pp. $1.95. Fascinating account of Franklin's early years in Philadelphia, recounting individual and civic self-help projects attempted and achieved.

Displaced Homemakers: Organizing for a New Life. Laurie Shields. 1981. 272 pp. $5.95. McGraw-Hill Paperbacks, 1221 Avenue of the Americas, New York, NY 10020. Records the genesis of a movement from 1974, when Tish Sommers (who coined the name) and a handful of older women began meeting as a small self-helf group, to the creation of a national network of Displaced Homemakers Centers. Shields, herself a displaced homemaker when she was widowed at fifty-five, tells how they overcame inexperience, poverty, naiveté, ageism, and sexism to reach their goal.

The Forgotten Heroes of the Montgomery Bus Boycott. Vernon Jarrett. 1975. 12 pp. $2. DuSable Museum of African American History, 740 E. Fifty-sixth Pl., Chicago, IL 60637. Inspiring story of ordinary people who organized the successful bus boycott in Montgomery, Alabama, in 1955. Features interviews with seamstress Rosa Parks, Pullman porter E. D. Nixon, professor Benjamin J. Sims, hair stylist Ann Smith Pratt, cook Georgia Gilmore, and insurance executive Robert Nesbitt. Recounts how these men and women organized the committees and raised the money to operate a car pool for 40,000 blacks for 381 days until they won desegregation of the buses.

How to Win Friends and Influence People. Dale Carnegie. 1936. 264 pp. $1.95. Pocket Books, 1230 Avenue of the Americas, New York, NY 10020. Now in its 104th printing, this is still the best advice on how to talk and listen to people. Recommended to any leader or staff person who works with the public.

The Hospice Movement: A Better Way of Caring for the Dying. Sandol Stoddard. 1978. 347 pp. $2.50. Vintage Books, 201 E. Fiftieth St., New York, NY 10022. A hospice is a patient-oriented system of care for dying people and their families. Stoddard's book covers the history, development, and alternative models of hospice care, all of which share the goals expressed by Dr. Cicely Saunders, founder of St. Christopher's Hospice: "You matter because you are you. You matter to the last moment of your life, and we will do all we can not only to help you die peacefully, but also to live until you die."

"The Organizer's Tale." Cesar Chavez. *Ramparts,* Vol. 5, No. 2, July 1966, pp. 43–50. First-person portrait of Chavez's first organizing experiences, beginning when Fred Ross took him off the apricot farm in 1950. Continues through his first terrifying (to him) house meetings for the Community Service Organization (CSO), his disillusionment with CSO as it got bigger and richer, and finally the decision to start the National Farm Worker's Association. Describes the groundwork from 1962 to the first strikes of rose grafters and grape pickers in 1965.

The Success System That Never Fails. W. Clement Stone. 1962. 280 pp. $2.50. Pocket Books, 1230 Avenue of the Americas, New York, NY 10020. Excellent book on how to motivate yourself and others to achieve your goals. Emphasizes the importance of on-the-job training, setting goals, and self-improvement; it's great for busy people, because it shows you that it takes less work to succeed than to fail. Especially recommended to the board, the fund-raising committee, and any fund-raising staff.

Success Through A Positive Mental Attitude. Napoleon Hill and W. Clement Stone. 1960. 302 pp. $1.95. Pocket Books, 1230 Avenue of the Americas, New York, NY 10020. Most popular book on how to motivate yourself and others to achieve your goals. Based on Napoleon Hill's principle, "Whatever the mind of man or woman can conceive and believe, it can achieve." Two legends share their tested advice for success and happiness. An excellent book to give your staff.

Twenty Years at Hull House with Autobiographical Notes. Jane Addams. 1910. 320 pp. $1.95. Signet Classics, 1301 Avenue of the Americas, New York, NY 10019. Wonderful account of Addams's youth, the formation of Hull House when three twenty-nine-year-old women moved into the house in 1889, and the story through its expansion to thirteen buildings, forty staff, and myriad programs twenty years later. Moving and marvelous stories with old-fashioned ideals and ideas as well as discussion of timeless problems such as burnout and character assassination.

OUT OF PRINT, BUT WORTH LOOKING FOR

A Flock of Lambs: A New Approach to the Care of the Mentally Retarded. Robert Terese with Corinne Owen. 1970. 225 pp. Henry Regnery Co., Chicago. Library of Congress Catalog Card Number 76-105119. Wonderful first-person account of how two people decided to invent a better way to care for the mentally retarded young adult. They tried and succeeded in a small pet store, then expanded to a farm with the goal of becoming a self-sufficient community. Almost too good to be true, this book will make you believe in good, old-fashioned values like courage, love, hard work, and even miracles.

The Not-So-Helpless Female. Tish Sommers and Bülbül. 1973. 240 pp. David McCay Co., New York City. Library of Congress Catalog Card Number 72-86968. Inspiring book written to motivate women to be more ambitious and more effective in running their own lives and communities. Excellent book for anyone who is eager to get more accomplished but is not sure where to start.

Chapter 9: Choose Method to Report Lobbying Expenses

The Internal Revenue Service explains lobbying, direct lobbying, grass roots lobbying, and exceptions in Publication 557 and in the instructions to Schedule A of Form 990. Both are available free from your local office of the IRS, listed in the telephone book, or by calling the IRS toll-free number listed in Chapter 23.

The best current publications are published by national organizations for the benefit of their own members. Ask your national network for current publications. One good example is:

Associations & Lobbying Regulation: A Guide for Non-Profit Organizations. George D. Webster and Frederick J. Krebs. 1979. 76 pp. $9. Association Division, Chamber of Commerce of the United States, 1615 H St., NW, Washington, DC 20062. Excellent booklet explaining both the 1946 Federal Regulation of Lobbying Act and the Tax Reform Act of 1976 — including definitions, IRS rulings, Supreme Court cases, record keeping, and reporting. How the laws affect 501(c)(6) organizations such as trade associations and chambers of commerce and 501(c)(3) organizations.

If you choose to lobby, do it well. Here are some books to help:

Public Affairs Handbook: A Guide to Achieving Good Government. 1976. 30 pp. 50¢. The Sperry and Hutchinson Co., Consumer Services, 2900 W. Seminary Dr., Fort Worth, TX 76133. Introduction to learning about and taking action in your community, state, Congress, or political party.

How You Can Influence Congress: The Complete Handbook for the Citizen Lobbyist. George Alderson and Everett Sentman. 1979. 360 pp. $9.95. E. P. Dutton, 2 Park Ave., New York, NY 10016. Complete information on lobbying by letter or face-to-face, with tactics for a legislative campaign and building long-term influence.

See also *Displaced Homemakers: Organizing for a New Life,* listed earlier in the section "Inspiration/Motivation," for a firsthand account of a successful grass roots lobbying effort to pass legislation in California and then the U.S. Congress despite many obstacles. As Displaced Homemakers leaders Tish Sommers and Laurie Shields have proven, "Where there's a bill, there's a way!"

RESOURCES

For information on national legislation, politicians, or campaigns, contact:

League of Women Voters of the United States, 1730 M St., NW, Washington, DC 20036

Democratic National Committee, 1625 Massachusetts Ave., NW, Washington, DC 20036.

Republican National Committee, 310 First St., SE, Washington, DC 20003

For information on state and local elected and appointed public officials, contact your state or local League of Women Voters. Also ask for their literature list and information on how a bill becomes law in your state legislature.

PART II: GETTING RESULTS

Chapter 10: Members, Committees, and the Board of Directors

The Effective Board. Cyril O. Houle. 1960. 174 pp. Single copy free. Communications Department, The W. K. Kellogg Foundation, 400 North Ave., Battle Creek, MI 49016. Discussion of different sorts of boards for nonprofit organizations and how to make them work.

Getting People to Help. AFSCME Education Department. 1973. 2 pp. $1. The Midwest Academy, 600 W. Fullerton Ave., Chicago, IL 60614. Best advice on how to recruit good people, build active committees, and keep everyone happy.

Membership Handbook: A Guide for Membership Chairmen. 1977. 24 pp. 50¢. The Sperry and Hutchinson Co., Consumer Services, 2900 W. Seminary Dr., Fort Worth, TX 76133. How to plan and run a campaign to get new members for your organization. How to keep them: "Use a member or lose a member." Useful survey forms and checklists.

On Being Board, or How Not To Be Dead Wood. 1973. 16 pp. $1. Rocky Mountain Planned Parenthood, 2030 E. Twentieth Ave., Denver, CO 80205. Best discussion of why and why not to serve on the board of a controversial organization.

Hint: Ask your national organization or network for publications about boards tailored for specific groups. Many offer good materials, such as the Child Welfare League of America's "Guide for Board Organization in Social Agencies."

See also *Displaced Homemakers: Organizing for a New Life,* listed earlier under "Inspiration/Motivation," for a sample of the Volunteer Contract pioneered by the Displaced Homemakers to record and recognize the work of volunteers.

Chapter 11: Program Planning and Evaluation

Community Action Tool Catalog: Techniques and Strategies for Successful Action Programs. Laura Horowitz et al. Second Edition. 1978. 252 pp. $7. American Association of University Women, Sales Office, 2401 Virginia Ave., NW, Washington, DC 20037. Most complete manual on how to plan and do programs to improve your community. Includes how to organize and carry out a successful action project, how to work with legislatures and courts, how to show support or opposition, fact finding, organization, and planning. The detailed, step-by-step format makes it especially good for beginners and easy to use for veterans. Recommended to low-budget, volunteer groups.

Chapter 13: Fund Raising—How to Ask for Money

CORPORATIONS

A Case Study of the C.O.P.S. Ad Book. Arnie Graf. 1980. 8 pp. $2. Organize Training Center, 1208 Market St., San Francisco, CA 94102. Excellent account of using an ad book campaign to raise money and teach organizational principles. Emphasizes that selling ads is not begging. It is (1) collecting dues from everyone in San Antonio who benefited from Communities Organized for Public Services (COPS) work and (2) developing relationships of mutual respect with major businesses. Graf was staff director of COPS when it did its first ad book in 1977, net $47,000, and 1978, net $60,000. Suggestions and training can be copied by any citizens' group.

Marketing a Non-Profit. Dr. Richard Steckel. 1980. 90-minute, ¾" color videotape. $100 rental. The Children's Museum of Denver, 931 Banock St., Denver, CO 80204. Videotape of Steckel workshop on marketing skills any volunteer organization can use to sell its programs and potential to the business community. Steckel is the best in the business — he has personally developed a sales system that can also work for you. This is the plan that changed the museum from being 100 percent grant dependent to 100 percent self-sufficient in five years, thus freeing the board and staff to "concentrate on program excellence rather than emergency fund-raising."

Special Events Fundraising. 1975 and 1977. 16 pp. $2.75. The Grantsmanship Center NEWS, 1031 S. Grant Ave., Los Angeles, CA 90015. Features "Ten Steps to a Million Dollar Fund Raiser," by Sally Berger. This is the best thing in print on how to go to corporations and big businesses for money. Sally directed a yearlong campaign to raise money for a hospital research program. As a volunteer, she asked for a minimum of $500 per company and raised more than $1.4 million. She explains her system for putting together a prospect list, getting appointments, researching the prospective donor, preparing persuasive sales material, closing the sale, and the importance of the thank-you note! Recommended to any group that wants to ask for corporate money.

See also *The Learning Exchange* listed earlier under "How to Start a Volunteer Organization — Adult Education" for a sample corporate fundraising brochure.

FOUNDATIONS

Ask an experienced local grant writer for advice on the best people at local foundations. Use the Regional Collections of the Foundation Center listed in Chapter 13 for the most up-to-date free information on foundations.

Foundation Fundamentals: A Guide for Grantseekers. Carol M. Kurzig. 1980. 148 pp. $4.95. The Foundation Center, 888 Seventh Ave., New York, NY 10019. The best book on how to research foundations, what they are, where they are, and how to apply for their money. Many samples and a good bibliography.

The Grantseekers Guide: A Directory for Social and Economic Justice Projects. Jill R. Shellow. 1981. 307 pp. $7.50 National Network of Grantmakers, 919 N. Michigan Ave., Fifth Floor, Chicago, IL 60611. A new book designed to help social change projects qualify for and obtain grants, includes helpful information on 112 foundations.

The Grantsmanship Center NEWS. Magazine published six times a year. $20. The Grantsmanship Center, 1031 S. Grand Ave., Los Angeles, CA 90015. Up-to-date information on foundation and government grant writing and helpful tips on management for agencies that take grants. Also sells useful reprints of earlier articles.

Program Planning and Proposal Writing. Expanded Version. Norton J. Kiritz. 1980. 48 pp. $2.55. The Grantsmanship Center, 1031 S. Grand Ave., Los Angeles, CA 90015. Recommended to all grant writers, this booklet is the core of the Grantsmanship training course. Easy to read with lots of good examples, it covers each step of writing a proposal, from the cover letter to the budget.

STEPS in Writing a Proposal. Q-16. 1976. 6 pp. 50¢. Citizens Information Service of Illinois, 67 E. Madison St., Chicago, IL 60603. Recommended for new groups planning and writing a proposal for the first time; features "Is your organization ready for a grant?"

GOVERNMENT AGENCIES

Ask an experienced local fund raiser for the best way to pursue government grants. For more information, check the resources at the regional Collections of the Foundation Center listed in Chapter 13, the staff of local elected officials, or the nearest large library that is a federal depository.

The Bucks Start Here: How to Fund Social Service Projects. Kathleen M. Fojtik. 1978. 142 pp. $6. Domestic Violence Project, Inc., 1917 Washtenaw Ave., Ann Arbor, MI 48104. How to open a high-overhead social service project such as a battered women's shelter. Good introduction to all the funding choices, especially federal money and grants. Excellent appendix with twenty-three examples of real bylaws, letters, budgets, job descriptions, etc.

GRASS ROOTS MONEY

Designs for Fund-Raising: Principles, Patterns, Techniques. Harold J. Seymour. 1966. 210 pp. $18.95. McGraw-Hill Book Co., 1221 Avenue of the Americas, New York, NY 10020. Best book on how to design, lead, and maintain a campaign to ask for money in person from large donors. Best section anywhere on how to motivate volunteer fund raisers and potential donors. This is the bible for professional fund raisers and a source of quotable quotes such as Seymour's (prophetic) quip, "No one ever bought a Buick because General Motors needed the money." Most examples are huge institutions such as Yale and Princeton, but you can adapt the advice to a group of any size.

Fund Raising Handbook: A Guide for Ways and Means Chairmen. 1980. 32 pp. 50¢. Consumer Services, The Sperry and Hutchinson Co., 2900 W. Seminary Dr., Fort Worth, TX 76133. Best introduction to grass roots fund raising, special events, and asking for money. Recommended to new fund raisers.

The Grass Roots Fundraising Book: How to Raise Money in Your Community. Joan Flanagan for the Youth Project. 1977. 224 pp. $5.25. The Youth Project, 1555 Connecticut Ave., NW, Washington, DC 20009. Best book for any group that wants to raise its own budget. Includes information on how to set up a fund-raising program, how to choose the right strategy for your group, and how to raise money and build your organization at the same time. Best available bibliography recommends another one hundred books and articles on fund raising.

Helping NOW Grow: Fundraising. 1975. 20 pp. $2. Chicago Chapter of the National Organization for Women (NOW), Suite 1524, 53 W. Jackson, Chicago, IL 60604. Good introduction to ad books, budgets, planning, raffles, and door-to-door canvassing by members.

Subscribe Now! Building Arts Audiences Through Dynamic Subscription Promotion. Danny Newman. 1977. 276 pp. $7.95. Publishing Center for Cultural Resources, 625 Broadway, New York, NY 10012. Foolproof system for building a dependable income for the performing arts through season subscription sales, the theatrical equivalent of dues. This fun, easy-to-read book is packed with ideas for all groups that want to get large numbers of people from their community to support their program. See especially his system for brochures, mailing lists, block sales, and door-to-door sales.

To Light One Candle: A Manual for Organizing, Funding and Maintaining Public Service Projects. Nora Jean Levin and Janet Dempsey Steiger. 1978. 162 pp. $6. American Bar Association, Division of Bar Services, 1155 East Sixtieth St., Chicago, IL 60637. Written to tell state and local bar associations how to raise money from lawyers over and above dues. Recommended to any organization that wants to generate dependable annual income from professionals of high salary.

See also *How to Grow a Parents Group* in the section on "How to Start a Volunteer Organization: Children/Families."

RESOURCES — FUND-RAISING TRAINING

Many national organizations offer workshops on fund raising at their national or regional conferences. If your delegate likes the workshop, ask the trainers if they do on-site training. If you receive grants from large foundations or government agencies, they may be able to provide or recommend successful trainers.

In your own community, you may be able to get good training or advice from the United Way, the Regional Collection of the Foundation Center (See Chapter 13), local colleges, or local foundations. In large cities, the Small Business Administration offers free workshops on starting businesses, marketing, record keeping, and taxes. These are designed for small, for-profit businesses, but they are also very helpful to small and medium-sized nonprofit groups. Best of all, ask the experts—leaders who have organized successful funding strategies for similar organizations or similar communities. You know which organizations in your own community are thriving; ask them for advice and where they go for training.

Chapter 14: Making Meetings Fair and Effective

Chairing. Paul Booth. 1974. 6 pp. $1.50. The Midwest Academy, 600 W. Fullerton Ave., Chicago, IL 60614. How to be a great chair, written by the best chair I know. Discusses the relationship between the chair and the audience, how to assert authority and create unity, and an explanation of simple parliamentary procedure.

Introduction to Parliamentary Procedure. Q-6. 1980. 4 pp. 40¢. Citizens Information Service of Illinois, 67 E. Madison St., Chicago, IL 60603. Written for the new chair, includes all the choices about making and amending motions, how to count votes, special emergency procedures to protect individual rights, and encouragement for the novice. Recommended to any person who chairs meetings or takes minutes. En Español: *Introducción Al Procedimiento Parlamentario.* F-29. 40¢.

Leader's Guide for Workshops on Effective Organizations. Q-7. 1975. 12 pp. 75¢. Citizens Information Service of Illinois, 67 E. Madison St., Chicago, IL 60603. A discussion of the purpose, leadership, and agenda of meetings, plus parliamentary procedure. En Español: *Guía Para El Líder De Seminarios Sobre Organización Efectiva.* F-35. 75¢.

Making Sense of Consensus. Don Wells. 1980. 11 pp. 30¢. Friends Council on Education, 1507 Cherry St., Philadelphia, PA 19102. Excellent overview of the values needed to make consensus work and a frank discussion of problems that will stop it from working. Good discussion for any group of the attitudes that will help or hinder an effective meeting.

Robert's Rules of Order, Revised. Gen. Henry M. Robert. 1915. 324 pp. $2.95. Morrow Quill Paperbacks, 105 Madison Ave., New York, NY 10016. How to use parliamentary procedure. This is the most widely used set of rules for fair and effective meetings. Available at your public library or you can probably find a copy at a used bookstore.

Chapter 15: The Publicity Committee

THE BASICS

The Elements of Style. William Strunk, Jr., and E. B. White. Third Edition. 1979. 85 pp. $2.25. Macmillan Paperbacks, 866 Third Ave., New York, NY 10022. Anyone who writes must have this book. It is the model for any work you do: short, clear, easy to read, full of memorable examples and good humor. A perfect marriage of English professor Strunk's concise commands on usage and composition with author White's eloquent approach to style.

Equality in Print: A Guide for Editors and Publishers. Beryl Dwight et al. 1978. 24 pp. $1.50. Chicago Women in Publishing, P.O. Box 11837, Chicago, IL 60611. A clear, useful guide to help all writers "eliminate obsolete sexist terms, gender assumptions, unnecessary labelling, and anachronistic usages" in letters, newsletters, and reports.

How to Do Leaflets, Newsletters and Newspapers. Nancy Bingham. Expanded version. 1981. 144 pp. $5.75. The New England Free Press, 60 Union Sq., Somerville, MA 02143. Wonderful, thorough manual covers, start to finish, the production and editorial work on publications reported and produced by volunteers. Indispensable for the novice; valuable for the veteran. Packed with examples.

If You Want Air Time: A Publicity Handbook. 1979. 18 pp. 75¢. Publications Department, National Association of Broadcasters, 1771 N St., NW, Washington, DC 20036. How to get your message on radio and television, written from the point of view of the stations.

Publicity and The Press. Don Rose. 1967. 20 pp. $2. The Midwest Academy, 600 W. Fullerton Ave., Chicago, IL 60614. Best "how-to" for community organizations written by the man who handled the press for Dr. Martin Luther King, Jr., the Chicago Seven, and numerous political candidates.

Publicity Handbook. 1979. 36 pp. 50¢. Consumer Services, The Sperry and Hutchinson Co., 2900 W. Seminary Dr., Fort Worth, TX 76133. Best introduction to press work for volunteers, including a sample press release, photo caption, and radio public service announcement.

SPECIALIZED BOOKS

To show films and lead discussions:
In Focus. A Guide to Using Films. Linda Blackaby, Dan Georgakas, and Barbara Margolis. 1980. 206 pp. $9.95. Cine Information, 419 Park Ave., S., New York, NY 10016.

To set up a speakers' bureau:
Speaking Out: Setting Up a Speakers' Bureau. #299. 1977. 2 pp. 65¢. League of Women Voters of the U.S., 1730 M St., NW, Washington, DC 20036.

To make a slide show:
Projecting Your Image: How to Produce a Slide Show. #296. 1977. 4 pp. 80¢. League of Women Voters of the U.S., 1730 M St., NW, Washington, DC 20036.

To make your own television shows:
Doing Community Video. Uptown Community Video Staff. 1979. 30 pp. $2.50. Alternative Schools Network Video Project, 1105 W. Lawrence Ave., Rm. 210, Chicago, IL 60640. Clear introduction to community television. Covers basic equipment and skills.

To give a speech or do an interview:

How to Talk with Practically Anybody about Practically Anything. Barbara Walters. 1970. 241 pp. $2.25. Dell Publishing Co., One Dag Hammarskjold Plaza, New York, NY 10017. Excellent practical advice for anyone from the experienced speaker to the novice "strangled with panic." Features "the care and handling of a guest speaker" and "you're the speaker."

To run ads that work:

Do You Know the Results of Your Advertising? SMA 169. Elizabeth M. Sorbet. 1979. 8 pp. Single copy free. Small Business Administration, P.O. Box 15434, Fort Worth, TX 76119. Written for small for-profit businesses, tells you how to plan and test the effects of your advertising.

To answer complaints:

Complaint Handling: Your Guide for Turning Liabilities into Assets. 1979. 28 pp. Single copy free. Consumer Services, The Sperry and Hutchinson Co., 2900 W. Seminary Dr., Fort Worth, TX 76133. How to set up a system to handle complaints on the telephone or in letters. Includes sample surveys, forms, and letters.

See also *How to Win Friends and Influence People* listed earlier under "Inspiration/Motivation." See especially Part Five, "Letters That Produce Miraculous Results."

Hint: Ask your own national organization or network for publications on publicity. Many offer good booklets tailored to their members, such as the B'nai B'rith *Publicity and Bulletin Handbook* or The National Council on the Aging's *Media Relations Handbook.*

Chapter 16: How to Hire and Supervise Paid Staff

FREE PUBLICATIONS

Once you hire staff, think of yourself as a small business. The Small Business Administration (SBA) offers several good, free booklets that will be very helpful to you. Order these before you hire staff to help you plan your budget, personnel policy, job descriptions, and work plans.

Order the following from SBA, P.O. Box 15434, Fort Worth, TX 76119. All are free.

MA 191. *Delegating Work and Responsibility.* 6 pp.

MA 171. *How to Write a Job Description.* 4 pp.

MA 233. *Planning and Goal Setting for Small Business.* 8 pp. Includes sample work plan.

MA 197. *Pointers on Preparing an Employee Handbook.* 7 pp.

MA 195. *Setting Pay for Your Management Jobs.* 7 pp.

MA 241. *Setting up a Pay System.* 7 pp.

SMA 142. *Steps in Meeting Your Tax Obligations.* 11 pp.

Free tax publications:

Before you hire staff, get these and understand your responsibility to pay taxes. Be sure your treasurer and your bookkeeper know about all the taxes, how to pay them, and when they are due. You will need this information to find out the cost of hiring your staff and to calculate how much the staff will get in take-home pay.

Internal Revenue Service publications:

All are free and published each year. Order from your local office of the IRS, listed in the telephone book, or call the IRS toll-free numbers listed in Chapter 23.

Circular E. *Employer's Tax Guide.* Publication 15. 48 pp. How to withhold, deposit, report, and pay federal income tax and Social Security (FICA) tax.

Publication 583. *Recordkeeping for a Small Business.* 16 pp.

Publication 509. *Tax Calendar for 19XX.* 12 pp.

Publication 505. *Tax Withholding and Estimated Tax.* 12 pp.

Publication 539. *Withholding Taxes and Reporting Requirements.* 16 pp.

Unfortunately, the federal government has not written any tax publications designed specifically for nonprofit groups. You will have to use the booklets put out for employers in general and adapt them to your group. The two major differences are:

A 501(c)(3) tax-exempt nonprofit corporation does not have to pay Federal Unemployment Tax (FUTA).

A 501(c)(3) tax-exempt nonprofit corporation is exempt from Social Security (FICA) taxes. See page 11 of Circular E.

State and city income tax publications:
Contact your state and city departments of revenue to get current state income tax forms and instructions.

Resources for advice on taxes and hiring staff:
Ask a local business to donate the services of a bookkeeper to help you plan your budget and a manager to teach you how to hire and supervise staff. A local corporation can give you samples of job descriptions, application forms, and personnel policies, too.

Contact your closest Small Business Administration (SBA) office and ask about the next tax workshop. These are offered for small business owners and are taught by the Service Corps of Retired Executives (SCORE). They are free and usually give you a chance to meet several SCORE volunteers and SBA staff members. Get the name of the best one, and arrange for ongoing help. The SBA may try to put you off because you are a nonprofit group, but if you persist the agency may be willing to help you or refer you to other help.

PUBLICATIONS FOR SALE

Advice on how to pay and reward employees:
Personnel Management Guides for Small Business. Ernest L. Loen. 1974. 79 pp. $1.10. Small Business Administration. Order from Superintendent of Documents, Washington, DC 20402. Stock number 4500-00126. The best introduction to hiring staff includes "getting new employees, personnel training, compensation, including fringe benefits, physical working conditions and employee services, employee relations, and management-union relations in small firms."

INSURANCE

For advice on insurance, ask your insurance agent and read:

Insurance Programs for Neighborhood Centers: A Guide. 1970. 20 pp. $1.10. National Federation of Settlements and Neighborhood Centers, 232 Madison Ave., New York, NY 10016. Good introduction to the insurance you will want, including employee benefits, property damage and liability insurance, fidelity bonds, and your responsibilities for reporting claims.

Insurance Checklist for Small Business. SBA 148. 1976. 16 pp. Free. Small Business Administration, P.O. Box 15434, Fort Worth, TX 76119. The questions to ask about fire, liability, automobile, and workers compensation insurance.

Research

Action Research: A Guide to Resources. James Katz. 1980. 24 pp. $4. The Institute, 628 Baronne, New Orleans, LA 70113. A former research director of Massachusetts Fair Share gives advice on how to get information on individuals, property, corporations, politicians, and government agencies. Recommended to community organizations that need research to breed winning issues, strategies, and tactics.

How to Read a Financial Report. 1979. 32 pp. Single copy free. Merrill Lynch, Pierce, Fenner & Smith, Inc., One Liberty Plaza, 165 Broadway, New York, NY 10006. An introduction to reading, understanding, and comparing the figures in a company's annual report, especially a balance sheet with assets and liabilities and an income statement. Recommended to researchers or investors.

The New York Times Guide to Reference Materials. Mona McCormick. 1971. 224 pp. $1.75. Popular Library, 1515 Broadway, New York, NY 10036. The former librarian of the *New York Times* tells you everything about reference books, dictionaries, directories, atlases, indexes, encyclopedias, and more. See especially "A Few Words on Writing a Paper" if you want to prepare a professional-style report, research, or testimony.

Survey Savvy: A Guide For Understanding Surveys. Marjorie

Getchell et al. 1979. 29 pp. 30¢. League of Women Voters of Massachusetts, 120 Boylston St., Boston, MA 02116. Best guide to planning and conducting surveys, verifying and analyzing data, and preparing reports. Includes how to use handmade punch cards for sorting data, popularly known as the poor person's computer. Written by and for skilled volunteers.

Tactical Investigations for People's Struggles. Barry Greever. 1972. 21 pp. $2.50. The Midwest Academy, 600 W. Fullerton Ave., Chicago, IL 60614. A veteran researcher for successful campaigns from Harlan County, Kentucky, to Portland, Oregon, Greever shares his tips on how to collect political and economic intelligence. He reminds us that, "1) You can always get the information you need, and 2) It's your right!" Recommended to community organizations and rural groups that need to check on political candidates, corporations, or individuals.

See also *How People Get Power,* listed earlier under the section on "How to Start a Volunteer Organization: Rural Organizing." Best advice on rural research from veteran Si Kahn.

Hint: Ask your national organization or network for more help. It may have a professional researcher in the national office to give you advice or special publications to help you. For example, the National Trust for Historic Preservation in the United States publishes excellent materials on researching historic buildings. The National Women's Political Caucus and both national political parties publish good advice on research for a winning political campaign.

Training:

Teaching Free: An Introduction to Adult Learning for Part-time, Independent, and Volunteer Teachers. Bill Draves. 1980. 16 pp. $4. Lifelong Learning Resources, 1221 Thurston, Manhattan, KS 66502. Excellent booklet to help adults teach adults. Recommended to anyone who wants to train new volunteers or staff, or run workshops.

Training Guide. 1979. 16 pp. $1.25. Federation of Southern Co-operatives, P.O. Box 95, Epes, AL 35460. Excellent booklet based on the Federation of Southern Cooperatives experiences in training. Emphasizes the importance of people's participation in planning and using effective training. Especially recommended to rural organizations.

Training Resources

If you would like to get more training for your officers or staff, ask local organizations and similar types of organizations in other communities who they recommend as trainers. Also ask your national organization or network to recommend trainers. Many national organizations employ full-time trainers who have special expertise in your field. Some larger cities have published directories of people who do training or give advice, sometimes called "technical assistance" or "management support." These directories are available at the Regional Collections of the Foundation Center listed in Chapter 13.

TRAINING SCHOOLS

There are several excellent training schools that were created by experienced organizers and volunteer leaders to help community organizations. These offer training at their headquarters, intern-style placement with a community organization, on-site training designed for your leadership or staff, and/or consultation for membership groups. All of these have been recommended by the leaders and staff they have trained. For information on the cost, curriculum, schedules, and criteria for admission, write:

Center for Third World Organizing (CTWO)
1459 Columbia Rd., NW
Washington, DC 20009

Center for Urban Encounter (CUE)
3416 University Ave., SE
Minneapolis, MN 55414

Highlander Research and Education Center
Rt. 3, Box 370
New Market, TN 37820

Industrial Areas Foundation (IAF)
675 W. Jerico Turnpike
Huntington, NY 11743

The Institute for Social Justice
628 Baronne
New Orleans, LA 70113

The Midwest Academy
600 W. Fullerton Ave.
Chicago, IL 60614

National Training and Information Center
1123 W. Washington Blvd.
Chicago, IL 60607

North Country Institute
Box 184
Woodsville, NH 03785

Organize Training Center
1208 Market St.
San Francisco, CA 94103

Pacific Institute for Community Organizing (PICO)
3914 E. 14th St.
Oakland, CA 94601

PART III: GETTING ORGANIZED

Chapter 19: The Job of the Treasurer

Best for beginners:
  Bookkeeping Handbook for Low-Income Citizen Groups. Na-

tional Council of Welfare. 1973. 104 pp. Single copy free. National
Council of Welfare, Room 566, Brooke Claxton Building, Ottawa,
Ontario K1A 0K9 Canada. Best book for the brand-new treasurer.
Covers books, opening the checking account, setting up journals
and a petty cash system, reconciling the bank statement, and setting
up files. Many helpful drawings of sample forms and journal pages.
En français: *Le Poids des Impôts/Le Partage des Bénéfices.*
Gratuit.

Recordkeeping for a Small Business. Publication 583. Internal
Revenue Service. 1979. 16 pp. Free. Internal Revenue Service
listed in your telephone directory or use the IRS toll-free numbers
listed in Chapter 23. Good introduction to setting up books for a
business that can be used for a volunteer group, too. Includes setting up records; single-entry or double-entry bookkeeping; and
sample of checkbook reconciliation, daily summary of cash receipts, monthly summary of cash receipts, check disbursement journal, depreciation record, and employee compensation record.
Good if you handle cash every day, pay staff, or run a business such
as a thrift shop.

Best all-purpose reference:

Financial and Accounting Guide for Nonprofit Organizations.
Malvern J. Gross, Jr., and William Warshauer, Jr. 1979. 568 pp.
$24. The Ronald Press Co., 79 Madison Ave., New York, NY
10016. This is everything you will need in a reference book. Good,
clear advice on concepts, financial statements, taxes, control,
audits, books, and budgeting. It is worth the price because you will
use it often. Indispensable for any medium-to-large organization.

Other books for the treasurer:

The Accountant's Manifesto. Luther H. Buchele. 1977. 86 pp.
$2.50. NASCO, Box 7293, Ann Arbor, MI 48107. Recommended
for volunteer groups because it was written for housing co-ops in
which the treasurer changes every few years. Includes excellent sections on closing the books, what the new treasurer can do before
and after training, and proven solutions for "domestic" accounting

problems like the long-distance phone bills. For any co-op or other group that depends on each member paying his or her fair share, there is "How to be an Effective Treasurer Without Losing Friends," which covers collecting money, support of the board, dealing with deadbeats, and confidentiality of the books.

Financial Management for the Arts—A Guidebook for Arts Organizations. Charles A. Nelson and Frederick J. Turk. 1975. 52 pp. $5.50. Associated Councils of the Arts, 1564 Broadway, New York NY 10036. This has the best explanation of how to estimate the "personnel cost by program," or how to figure how much each program costs you in terms of the staff's salaries. Since organizations that employ staff spend 60 to 90 percent of their budgets on salaries, this is the best way to find out if your money is really being spent to accomplish your goals. Explanation of planning, budgeting, cash management, fund accounting, general accounting, and financial organization.

See also books on budgets and financial reports for the board in the next section.

Chapter 20: Budgets and Financial Reports for the Board

The Audit Committee: The Board of Trustees of Non-profit Organizations and the Independent Accountant. 1978. 8 pp. Single copy free. Price Waterhouse & Co., 1251 Avenue of the Americas, New York, NY 10020. How to set up and operate an audit committee.

Effective Internal Accounting Control for Nonprofit Organizations. A Guide for Directors and Management. 1980. 26 pp. Single copy free. Nonprofit Industry Services Group, Price Waterhouse & Co., 1801 K St., NW, Washington, DC 20006. Thorough manual written in very technical language. Recommended to organizations that handle large amounts of money or who hire paid staff to handle their money.

How to Grow a Parents Group. Diane Mason, Gayle Jensen, and Carolyn Ryzewicz. 1979. 212 pp. $5.95. CDG Enterprises, P.O. Box

97, Western Springs, IL 60558. Best explanation of planning, budgets, and fund raising by volunteers. Appendix B includes an excellent introduction to accounting and budgeting procedures for a nonprofit organization. Includes chart of accounts, income ledger, expense ledger, monthly cash report, and comparing budget and actual figures.

Where Do All the $ Go? What Every Board & Staff Member of a Non-Profit Organization Should Know About Accounting and Budgeting. Gerald G. Bowe, Jr. 1975. 40 pp. $3.75. The New Hampshire Charitable Fund, P.O. Box 1335, Concord, NH 03301. Covers accounting, budgets, and internal control; especially good on clarifying the vocabulary of accounting and introducing double-entry bookkeeping.

Chapter 22: Calendars: How to Get Control of Your Time

Chases' Calendar of Annual Events: Special Days, Weeks and Months in 19XX. William D. Chase. Published annually. 128 pp. $12. Apple Tree Press, Inc., Box 1012, Flint, MI 48501. Every holiday, festival, commercial promotion, and famous person's birthday. You can find an excuse for a party or a theme for a meeting on *any* day from this book.

How to Get Control of Your Time and Your Life. Alan Lakein. 1973. 160 pp. $1.95. Signet Paperbacks, 1301 Avenue of the Americas, New York, NY 10019. Best book on how to stop procrastinating and start getting results. Features Lakein's question "What is the best use of my time right now?" and "How to judo fear."

25

Notes

CHAPTER ONE: DO'S AND DON'TS

1. *Introduction to Parliamentary Procedure* (Chicago: Citizens Information Service of Illinois, 1977), p. 4.
2. Nicholas von Hoffman, *Finding and Making Leaders* (Chicago: The Midwest Academy, 1976), p. 7.
3. Jane Addams, *Twenty Years at Hull House with Autobiographical Notes* (New York: Signet Classics, 1910), p. 15.
4. Cesar Chavez, "The Organizer's Tale," *Ramparts,* vol. 5, no. 2., July 1966, p. 44.

CHAPTER TWO: FROM ONE PERSON'S IDEA TO A PLANNING COMMITTEE

1. *Fair Housing Keys,* vol. 4, no. 1 (Milwaukee: Metropolitan Milwaukee Fair Housing Council, Winter, 1981), p. 12.
2. Diane Mason, Gayle Jensen, and Carolyn Ryzewocz, *How to Grow a Parents Group* (Western Springs, Ill.: CDG Enterprises, 1979), p. 120.

CHAPTER THREE: CHOOSING A STRUCTURE

1. *The American Heritage Dictionary of the English Language* (New York: Dell Publishing Co., 1973), p. 100.

CHAPTER FIVE: SHOULD YOU BECOME
A TAX-EXEMPT NONPROFIT CORPORATION?

1. Publication 561. *Determining the Valuation of Donated Property* (Washington, D.C.: Internal Revenue Service, 1979), p. 1.

CHAPTER SEVEN:
STEPS TO INCORPORATION AND TAX EXEMPTION

1. Publication 557. *How to Apply for and Retain Exempt Status for Your Organization* (Washington, D.C.: Internal Revenue Service, 1980), p. 13.
2. Publication 557, p. 15.
3. Publication 557, p. 14.
4. Publication 557, p. 16.
5. Publication 557, p. 17.
6. Publication 557, p. 16.
7. *Instructions for Form 1023* (Washington, D.C.: Internal Revenue Service, 1979), p. 2.
8. *Information on the Formation of Charitable Organizations* (Springfield, Ill.: Attorney General's Office, 1979), p. 1.
9. Publication 557, p. 14.
10. Publication 557, p. 7.

CHAPTER NINE: CHOOSING A METHOD
TO REPORT LOBBYING EXPENSES

1. Instructions for Schedule A (Form 990) (Washington, D.C.: Internal Revenue Service, 1980), p. 4.
2. Publication 557. *How to Apply for and Retain Exempt Status for Your Organization* (Washington, D.C.: Internal Revenue Service, 1980), p. 15.
3. Publication 557, p. 59.
4. Publication 557, p. 59.

CHAPTER TEN: MEMBERS, COMMITTEES,
AND THE BOARD OF DIRECTORS

1. Si Kahn, *How People Get Power: Organizing Oppressed Communities for Action* (New York: McGraw-Hill Paperbacks, 1970), p. 10.

CHAPTER ELEVEN:
PROGRAM PLANNING AND EVALUATION

1. Peter F. Drucker, "Managing the Public Service Institution," *The Public Interest,* Fall 1973, p. 21.
2. Adapted from Heather Booth and Steve Max, *Direct Action Organizing* (Chicago: The Midwest Academy, 1977), pp. 37–38.

3. "The origins of the 'Make No Little Plans' motto are ambiguous and difficult to document. Burnham apparently never wrote out or delivered the piece in the exact, now famous, sequence quoted by Charles Moore in *Daniel H. Burnham, Architect, Planner of Cities, II* (Boston, 1921), 147. Moore's version, according to Daniel Burnham, Jr., was copied from the one used by Willis Polk, Burnham's San Francisco friend and junior associate, on Christmas cards sent out in 1912, following Burnham's death the previous June. Most of the statement was drawn directly from Burnham's address at the 1910 London Town Planning Conference. . . . Since Polk ascribed the entire statement to Burnham, the additional lines were probably drawn by Polk from conversations or correspondence with Burnham that are now lost. The entire statement is consistent with and appropriate to Burnham's views and values." Thomas S. Hines, *Burnham of Chicago. Architect and Planner* (New York: Oxford University Press, 1974), p. 401.

CHAPTER TWELVE:
STRATEGY FOR SELF-SUFFICIENCY

1. Sue Gould and G. C. Guard, "Chimera Self Defense for Women," *Kuchi Waza News*, Winter-Spring 1980, p. 23.

2. Fred Schnaue, *Giving USA: 26th Annual Issue. A compilation of facts and trends on American philanthropy for the year 1980* (New York: American Association of Fund-Raising Counsel, Inc., 1981), p. 6.

3. *Giving USA*, p. 6.

4. Marianna O. Lewis, ed., *The Foundation Directory*, 7th ed. (New York: The Foundation Center, 1979), p. xii.

5. *Giving USA*, p. 6.

6. *The Foundation Directory*, p. xiv.

7. Carol M. Kurzig, *Foundation Fundamentals: A Guide for Grantseekers* (New York: The Foundation Center, 1980), pp. 6–7.

8. *Giving USA*, p. 6.

9. "A Triple Whammy on Charities," *Business Week*, March 23, 1981, p. 121.

10. Interview with Sally Barnum, librarian, United Way of Metropolitan Chicago, June 16, 1980.

11. *Alcoholics Anonymous: The Story of How Many Thousands of Men and Women Have Recovered from Alcoholism*, 3rd ed. (New York: Alcoholics Anonymous World Services, Inc., 1976), p. xxii.

12. Susan D. Armstrong, ed., *Moneyplan, The Newsletter of Political Fund Raising Ideas*, vol. 1, no. 2 (Wichita: Moneyplan, September 1975), p. 3.

CHAPTER THIRTEEN:
FUND RAISING: HOW TO ASK FOR MONEY

1. Kathleen M. Fojtik, *The Bucks Start Here: How to Fund Social Service Projects* (Ann Arbor: Domestic Violence Project, Inc., 1978), pp. 28–30.

2. *The Bucks Start Here*, pp. 58–59.

3. Jessye G. Payne, "How to Write a Grant Proposal by Really Trying," *Caring,* vol. 5, no. 1, Spring 1979, pp. 2-4. Reprinted with permission of the publisher, The National Committee for the Prevention of Child Abuse, 332 S. Michigan Ave., Suite 1250, Chicago, IL 60604.

4. Benjamin Franklin, *The Autobiography of Benjamin Franklin* (New York: Washington Square Press, Inc., 1955), pp. 151-52.

5. *The Autobiography of Benjamin Franklin,* p. 153.

6. Jane Addams, *Twenty Years at Hull House with Autobiographical Notes* New York: Signet Classics, 1910), p. 138.

7. Robert Therese with Corinne Owen, *A Flock of Lambs: A New Approach to the Care of the Mentally Ill* (Chicago: Henry Regnery Company, 1970), p. 190.

CHAPTER FOURTEEN:
MAKING MEETINGS FAIR AND EFFECTIVE

1. The Co-op Handbook Collective, *The Food Co-op Handbook: How to Bypass Supermarkets to Control the Quality and Price of the Food You Eat* (Boston: Houghton Mifflin Co., 1975), p. 131.

2. Don Wells, *Making Sense of Consensus* (Philadelphia: Friends Council on Education, 1980), p. 4.

3. *Making Sense of Consensus,* p. 3.

4. Clarence Petersen, "Order! If you plan a power game, better know new (Robert's) rules," *Chicago Tribune,* Aug. 13, 1980, sec. 3, p. 1.

5. *State of Illinois General Not-For-Profit Corporation Act* (Springfield, Ill.: Secretary of State's Office, 1979), p. 11.

CHAPTER FIFTEEN: THE PUBLICITY COMMITTEE

1. *The American Heritage Dictionary of the English Language,* (New York: Dell Publishing Co., 1973), p. 570.

2. Vernon Jarrett, *The Forgotten Heroes of the Montgomery Bus Boycott* (Chicago: DuSable Museum of African American History, 1975), pp. 6-7.

3. *The American Heritage Dictionary of the English Language,* p. 570.

4. Don Rose, *Publicity and the Press* (Chicago: The Midwest Academy, 1967), p. 1.

CHAPTER SIXTEEN:
HOW TO HIRE AND SUPERVISE PAID STAFF

1. Peter F. Drucker, *The Effective Executive* (New York: Harper & Row, 1967), p. 86.

2. *Circular E. Employer's Tax Guide* (Washington, D.C.: Internal Revenue Service, 1979), p. 6.

3. Bill Draves and Cathy MacRunnels, eds., *The Free U Manual: A National*

Guide to Operations of a Free University (Manhattan, Kan.: Free University Network Publication, 1976), p. 510.

CHAPTER NINETEEN: THE JOB OF THE TREASURER

1. *State of Illinois General Not-For-Profit Corporation Act* (Springfield, Ill.: Secretary of State's Office, 1979), p. 11.

Index

post office, 281, 320
SBA, 320
Publicity, 226, 239–41
Publicity committees, 112, 225–42,
  347–49
  duties of, 226
Purposes, 8–9, 20, 71

Q

Qualifications, board members', 22
Quality of life, 135
Quarterly reports, 234
Quorum, announcing, 218–19
Quotas, committee, 134

R

Raffles, 200
Reading, XVI–XX
Reason, XVI
Reasons for organization, 8–12
Reassurance, 127
Record keeping, XXIII, 26, 168,
  279
Recruiting, 5, 19, 22, 106–11, 213
  year-round, 109–10
Referrals, 43–44, 46, 49
Registered agent, 74
Registration, charitable
  organization, 57
Renewable money, 163–64
Renewals, subscription, 230–31
Replacing nonrenewable funds,
  165–68
Reporting methods for lobbying
  expenses, 96–101
Research
  books on, 352–53
  original, 281
  starting, 12–14, 17
Resources, 325–58
  basic, 327–28
Reviewing reading, XVIII
Rewards, 5

Robert's Rules of Order, 202
Roll calls, 219
Rotating officers, 124
Rules. *See also* Bylaws
  fund-raising, 170–71
  meeting, 201–4, 219–20
  standing, 33–34
Rural organizing, 333

S

Salaries, 39, 72, 265
Sales, 167
  subscription, 229–30
Sales goals, listing, 146
Sales tables, 215
Salespeople, 108, 148–52
  qualities of, 149
Savings accounts, 286
  opening, 55, 287
Scheduling, 307–9
Secretaries, 26–27, 48
  choosing, 15
  duties of, 205, 279–82, 305
  equipment for, 215
Secretary of State, 75, 321
Seed money, 168
Self-help books, XIII–XIV, XVI–
  XX, 333–34
Self-image, XVII
Self-motivators, XVI, XIX
Self-starters, XVI
Self-sufficiency
  achieving, 164–65
  strategy for, 145–68
Sense of humor, 127, 272
Services, XXIII, 167
  banking, 54, 93
  free government, 313–23
  lawyer referral, 43
  special, 248
Sharing costs, 16
Sharing leadership, 25
Sign-in table, meeting, 214
Size, organization, 269–70, 270–71